NATURAL ALLIES?

NATURAL ALLIES?
CANADIAN AND MEXICAN
PERSPECTIVES ON INTERNATIONAL SECURITY

CHANGING AMERICAS
Volume 2

edited by
H.P. Klepak

Carleton University Press
&
Canadian Foundation for the Americas

© Carleton University Press Inc., 1996

Printed and bound in Canada

Canadian Cataloguing in Publication Data

Main entry under title:

Natural allies? ; Canadian and Mexican perspectives on international security

(Changing Americas ; #2)
Includes abstracts in French.
Includes bibliographical references.
ISBN 0-88629-277-8

1. National security—Canada. 2. National security—Mexico. 3. Security, International. 4. Canada—Relations—Mexico. 5. Mexico—Relations—Canada. I. Klepak, H. P. (Harold Philip), 1946- II. Series.

UA600.N38 1996   327.71072   C96-900376-5

Cover illustration: Original Art, *Paisaje con escaleras*, 1991 by Paloma Torres. The publisher thanks Michael Bell for suggesting this artwork from the "Terra Incognita" exhibit, shown at Carleton University Art Gallery in 1993.

This edition is published as a collaboration between Carleton University Press and the Canadian Foundation for the Americas (FOCAL).

Carleton University Press gratefully acknowledges the support extended to its publishing program by the Canada Council and the financial assistance of the Ontario Arts Council. The Press would also like to thank the Department of Canadian Heritage, Government of Canada, and the Government of Ontario through the Ministry of Culture, Tourism and Recreation, for their assistance.

CONTENTS

ACKNOWLEDGEMENTS *vii*
PROLOGUE *Jorge Castro-Valle K.* *ix*
LIST OF ACRONYMS *xiii*
INTRODUCTION *H.P. Klepak* *xv*

I FAR FROM A *TABULA RASA*: THE CONTEXT FOR MEXICAN AND CANADIAN THINKING ON INTERNATIONAL SECURITY AFFAIRS

1 *Los Desconocidos se Conocen:* Bridging the Knowledge Gap Between Mexico and Canada *H.P. Klepak* *3*

2 National Security in and of Canada, 1775-1989, with Some Thoughts on the Current Context *H.P. Klepak* *29*

3 Sovereignty, Foreign Policy, and National Security in Mexico, 1821-1989 *Raúl Benítez Manaut* *57*

II CURRENT PERSPECTIVES ON INTERNATIONAL SECURITY ISSUES

4 Canada's Long-Term Strategic Situation: Implications for Canadian International Security Policies *Paul Buteux* *91*

5 National Security and the Cold War: Some Conceptual Interpretations *Jorge Chen Charpentier* *109*

6 Recent Developments in the Concept of Hemispheric Security *Luis Herrera-Lasso* *121*

7 Cooperative Security and Canada's Role in Inter-American Security Reform *Brian J.R. Stevenson* *133*

8 Canada's International Security Policy *Jill Sinclair* *155*

III THE WAY AHEAD

9 Prospects for Increased Mexican-Canadian Collaboration in the Security Field *H.P. Klepak* *169*

10 What Conclusions? *H.P. Klepak* *191*

SELECT BIBLIOGRAPHY *193*
LIST OF CONTRIBUTORS *208*

ACKNOWLEDGEMENTS

THE GREATEST THANKS in a work such as this must go to those who not only contributed their time and energy to the Workshop on Mexican and Canadian Perspectives on International Security, held in Mexico City, 5-6 May 1994, but also found the time to write up the results of their presentations and the comments received at the event itself. Therefore, I would like to thank all the authors whose final papers on the various themes discussed are collected here. These include the Mexican team of Raúl Benítez Manaut of the *Universidad Nacional Autónoma de México*; Ambassador Jorge Chen Charpentier, Director General for Asia and Africa at the *Secretaría de Relaciones Exteriores*; Luis Herrera-Lasso, now Mexican Consul in San Diego, U.S.A.; and our Mexican-Canadian bridge between the two teams, Brian Stevenson, now of the University of Alberta as well as the *Instituto Tecnológico Autónomo de México* (ITAM).

The Canadian team comprised Paul Buteux, Director of the Centre for Defence and Security Studies at the University of Manitoba; Jill Sinclair of the Department of Foreign Affairs and International Trade (DFAIT) in Ottawa; and myself.

Additional recognition is due to other presenters at the workshop who were not able to prepare formal papers for inclusion in this book. These include Ambassador Jean-Paul Hubert, Canada's first ambassador to the Organization of American States, and now ambassador to Belgium; Rafael Fernández de Castro, Director of the Department of International Relations at ITAM; and Brian Job of the University of British Columbia.

The stalwart backers for the project were DFAIT and ITAM, which allowed the Canadian Foundation for the Americas (FOCAL) initiative to come to fruition. DFAIT was extremely generous, not only with financial support for the idea, but also with the time and energy provided by their staff in both Ottawa and the embassy in Mexico City. Especially helpful were Michael Smart and Nic Coghlan. ITAM could not have been a more gracious host for the event, bending over backwards to provide the best of administrative support and hospitality. In this regard, Brian Stevenson, Rafael Fernández de Castro, Jean-Paul Hubert and Jill Sinclair must be thanked again. At the Collège militaire royal de Saint-Jean (CMR), Pierre Babinsky, in conjunction with Carlos Escobar of ITAM, made everything happen.

From the editorial perspective, I would like to acknowledge the invaluable help of Jean Daudelin, a pillar on the publishing side of the house at FOCAL and an academic well-versed in Latin American security issues. Michelle Hibler showed her usual patience with my infelicities. Special thanks go to Denis Berthiaume of the Governance and Security Program, who did sterling work on the text as part of his excellent ongoing work with me. Rebecca Nelems provided critical assistance in the editing process. Juanita Montalvo and Wendy Drukier of FOCAL were wonderful supporters and kept the administrative wheels moving.

Last, but far from least, I would like to thank Glen Hartle for help in resolving the computer difficulties that I, an artsman, found so baffling.

PROLOGUE

THROUGHOUT CONTEMPORARY HISTORY, security has been a controversial issue. In its broader geopolitical sense this term has sometimes been used to justify, or even cover up, overt expansionism or unilateral promotion of particular interests over the basic rules of international law. Hence the need to approach it cautiously, with special emphasis on the intrinsic right of each state to ensure its own security, as well as on the commitment of all to finding a balance between their national aspirations and their international obligations.

This fact takes on special relevance in the post-Cold War era. The dismemberment of the Soviet Union and the resulting extinction of the bipolar system has led to an international scene that is much more tense and complex. We are living in a period of dynamic tension between contradictory forces—on one hand, the trend toward economic integration resulting from the process of globalization and, on the other, the trend toward political and social fragmentation, the result of a resurgence of exclusive nationalism, inter-ethnic conflict, and religious fundamentalism. More often than not, these inherent contradictions have exceeded the mechanisms which the international community has available for tackling challenges to global security.

Therefore, each state has been faced with the imperative of thoroughly rethinking its view of national security, starting from the undeniable fact that domestic decision-making capability today contains an inevitable international component. No country can isolate itself from this reality, especially where geographic proximity is combined with economic interdependence.

For Mexico, sovereignty is the most important value of its nationality, and its defence and strengthening is the primary aim of the state. One of the major aims of Mexican foreign policy, set forth in the National Development Plan 1995-2000, is precisely the strengthening of that country's ability to ensure its national security, along with active promotion of its interests through international cooperation and growing links with the centres of world economy. In this context, Canada is both an essential component of Mexico's strategy for diversifying its international relations and a factor of equilibrium in North America.

After more than half a century of formal diplomatic relations, characterized by respect and cordiality, Mexico and Canada have met again in a world in transition, full of challenges but also opportunities, in which both countries have more solid bases for rich and fruitful cooperation. To their traditional friendship are now added concrete shared interests that give greater consistency to their bilateral links.

From being distant and mutually unknown countries, we are today moving toward an authentic strategic alliance which, to yield the desired results, must be based on making the most of our similarities and complementarities while fully respecting national differences and individuality.

Belonging to the same geographic and economic space, being neighbours of the only global superpower, and growing identification in various areas of international policy are all factors that have strengthened communication and bilateral links in all spheres. Better knowledge of one another has also contributed to this relationship; we have learned to look at each other directly and no longer solely, as in the past, through the prism—sometimes opaque or distorting—of our powerful common neighbour.

Undoubtedly, the North American Free Trade Agreement was the initial impetus for this new stage of rapprochement. However, the emerging Mexican-Canadian strategic alliance goes far beyond trade. Our increasingly rich and diversified agenda takes in bilateral, trilateral, regional, and global issues. It is no exaggeration to say that in the past five years, of all Mexico's bilateral relations, those with Canada have experienced the greatest growth and dynamism.

The undeniable progress made in this process of linkage for the benefit of both nations calls for a redoubling of our efforts to consolidate and increase our ties. In addition to constancy and continuity in our endeavours, a forward-looking vision of our priorities is required. It was for this purpose that, at the last meeting of the Ministerial Committee, held in Ottawa in April 1995, the two governments undertook the drawing up of a Declaration of Principles and Objectives that will provide a framework and direction for our strategies and actions into the twenty-first century. In this task, as in many others, the active participation of diverse representatives of our societies—including the private sector, the academic community, and non-governmental organizations (NGOs)—is of the greatest importance.

While it is true that there are a large number of common goals to be achieved, there are still major differences in approaches and means, specifically, the very different views which the two countries have of questions of international security, especially regarding the defence and promotion of democracy in the world.

This aim is an unalterable priority of Canada's foreign policy. The Canadian government has maintained a position of stalwart support for all regional and world initiatives aimed at establishing mechanisms for the cooperative defence of democracy. Its committed action in United Nations peacekeeping operations is only one expression of this position. For its part, Mexico holds that the consolidation of democratic systems must be the ultimate result of internal processes which, though supported from outside, must first and foremost respond to and reflect the legitimate aspirations of each national society in the exercise of its right to self-determination.

However, it is important to recognize that differences in approach—some fundamental, others minor—are an integral and natural part of a partnership such as the one Mexicans and Canadians are building.

We will have to confront many complex challenges in the immediate future on the world stage and, particularly, within our own hemisphere. These challenges will demand active contributions from Mexico and Canada, both individually and in concert. Perhaps the most important are follow-ups to agreements resulting from the Summit of the Americas, held in Miami in December 1994, on the preservation and strengthening of democracy, the promotion of economic integration and free trade, the eradication of poverty and discrimination in the hemisphere, and sustainable development and the conservation of the environment.

Along the same lines is the project initiated by the United States to increase cooperation and information exchanges between armed forces on the continent. Because of their importance and implications, commitments resulting from the meeting of Defence Ministers of the Americas, held in July 1995 in Williamsburg, Virginia, also require in-depth analysis. Countries such as Mexico and Canada can make a valuable and constructive contribution to these initiatives.

Moreover, it is essential to decide if this ambitious process is to be carried out within the framework of the Organization of American States (OAS), or whether—new institutional mechanisms for regional cooperation are to be established.

What is certain is that following the model that came out of Miami, political and economic integration, along with cooperation in the military sphere, cannot and must not be the result of unilateral decisions or directives. The differences in political, economic, and social conditions between the countries of the region and the diversity of geostrategic conditions necessitate a broad process of consultation.

Ultimately, hemispheric security is the right and responsibility of all; it cannot be consolidated apart from the basic rules of international law. Neither the defence of democracy and the promotion of human rights, nor the fight against the greatest threat to the security of many states—drug trafficking with its train of crime, corruption, arms smuggling, and money laundering—justify actions that violate universally established principles, such as respect for sovereignty, non-intervention in the internal affairs of states, and self-determination of peoples. In short, hemispheric security is a common objective that requires the support of all countries in the region. It cannot be based on the view that the national interest of some states takes precedence over that of others.

In the new stage of linkage between Mexico and Canada, issues that were considered untouchable yesterday are today widely discussed by our governments and societies—further proof of the maturity that relations between our two countries have reached. Mutual trust and recognition will help consolidate our potential as "natural allies."

Therein lies the relevance and timeliness of the workshop on Canadian and Mexican perspectives on international security, organized jointly by the Canadian Foundation for the Americas (FOCAL) and the *Instituto Tecnológico Autónomo de México* (ITAM). This book is but one product of that forum, and it is my privilege to present it as a signal of our shared, and future, interests.

Jorge Castro-Valle K.

LIST OF ACRONYMS

APEC	Asia-Pacific Economic Council	IADC	Inter-American Defense College
ASEAN	Association of South-East Asian Nations	ITAM	*Instituto Tecnológico Autónomo de México*
AWACS	Airborne Warning and Control System	JID	*Junte interaméricaine de défense* (IADB)
CF	Canadian Forces or Canadian Armed Forces	NACC	North Atlantic Cooperation Council
CIA	Central Intelligence Agency (United States of America)	NAFTA	North American Free Trade Agreement
CICAD	Inter-American Drug Abuse Control Commission	NATO	North Atlantic Treaty Organization
CMR	*Collège militaire royal de Saint-Jean*	NCOs	Non-Commissioned Officers
		NGOs	Non-Governmental Organizations
CSCE	Conference on Security and Cooperation in Europe	NORAD	North American Aerospace Defence Agreement
DEA	Drug Enforcement Administration (United States of America)	OAS	Organization of American States
DFAIT	Department of Foreign Affairs and International Trade (Canada)	ONUSAL	United Nations Observer Mission in El Salvador
		OSCE	Organization for Security and Cooperation in Europe
DND	Department of National Defence (Canada)	PAN	*Partido de Acción Nacional* (Mexico)
EEC	European Economic Community	PEMEX	*Petróleos Mexicanos*
EU	European Union	PNR	*Partido Nacional Revolucionario* (Mexico)
FDR	*Frente Democrático Revolucionario* (El Salvador)	PRI	*Partido Revolucionario Institucional* (Mexico)
FLACSO	*Facultad Latinoamericana de Ciencias Sociales*	PRM	*Partido de la Revolución Mexicana*
FMLN	*Frente Farabundo Martí de Liberación Nacional* (El Salvador)	RCAF	Royal Canadian Air Force
		RCMP	Royal Canadian Mounted Police
FOCAL	Canadian Foundation for the Americas	RCN	Royal Canadian Navy
FSLN	*Frente Sandinista de Liberación Nacional* (Nicaragua)	SRE	*Secretaría de Relaciones Exteriores* (Mexico)
FTA	Free Trade Agreement	TLC	*Tratado de Libre Comercio* (FTA)
GATT	General Agreement on Tariffs and Trade	UN	United Nations
GDP	Gross Domestic Product	UNAM	*Universidad Nacional Autónoma de México*
G-7	Group of Seven Largest Industrialized Countries	USAF	United States Air Force
G-8	Group of Seven Largest Industrialized Countries plus Russia	WHFTA	Western Hemisphere Free Trade Agreement
		WTO	World Trade Organization
IADB	Inter-American Defense Board		

INTRODUCTION

AS THE TITLE SUGGESTS, this book intends to answer—insofar as a number of distinguished Mexican and Canadian academics and diplomats can—the question of whether and/or to what extent Canada and Mexico are "natural allies." Historically, there certainly were moments when Canada, or British North America, was seen as a potential ally for Mexico. And as will be seen, such a role for Mexico was also sometimes envisaged in British and Canadian strategic thought. Yet such a connection never seemed to work out. This book hopes to address whether it might do so in the very different context of the present and the not-so-distant future.

I must first apologize for the extent to which the book is my own creation. The demands on the time of some participants at the workshop held in Mexico City in 1994 were such that not all could follow their oral presentations with written papers. To some extent, I, as the editor, have had to deal with that issue by blending their ideas with my own.

In the first chapter I have tried to introduce the subject of the book and set the stage for the chapters to follow. Canadian and Mexican readers, even in the international security fields, are by no means necessarily familiar with one another's concerns, and this chapter attempts both to describe and to address those concerns.

The two historical chapters that follow take this process further. In my own chapter, I endeavour to trace the evolution of national security concerns in Canada. With Dominion status and Confederation achieved only in 1867, and full control over foreign and defence policy not for several more decades, it proved necessary to go back to the decisive events of 1775 to begin to follow this story from modern Canada's true beginnings. The crucial year of 1989 is used as the endpoint of this historical introduction.

Raúl Benítez Manaut's chapter similarly describes the historical roots of national security in Mexico. Taking the formative date of 1821 as his starting point, Dr. Benítez traces the links between sovereignty, foreign policy and national security through the troubled early decades of independence, into the long peace of Porfirio Díaz, across the years of upheaval known as the Mexican Revolution, and into the period of the modern Mexican state. Here too, 1989 is used as the cut-off year.

The following two chapters deal with perspectives on national security in the two countries. Dr. Paul Buteux of the University of Manitoba addresses Canada's long-term security context and its challenges, as well as their implications for the international security policies the country must choose. Ambassador and Professor Jorge Chen Charpentier of ITAM then discusses national security in the Mexican context, especially some conceptual thoughts on the Cold War and its aftermath.

Another Mexican diplomat and academic, Luis Herrera-Lasso, follows this discussion with his own contribution, placing the emphasis on hemispheric security matters. He discusses Mexico and recent developments in thinking on security related to the Americas.

Brian Stevenson of ITAM, a Mexican and Canadian academic and one of the most important bridges between the two countries in the security and other fields, then takes a look at the concept of cooperative security in Canadian foreign and defence policy with a view to explaining how it might play out in the inter-American security arena. Jill Sinclair, a Canadian career diplomat, follows this with a chapter on current Canadian perspectives on hemispheric, and wider, security.

I then attempt both to pull together some of the threads of the various individual chapters and to reflect the wider debate of the workshop by examining the prospects for future cooperation between the two countries in the international security field. Some brief reflections on the conclusions reached round off the debate.

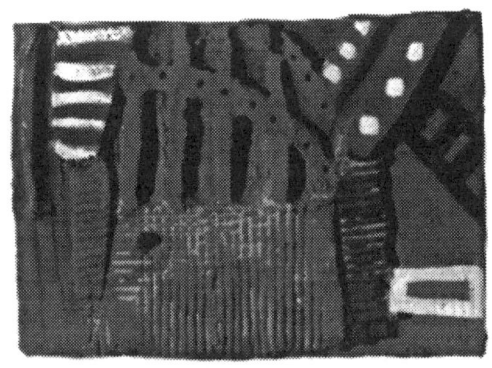

I

FAR FROM A *TABULA RASA*

THE CONTEXT FOR MEXICAN AND CANADIAN THINKING ON INTERNATIONAL SECURITY

1

LOS DESCONOCIDOS SE CONOCEN
BRIDGING THE KNOWLEDGE GAP BETWEEN MEXICO AND CANADA

LE MEXIQUE ET LE CANADA FONT CONNAISSANCE

H.P. Klepak

Abstract: If Canada and Mexico are now partners in many fields, the road to this privileged relationship has been strewn with obstacles, the asymmetries of North American relations and other factors having long prevented a close relationship. It was almost despite themselves that Canada and Mexico discovered one another. First, the Cold War brought the two countries a little closer as they sought to distance themselves from the somewhat intransigent policies of the United States. The end of the Cold War then stimulated a climate conducive to the continentalization of economies. Finally, the multiplication of political and economic links fostered links between the populations themselves. Thus, Canada and Mexico have become political, economic and social partners.

This partnership entails a bureaucratic structure adapted to the priorities of each as Canada and Mexico are important, but not essential, to each other. There is also a convergence of interests or advantage when cooperating in the management of their bilateral relations with the U.S., a difficult task given the different visions—given their different histories—each has of its gigantic neighbour.

Although neglected in the past, the security dimension should not be excluded from this Canada-Mexico partnership. After all, Canadian and Mexican perceptions of a large number of evolving traditional and non-traditional security threats are very similar. Both countries will, however, need to reconcile their desire for closer security relations with the realities of U.S. predominance in this area.

Sommaire : Le Canada et le Mexique sont aujourd'hui des partenaires dans plusieurs domaines. La route vers cette relation privilégiée a toutefois été semée d'embûches, l'asymétrie des relations nord-américaines, et d'autres facteurs, ayant longtemps empêché le Canada et le Mexique de bien se connaître.

C'est un peu malgré eux que le Canada et le Mexique se sont mutuellement découverts. D'abord, la Guerre froide a amené les deux pays à se rapprocher, pour mieux s'éloigner des politiques plutôt intransigeantes des États-Unis. Ensuite, la fin de la Guerre froide a permis l'instauration d'un climat propice à la continentalisation des économies. Finalement, la multiplication des liens politiques et économiques a favorisé l'établissement de liens au niveau même des populations. Le Canada et le Mexique sont ainsi devenus des partenaires politiques, économiques et sociaux.

Ce partenariat se traduit par un appareil bureaucratique qui reflète bien les priorités de chacun: le Canada et le Mexique sont importants, l'un pour l'autre, sans être essentiels. Cela démontre bien la communauté d'intérêts, soit l'avantage qu'ont les deux pays à coopérer en ce qui a trait à la gestion de leurs relations bilatérales avec les États-Unis. Cela ne s'avère guère une tâche aisée puisque le Canada et le Mexique entretiennent des visions différentes du géant voisin, visions découlant d'un passé tout aussi différent.

Bien que laissées pour compte dans le passé, les qestions de sécurité doivent être incorporées à ce partenariat canado-mexicain. Déjà, les deux pays partagent plusieurs priorités, tant du point de vue traditionnel que d'un autre, non-traditionnel. Les deux pays devront toutefois concilier leurs désirs d'étendre ce partenariat au secteur de la défense à la prédominance des États-Unis dans ce domaine.

NATURAL ALLIES?

CANADA AND MEXICO are finally coming to know each other in this last decade of the 20th century. This long-delayed meeting of *los dos desconocidos*—the two strangers—has not been without pitfalls and misunderstandings, but the reality is that the two countries are more interconnected, and know each other better, than anyone could have imagined little more than half a decade ago.

The catalyst for this, of course, has been the negotiation and signing of the North American Free Trade Agreement (NAFTA), but the extent of the growth in the bilateral relationship has been much more than simply in trade.[1] In the investment, cultural, academic, and politico-diplomatic fields, the expansion of the connection has likewise been vast. Thus, although trade tends to steal the headlines with increases of over 400 percent in the first two years of NAFTA and its negotiation, this is only part of the story.

THE PAST

As many observers have remarked, it is not that there has never been much interest in Mexico about Canada, or in Canada about Mexico. Rather, the difficulties in establishing a closer relationship have been ever-present, while the drives to overcome them have been sporadic and often half-hearted.[2]

The existence and dominant position of the United States in North America, situated between the two countries, formerly tended to work against a coming together of its two neighbours. This may now be seen as rather curious since it can be argued that it is just this neighbour that is currently forcing the other two to start getting together.[3]

For a long time, Canada's constitutional tradition of at least partial dependence on the United Kingdom also tended to reduce the degree and likelihood of closeness. Imperial unity, especially in the diplomatic field, was too advantageous for Canada to be given up easily. And often, Britain's troubled relationship with Mexico may have tended to hinder Canada's connection with that country.[4]

Mexico's chronic political instability also reduced any likelihood of Canada developing a sustained interest in the country. Indeed, the very first Canadian mission sent to Latin America and the Caribbean in 1865-66 to study and stimulate Canadian trade with, among other countries, Mexico, was unable to visit that nation because of an insurgency against the French-backed but ill-starred monarchy of Maximilian.[5] It would be another four decades before the first Canadian commercial office was opened in Mexico.[6]

This did not mean that Canadian investment—often linked with that from other parts of the Empire and particularly Great Britain itself—could find no place in Mexico. Indeed, Canadians found it enticing to place their money in Mexico: in railways, urban public transport, electricity, banking, shipping, and to some extent petroleum.[7] But Canada shared the disappointment of the rest of the British Empire in the fall of Porfirio Díaz in 1911 and the disruptions caused by the long struggles known collectively as the Mexican Revolution.

Instability also meant that moments that seemed tailor-made for British (or Anglo-Canadian) cooperation in curbing United States' pretensions in North America were lost. Despite the terrible relations existing between London and Washington for much of the first 125 years of U.S. independence, and the even worse condition of Mexico-U.S. relations from independence in the 1820s until the Roosevelt administration of the 1930s, there were few moments when London or Ottawa could feel confident in seeking Mexican help to produce a counterpoise to Washington.[8] It comes thus as a surprise that, despite the resulting frustrations in Mexico, modern Mexican historians are apt to side with the analysis made by statesmen of the British Empire[9] of the Mexican political situation, and indeed of Mexico's diplomatic and military potential.

Thus, for a variety of reasons, not the least of which were real distance, less than attractive stereotypes of one another, and no obvious points about which to coalesce, the two countries did not develop a closer relationship—or indeed establish diplomatic relations—until World War II was well under way. If in 1865 it was the threat of the loss of the U.S. market that drove Canadians to look farther south for others, in World War II it was the loss of virtually all the European markets that shocked Canada into a determined attempt to find replacements.[10] With much of the world in Axis hands, Latin America—especially Argentina, Brazil, and Mexico—looked very good indeed.[11]

The closing of legations in occupied Europe meant that the small but expanding professional diplomatic staff of the Canadian Department of External Affairs could now contemplate new missions, while Mexico's *Secretaría de Relaciones Exteriores*, which had enjoyed a significant staff for many years, looked forward to a full operation in Ottawa.[12] The exchange of ministers took place in 1944.

THE POST-WAR WORLD

Much progress was made once relations were established formally, but the end of the war reduced the urgency of the linkage. European markets were slowly reopening. Europe and the United States remained the main focus of Canadian foreign policy. Wartime interest in the Pan-American Union temporarily died out, at least partially because of U.S. reluctance to see Canada in the organization during the war. The Cold War not only forced Canada to concentrate its efforts and attention elsewhere, but also reinforced long-existing stereotypes about Latin America, and even Mexico.

Mexico benefited from the return of something like normality to international markets, and its own European connection loomed large again. Canada could not but lose ground with Mexican decision makers under these circumstances.

Economic relations did not die, however. A year after the war, another trade mission from Ottawa visited Mexico. The country had become, and remained, a significant customer of Canada within Latin America even though that region did not rank high as a destination for Canadian exports (always well under 4 percent of the total). The Latin American share of imports was for a while considerably higher, although this had fallen off as well by the 1960s.[13] Prime Minister John Diefenbaker's attempt to diversify Canadian trade gave a further boost to the connection in the late 1950s and early 1960s, but links were once again too sporadic and disjointed to create much of a lasting impression in either Canada or Mexico.

Mexico's own attempts to diversify its trade, in the context of a steady drift to what successive governments in Mexico City felt was excessive dependence on one market and source of supply, namely the United States, included Canada as a target along with the rest of the world.[14] Mexico's attempts in this area had also begun after World War II. Later on, in the administration of Adolfo López Mateos (1958-64), this objective once again became a priority. This level of interest increased further during the *sexenios* of Luis

Echeverría and José López Portillo.[15] The language of Canadian and Mexican concerns on this matter was extraordinarily similar.

Neither country loomed large from the other's standpoint when these attempts at trade diversification were made. Both Mexico and Canada aimed at bigger fish such as Japan (and Asia more widely), Germany and Europe, and Latin America in general.[16] While assessments of the other country were always made and its potential included in analyses of trade and other potential, neither considered the other a priority. The size of the market and the types of economy were key to such a relative lack of interest.

The interest quickened under Prime Minister Pierre Trudeau because of both political factors and Mexico's sustained economic growth. As Stephen Randall has observed, Mexico and Canada were felt to share a similar attitude to the value of multilateralism in their international relations, a vital need for access to U.S. markets and investment, a keen requirement for more non-U.S. markets, a feeling that they should do something to moderate U.S. Cold War policies, and a need to protect their own natural resources.[17] Although at a very reduced level, Canadian and Mexican politicians began to get to know each other, a development marked most emphatically by Trudeau's visit to Mexico in 1976. The limits of the connection were quickly visible, however, as even such a high-level contact resulted in little of a concrete nature.

Despite growth in trade over the next few years, the connection was still rather tenuous when the 1982 Mexican financial crisis occurred, dispelling much of the interest that had been built up.[18] And in spite of further interests linking the two countries—not the least of which proved to be similar approaches to the Central American wars of the 1980s—as the decade continued, this economic context overshadowed all efforts to build a truly close relationship.[19]

NAFTA

The globalization and concurrent, if rather contradictory, "blocism" of the past few years changed all this. Joined to these trends was the remarkable Mexican economic recovery of the late 1980s and early 1990s. Once again, however, the role of the United States in the new context of closer relations between Mexico and Canada was to prove crucial.

For a variety of reasons, Washington began to perceive the need to head an economic bloc of its own, largely in response to the spectacular success of such a grouping in Europe and the prospects of similar ones in East Asia and elsewhere. In the late 1980s, proposals were launched for a Canada-U.S. free trade area, and in 1990 for a larger Initiative of the Americas which might lead to a single free trade area from Canada to the Southern Cone.

It would be an exaggeration to say that the free trade area with the United States was universally well received in Canada. Indeed, it is probable that at no time did a majority actually want it, and this would certainly be in keeping with Canadian views on such accords historically.[20] But by 1988 Ottawa had signed and had battened down the hatches for what was to prove a very rough patch for Canadian industry and employment. It is more than likely that the shattering defeat of Prime Minister Mulroney's Conservatives in the 1993 elections was more than slightly connected to the agreement and its short-term impact on Canadian industry.

Be that as it may, Canada soon found that the United States was involved in another bilateral free trade negotiation, this time with Mexico. Rather to its annoyance, the Canadian government was obliged to join these negotiations if it did not wish to find itself at a disadvantage. Thus, the growth in Canada-Mexico relations occasioned by NAFTA cannot really be seen as the result of a distinct initiative on the part of the two U.S. neighbours to get to know one another. Rather, such growth was itself a spin-off of the two countries' desperate attempts to ensure that they were as well placed as possible to operate in the American market, and indeed to fend off the threat of protectionism that was steadily raising its ugly head in important U.S. circles.[21]

In any case, the NAFTA negotiations and sequel have made the relationship grow apace. New Canadian studies programs have sprouted in a number of Mexican universities, and courses on Mexico have multiplied in Canada. In some cases, registration in Spanish courses in Canada doubled in one year as NAFTA became more of a certainty. And, as mentioned elsewhere, trade began to grow.

Canada held the biggest overseas trade show in its history in Monterrey in March 1994.[22] From 1991 to 1994, the Canadian Embassy staff in Mexico City dealing with trade and economic matters rose from 15 to 34.[23] High-level visits between the two countries have proliferated, and both heads of government have found time, at difficult moments for each country, to visit their counterpart. Indeed, in 1994, Prime Minister Jean Chrétien went to Mexico, not to the United States or the United Kingdom, on his first official visit to another country. The significance of this gesture was not lost on Mexicans.[24]

And while press representation in the other country is still poor for both Mexico and Canada and many stereotypes persist, Mexico is now definitely "news" in Canada and vice versa. As shown by the Zapatista rising, the political assassinations of 1994, the Quebec referendum debate, and the Mexican financial crisis of late 1994-early 1995, the publics of both countries now tend to take the other seriously and follow key events with some attention.

The process of getting to know one another has, of course, had its ups and downs. The timing of the Zapatista revolt could not but place Mexico in an awkward light at precisely the moment when elements of NAFTA began to come into effect. Political instability leading up to the presidential elections of August 1994 also added much grist to the mill of those Canadians who were dubious about the advantages of the accords. The financial crisis of December 1994 did even less to help the NAFTA cause and, although Canada's share of the emergency assistance was only a small percentage of that offered by the United States, critics were vociferous about what they saw as a "bailing out" of Mexico so early in the relationship.

Worse yet, many non-governmental organizations (NGOs), especially those most concerned with human rights, stridently criticized the Mexican government. This could not fail to annoy those in Mexico City desperately trying to grapple—in what most serious observers considered a remarkably correct fashion—with legacies of the past. That not everything was ideal is not in question here. Many NGOs did not appear to understand, however, that the baby should not be thrown out with the bath water: the Canada-Mexico relationship had much to offer, although it could hardly begin with perfection on either side.[25] Thus, the first year of the new relationship did not start smoothly.

Despite this, however, Canadians did not lose faith in Mexico, and Mexicans were not excessively annoyed at the reactions of Canadians who believed the worst of the reports about their new partner. Canadian confidence in the Mexican economy was damaged severely, but few businesspeople seemed to give up entirely. Nor did Mexicans give way to despair and a sense of hopelessness in the face of these difficulties. In the end, NAFTA, while obviously much more questionable than before, was not brought tumbling down.

THE FOREIGN POLICY DIMENSION

Meanwhile, a considerable change was being effected in the foreign policy bureaucracies of both countries. Although some had called for a stronger diplomatic relationship between the two for several decades, they had largely been crying in the wilderness, as the main targets of both countries' foreign policies remained clearly the United States, followed by Europe.

Once forced to begin to negotiate with one another seriously on NAFTA, Mexican and Canadian diplomats learned quickly that they had much to gain by cooperation. In the past six years, over thirty bilateral accords have been signed. As Ambassador Castro-Valle, former minister-counsellor to Canada from Mexico and then director for North America within the Mexican Foreign Ministry, has observed:

On the bilateral level, Mexico and Canada are in a dialogue in areas as diverse as foreign policy, commerce, finance, agriculture, transport, tourism, the environment, education and culture, labour and social security, assistance to judiciaries, fighting the drugs trade, energy, mining, and fisheries, to name only some.[26]

In seminars, workshops, formal and informal discussions, and the NAFTA negotiations themselves, each learned that the other had something of value to say, and that there was much to be gained from a frank exchange of views. It became clear to both that the central reality of the focus of both countries' foreign policies was handling the bilateral U.S. relationship. While both sides knew instinctively that this must be so, many diplomats and persons in power have commented on their surprise at the extent of shared views of the implications of this state of affairs for their two countries.

As each country began to study the other's history, similar patterns emerged on key fronts, even though the experience of each was different. The role of Europe in ensuring counterpoise, non-American markets, and the possibility of multilateralist policies had clearly been crucial to both in the past. The relative failure of maintaining Europe in that role was equally clear to both.

Although the Cold War was over, memories of it were still fresh. Both sides could see how closely linked their policies were in terms of attempts to calm what each considered excessive reactions on the part of Washington to the East-West struggle. And if Central America was already fading as an important focus of both countries' policies, Cuba was not. Indeed, more than ever, the island became a point of convergence for the political statements of both foreign ministries. Cuban policy became a way for both countries to mark their divergence from any drift toward the idea of a common foreign policy for the three North American nations. And while such coherence has been difficult to maintain in the face of the growth of even more ferocious U.S. opposition to Castro than during the Cold War, Mexico City and Ottawa have done their best to remain consistent with their past policies of ideological pluralism in the hemisphere.[27]

As will be seen from the historical chapters of this book, Mexico and Canada have very different experiences with the United States. Despite poor relations and dangerous circumstances in the late 18th and entire 19th centuries, Canada's membership in the British Empire ensured its survival, and Anglo-Canadian efforts repeatedly defeated invasions in 1775-81 and 1812-14. Those victories gave Canadians at least some degree of self-assuredness in their early dealings with the Americans. They also ended the dreams of all but the keenest U.S. expansionists of incorporating the north of the continent into the United States. Canada was able not only to hold its own, but also to expand into the vast northern and northwestern regions of the hemisphere, despite the ambitions of the United States.

Mexico by itself was in no position to offer such resistance to the "Colossus of the North." Although Spanish power could long hold in check the worst elements of what was to become known as Manifest Destiny, even it was hard-pressed to do so after the War of 1812, especially as defeat in the North forced U.S. expansionists to take a closer look to the south. An independent but far from consolidated Mexican state proved powerless in the unequal struggle that followed. And such was that weakness that some Mexicans continued to hope for a Bourbon monarchy for their country—and later monarchy *tout court*—to address the domestic chaos that made the country easy prey for the forces to the north. Half of the national territory was sacrificed in humiliating wars with Texas, backed by the United States, and later with the United States itself. Far from expanding in the face of the U.S., Mexico was forced to shrink drastically. This left Mexicans with a sense of both bitterness and powerlessness where relations with the Americans were concerned.

By the mid-20th century, however, difference again seemed to be the norm in the U.S. aspect of Canadian and Mexican foreign policies. As British power waned, Canada found that, despite obvious asymmetries, close relations with the United States were not necessarily catastrophically dangerous for the country's independence and that, if watched closely, both close relations and independence could be maintained. There resulted all manner of North American defence arrangements, culminating in the North American Air Defence Command, later renamed the North American Aerospace Defence Command (NORAD), the St. Lawrence Seaway accords, extensive special economic connections, and finally the Canada-U.S. free trade area.

Mexico, meanwhile, found that it preferred a policy of maximum distancing from its northern neighbour. With the exception of World War II, links were kept at a formal minimum even though, as mentioned previously, trade and investment could not forever be denied. Nationalist policies were indeed actually designed to limit U.S. influence in the country.

Thus, Mexicans and Canadians came to the task of ensuring that they got the most out of their key U.S. relationship from very different traditions and experiences. That difference seems to have considerable potential to enliven and enrich the debate among the countries' citizens on the question of a bilateral relationship.

There is a sense of the passing of an era in both countries. The economic and even cultural context, however, has made for what must surely be seen as a muffled questioning of the stronger relationship with the United States which the two governments—and now their whole societies—have opted for in the 1990s. Fearing the impact it will have on national identity, democracy, culture, sovereignty, cost of labour, industry, or whatever else, many intellectuals have denounced the drive for what will be essentially a single North American economy. Rejection by ordinary people of the dramatic shifts in national policy implied in the new direction, however, has been muted, to say the least.

CANADA AND THE FTA QUESTION

In Canada, the main battle was not over NAFTA, but rather over the first free trade accords with the United States. This two-country Free Trade Agreement (FTA) was fought with some vigour by sectors that felt they had much to lose economically by the exposure to U.S. competition. What was noticeable to some observers, however, was the lack of traditional nationalist reaction. The asymmetries of power in North America have always kept Canadians on the *qui vive* where economic, as well as political, relations with the United States are concerned. There was in the past a well-established, almost knee-jerk reaction to what could be called excessive closeness to the United States. And despite the slow incorporation into what was in many ways already a North American economy before 1988, Canadians were loath to admit that this was inevitably to push them into the total embrace of their neighbours.

Some historians and sociologists did point to the dangers. But even they, once the debate ended and the deal was signed, appeared to accept their fate. Foreign policy analysts did, on occasion, pour scorn on the idea that such an arrangement could be anything but one of total dependence rather than of interdependence, but they also seemed to go about their business after Prime Minister Mulroney's Conservatives—the main proponents of the deal—were re-elected with a massive majority in 1989. A symbol of just how much Canada had changed was surely the very fact that it was the Progressive Conservative Party—the party of the architects of Macdonald's "National Policy" of the post-Confederation era, former arch-representatives of the Loyalist tradition in Canada, and long-time opponents of free trade and of a close connection with the United States—that now proposed the closest link ever imagined short of outright annexation.

Part of this change was economic, of course, and relates to the shifts in trade and investment discussed briefly above and that will be referred to by various authors in this work. Another part relates equally to the shifts in national self-image that had occurred since World War II and, in some senses, even before. Canada had been based on conservative, monarchical, and often Catholic principles to which had been added an agreement on moderation in order to preserve unity, both before and after Confederation. Those principles, moreover, had been reinforced by the National Policy which aimed to make the country's life lines run east-west rather than on the perhaps more natural north-south axis. Superb national railways, varied but cohesive provincial education systems, highly specific tariff arrangements, monarchical institutions, massive borrowing from the United Kingdom in myriad fields of national life, and a host of national myths—all were put in place to shore up a national system whose future depended on being different from the United States if there was to be any reason for the nation to survive.

Few Canadians are sure they would agree to all of this today. The monarchy, while revered by many, is no longer able to reinforce national unity in the way it did until the Quiet Revolution of the 1960s in Quebec and what George Grant, one of Canada's primary philosophers, has termed "the end of English-Canadian nationalism" through the loss of faith in itself at roughly the same time.[28] And while deep-rooted Canadian conservatism and resistance to those things viewed as somehow "new-fangled" and unproven are probably alive in some forms, the impact of consumerism is now very strong. So is the U.S. influence on Canadians through exposure to their arts, film, television and radio, and even the printed press and books. The loss of British cultural power is as evident as that of British economic strength. Nor do Canadians appear to have confidence in, or a willingness to pay for, institutions such as the Canadian Broadcasting Corporation and the systems of national arts subsidies that have sustained the creation of what many see as an embryonic national culture. Likewise, the national railways are a shambles and cannot in any real sense be considered the solid east-west linkages they were for nearly a century.

Catholicism, bedrock of French Canadian nationalism alongside language and culture, has been even more soundly routed, at least in this generation. If it mentions the Church and faith at all, French Canada's elite usually does so with derision or worse. And if the public is sometimes uneasy about the rejection of the Church's past role, the dominance of one, almost exclusively negative, view of this part of French Canada's heritage is undeniable. As many prominent intellectuals have pointed out, into this spiritual *vide* the once-scorned business ethic and consumerism have poured.

Thus, the very principles on which Canadian life, and indeed nationhood, have been based are no longer shared, cohesive elements of the country's political and cultural life. If one adds the extremely serious questioning by Quebec of its interest in staying in Confederation, the future becomes potentially dark indeed. It is no longer true that the provincial education systems fully act to support national unity. Nor is history given a particularly prominent place in the curriculum of any of the provinces. Survey after survey has shown that Canadians are woefully unsure of their past and its achievements.

British traditions and practices are frequently challenged—or have already been abandoned—in the face of pressures from a variety of groups. Some of what has been dropped has been replaced by truly Canadian approaches, but few would dispute that this has happened most of the time in a North America absolutely dominated by the culture, in the largest sense of the word, of the United States[29] and that, as a result, the temptation of "new approaches" has often proven to lead to mere acceptance of American ideas.

National myths have also taken a pounding, even deep into national territory. Unlike previous generations, few younger Canadians are familiar with the "militia myth," for example, which holds that the Canadian militia virtually single-handedly defeated the Americans in 1775-81 and 1812-14 and deterred further attack for a century afterward.[30] And while, no doubt, many would still vaguely understand other myths, such as the basic Canadian myth of the good Loyalist versus the bad rebel in 1776, national mythology in Canada is far weaker than that south of the border.

Thus, the sources of perceived differences between Canadians and Americans are becoming rarer while other forces propel them together—easy travel, strong trans-border family connections, cultural links, common social concerns, and so on. And while Canadian nationalists still point to many differences, these increasingly tend to be rather intellectualized and less clearly defined than in the past.[31]

It was in this context that the FTA debate was launched. The government was convinced that the Third Option was unworkable, indeed dead, and that the mounting protectionist tendencies in the United States, combined with the spread of regional free trade areas and common markets to much of the planet, meant that Canada would have to accept the inevitable and join with the United States. The reality of the debate, as several commentators remarked, was sometimes difficult to assess. After all, the actual tariff walls that were to come down were no longer very impressive. Indeed, the debate for many was more about the power of multinational enterprises to model a world to their liking than it was about free trade between a particular pair of countries. Be that as it may, the symbolism was as important as the reality. And for much of small and medium Canadian industry and business generally, the threat of increased U.S. competition was real enough.

The protection that remained in the tariff system, set up over many decades after Confederation and then taken down in succeeding years, was essentially to end altogether. And the idea of a North American economy (not, at the time, felt to include Mexico) was to apply in the future with all its promise and problems. The expression "North American society" was also to gain ground, to the horror of Canadian nationalists. And the reworking of Canadian industry was to be fraught with pain and misery for many thousands of Canadians as unemployment, plant closings, and office redundancies became the rule across much of the country, most notably in the largest and key province, Ontario.

After the shocks of readjustment had passed, the promise of better days to come was essentially accepted by the Canadian business community which had, over many decades, been weaned away from its reliance on its own tariff and protection system. And some cultural protection measures were set in place which quietened somewhat the perceptions of grave danger held in many non-business circles.

The battle for FTA acceptance was long but, in the view of many historians and political scientists, less so than expected given Canada's past and former dislike for such proposals. The relative ease with which NAFTA, and thus the expansion of the Mexican relationship, was later accepted in Canada can only be understood against this background. The main issues of North American free trade had already been fought over in the FTA debate. That instrument was the chief source of controversy in Canada because it posed the questions of Canadian sovereignty, cultural survival, and future economic prosperity.

With the FTA a reality, Canadian thinking about North American trade evolved. An expansion to a NAFTA that would include Mexico, although looked on with some apprehension in the early stages of U.S.-Mexico negotiations, was soon seen by most key players as a chance to bring at least part of Canada's preference for a multilateral approach into North American affairs.[32] Even the Liberal Party, in opposition during the FTA and NAFTA debates and loud in its criticisms of the agreements, supported the larger accord once the party came to power in late 1993. As a result of this evolution of thought, NAFTA—and indeed its expansion beyond the three initial partners—came to be seen as the best available means for handling the future of the Canada-U.S. relationship. This background needs to be recognized to explain Ottawa's interest in pushing for a relatively easy accession clause for NAFTA.

MEXICO AND NAFTA

If Canada's great debate took place early over the FTA, Mexico's was to await NAFTA. Yet the similarities between the debates in the two countries are striking and illustrate why cooperation between these two countries seems to many observers such an obvious route to take.

As mentioned, for Mexico as for Canada the crucial question was the handling of the U.S. relationship. And for Mexico, too, circumstances were closing options at a rapid rate. This was especially true for trading patterns and the percentage of the country's international commerce conducted with the United States.[33] Most worrying about this state of affairs was the thorny issue of the growth of protectionist pressures within the United States.

The immediate context, of course, was the ferocious and lengthy generalized economic crisis that had struck Mexico in 1982. Essential to the plan for recovery of Salinas de Gortari's government was the prospect of a closer connection with the United States' economy, and thus of restoring confidence in Mexico's future and economic stability: if this confidence was won, Mexico could recover; if not, prospects were far from bright.[34]

Mexico was, however, not even as well placed as Canada to carry out such discussions with the United States. Since the events of and following the Mexican Revolution of 1910-20, the country had developed an economy based on high levels of protection, tough rules governing foreign investment—especially in natural resources—and a strong dose of statism. None of this matched U.S. perceptions of what closer regional economic integration would entail.

If this was true for the economy, the political traditions of the post-revolutionary republic were even less welcoming for an initiative to tie Mexico's future to that of the United States. For decades, the country's policies had been based on a strong defence of sovereignty, especially in its relations with the United States; an independent foreign policy actively seeking to distance itself from Washington; and the continuous use of Latin American, European and, to some extent, Asian dimensions of that policy to further the attempt at distancing. Mexico City had developed policies that differed from those of the United States on major issues such as Central America, Cuba, the international economic order, interventionism, and many other points.[35]

President Salinas had the unenviable task of countering decades of this tradition and of doing so with a population that had been raised to distrust the United States and that remembered only too well the impact of past U.S. interventions. Mexicans also prided themselves on a strong national culture, the defence of which had, for decades, been a major part of Mexican domestic and foreign policy.[36]

Here again, however, the struggle to convince Mexicans to throw in the national lot with that of the United States was both shorter and smoother than had been expected by many long-time observers.[37] The economic shocks of the 1980s seem to have sufficed to cause a rapid and deep re-evaluation of the national context, even by some of the most careful of Mexicans insofar as the U.S. relationship was concerned.[38] And while many voices questioned the dominant trends, the reception reserved for such criticisms was infinitely less supportive than most would have imagined, even though Mexico's national future was in the balance.[39] As one Canadian observer put it, Mexican support for NAFTA was based on an almost desperate hope that "better times must come, that nothing could be worse than the economic situation presently facing them."[40]

Thus, despite the disapproval of a number of nationalists, intellectuals, opposition party members, some agricultural sectors, some

NGOs, and quite a number of smaller business entrepreneurs, the general impression is that the debate in Mexico was stunted and hardly serious in its implications. As the polls consistently showed, the government had convinced the bulk of public opinion that free trade was the only option available to Mexico and that it would be pursued to good effect.

It should be said that, even before the treaty "debate," the overhaul of the Mexican economy in ways appealing to the new economic orthodoxy was taking place at a rapid rate. The opening of the economy to foreign investment in general, and in a number of formerly reserved sectors in particular, was occurring despite misgivings in some nationalist circles. State intervention in the economy was lessening and was increasingly considered inadvisable. With the debt crisis, Mexico learned some harsh lessons about getting its house in an order that the World Bank and the International Monetary Fund considered proper. And the general opening up of Mexico to a variety of trends generally referred to as globalization was well under way. The positive aspects of this trend, evident in a new prosperity in the late 1980s and early 1990s, were difficult to deny even for those most opposed to taking the next step toward free trade.

Political factors also came into play. Mexico's relations with the United States were showing their traditional patchwork of good and bad. Border issues, the anti-drug effort, migration, and other highly volatile matters were far from solely favourable as the last decade of the century dawned. NAFTA offered a way for Mexico to exert more influence in Washington, or so the argument went. In any case, no options other than NAFTA were open. Here, as so often elsewhere in the post-Cold War era, a closer U.S. connection was "the only game in town."

THE CONVERGENCE OF INTERESTS

It was under these circumstances that the Canada-Mexico relationship entered high gear. As mentioned, diplomats, businesspeople, academics, and sometimes mere tourists were able to discover more in common between the two countries than ever before.

Common difficulties with asymmetries in North America were basic to these discoveries. But other factors were entering into play.

Exporters were indeed discovering that there were interesting prospects in the Mexican market. Academics in both countries were expanding their connections and fostering a perception that a healthy North American trilateral arrangement depended on a healthy bilateral one between Canada and Mexico. Otherwise, they argued, it would not address the problems of asymmetries, but merely reinforce them as both countries maintained their dependency vis-à-vis the regional giant, a situation that Edgar Dosman, a Canadian specialist on these issues and former executive director of FOCAL, has termed a "nightmare scenario."[41]

Thus, the growth of the Canadian diplomatic presence in Mexico City and elsewhere in the republic, as well as its Mexican counterpart in Ottawa and in other parts of the country, is a very healthy sign.[42] Mexico restructured its Directorate General for North America in order to create a Directorate for Canadian Affairs. And although Canada has found it more difficult to find the right bureaucratic structure to accommodate the special nature of the Mexican connection, the final government document of the major foreign policy review conducted in 1994 left no doubt about Mexico's new place in Canadian foreign policy: referring to the country as "a partner of growing importance," it said the two countries have "much to gain and learn from each other through further cooperation in NAFTA," and insisted that "this relationship holds promise over time in other spheres as well, including close cooperation in a broad range of multilateral institutions such as the UN."[43]

The 50th anniversary of Canadian-Mexican diplomatic relations in 1994 also offered an occasion to deepen the connection in these areas. Among myriad other events, the *Universidad Nacional Autónoma de México* hosted two conferences on Canadian-Mexican relations, one by the Mexican Association of Canadian Studies and the other by the university's Institute for Studies of North America. Canadian-Mexican issues also loomed larger than ever in the Conference on History of the Three Nations, in Mexico City in October 1994.

It must be understood, however, that these efforts must be sustained, given the natural U.S. dominance of North American affairs inherent in a free trade area where one country represents about 88 percent of gross community product while the other two *combined* make up only 12 percent.[44] If they are not, the pitfalls of lost opportunities, already seen in the Mexico-Canada relationship after 1944, will again become painfully obvious.[45]

IS THERE A SECURITY DIMENSION?

The question then arises as to whether there is, or indeed should be, a security dimension to Canadian-Mexican relations. Given the two countries' very different experiences in the defence field, it is hardly surprising that this question elicits very differing responses.

Arguments against such a dimension point to what is viewed as the inevitable linking of any such bilateral connection to a larger one with the United States, if only because that superpower would insist on being brought into any arrangement that mattered. This, given Mexico's extreme—and extremely understandable—concerns about sovereignty, is fraught with potential difficulties.[46]

As mentioned elsewhere in this book, Canada and Mexico view defence and security cooperation with the United States in very different ways, reflections of their historical situations vis-à-vis that country. On the Canadian side, there is still a feeling, often based on little knowledge of Mexican realities, that civil-military relations in that country are very similar to those in other Latin American states and that it is therefore best not to link oneself too closely with Mexico in this field.[47] This position was somewhat reinforced by the often bad press that the Mexican security forces received during the first widely covered Zapatista actions of January 1994.

Arguments in favour suggest that, in order to deepen the relationship between Canada and Mexico, an area of such great common interest as security should not be excluded. After all, this argument runs, Canadian and Mexican perceptions of a host of evolving traditional and non-traditional security threats are very similar. Canada and Mexico see non-proliferation issues in very similar ways and are very active in multilateral fora on related matters. Ottawa and Mexico City also view the reinforcement of peace in Central America in much the same way.[48]

The impact on regional security of a mishandling of the Cuban transition is also a matter of shared perceptions between Canada and Mexico.[49] This has been reflected in joint discussions at high diplomatic levels and by similar speaking and voting patterns on related issues in the United Nations (UN) and the Organization of American States (OAS).

Although Mexico officially considers the battle against drug trafficking as a security issue and Canada does not, this does not mean that the two countries do not still have remarkably similar views on the matter.[50] Indeed, cooperation in this area has already been the subject of accords between the two capitals. And while peacekeeping in its current forms is viewed by many in Mexico City as a threat to national sovereignty and a potentially serious intrusion in domestic affairs, these attitudes are changing in Mexico, just as sensitivity to Mexico's concerns is growing in Ottawa.

The economic security issues related to NAFTA are also not without reflections in both capitals, especially in Mexico City.[51] And the links between environmental issues and security have escaped neither country. Ottawa is well aware of Mexican views of the security implications of massive uncontrolled immigration, and there seems to be considerable commonality of views on this vexing problem.[52]

On the other hand, there are quite distinct differences on other security matters. Mexico City and Ottawa clearly do not yet feel the same way about the changes required in the current inter-American security arrangements. Nor do they view the future context and responsibilities of the Inter-American Defence Board (IADB) in the same way. Thus, today, there are many issues in the broadly defined security field that bring the countries together. But there are still fundamental issues that divide the two.

At the moment, there are few bilateral linkages in this field. The Mexican armed forces are represented in Ottawa by senior officers of both the Army and the Navy. Ottawa reciprocated in 1993 with its own defence attaché in Mexico City, the first ever in a Latin American country. In addition, a Royal Canadian Mounted Police officer acts as liaison with Mexican authorities in Mexico City.

Although there were proposals for a trilateral defence commission in North America during World War II, this idea was not acceptable to Washington, and direct Canadian-Mexican cooperation in the defence area did not begin at that time. There was, however, considerable appreciation in Canada for Mexico's role in selling the need for a united war effort to other Latin American countries and for its economic and wider political support in the conflict.[53]

Mexican natural resources, agricultural products, even human resources, were given to the Allied cause under special circumstances which received favourable Canadian attention on more than one occasion.

Instead, North American defence has remained very much a "hub and spoke" affair: Canada and the United States have a very close relationship, necessary in the East-West conflict given the geography of North America, while Mexico stands somewhat aloof although formally a member of the inter-American arrangements for hemispheric security. In that sense, while World War II was a watershed in Canada's defence relations with the United States and opened the door to close collaboration, wartime cooperation with the United States was a one-time affair for Mexico, not to be repeated, at least to the present.

It cannot have been pleasant for Mexico City to see the first initiatives for bilateral discussions of security issues, undertaken informally in Mexico City with the workshop that produced much of this book, quickly overtaken by the United States' wish to broaden the discussion to a trilateral basis. Once again, history has taught Mexico that it must move with great caution in such matters. It is perhaps telling that some Canadians were also more than a little disappointed to see a rather promising bilateral dialogue become awkward when pushed too quickly to encompass more. Only time will tell if there is room for a reinforcement of the bilateral effort.

To summarize, this chapter has attempted to show that two mutually unfamiliar countries, Canada and Mexico, have been quickly getting to know one another. This phenomenon, never before seen in Canada's relations with any country of Latin America, shows no signs of slowing down, even with the recent difficulties of 1994 and 1995.

From very different historical experiences, the two countries have come to see that they have much more in common than in the past. In the tough times at the end of this century, it has become clear to many that there is great potential in combining efforts in a number of areas of mutual concern. Economically and politically, much progress has already been made and, despite more than one major setback, the future looks promising. In security terms, other factors come into play.

The following chapters will show readers in both countries what the national experiences have been in the security area, how perceptions are changing, and whether there is potential for looking at a Mexico-Canada dialogue in the security field.

NOTES

1. A useful table of what bilateral accords exist between the two countries is provided in Edgar Dosman, "Managing Canadian-Mexican Relations in the Post-NAFTA Era," in Jean Daudelin and Edgar Dosman, eds., *Beyond Mexico* (Ottawa: Carleton University Press, 1995) 81-98.
2. This is, of course, also true for Latin America in general. See J.C.M. Ogelsby, *Gringos from the Far North: Essays in the History of Canadian-Latin American Relations, 1866-1968* (Toronto: Macmillan, 1976); James Rochlin, *Discovering the Americas: The Evolution of Canadian Foreign Policy towards Latin America* (Vancouver: University of British Columbia Press, 1994).
3. Gustavo del Castillo V., "Rediscovering the Neighbourhood: Post-NAFTA Mexican-Canadian Relations," in Daudelin and Dosman, *Beyond Mexico* 35-52, esp. 36-38.
4. For the story of the U.K.-Mexico relationship in this century, with much to learn about Canadian connections with that country, see the excellent Lorenzo Meyer, *Su Majestad Británica contra la Revolución Mexicana, 1900-1950* (Mexico: El Colegio de México, 1991). See also Ogelsby, *Gringos* 154-81.
5. See Ogelsby, *Gringos* 10-16.
6. David Winfield, "Las relaciones bilaterales Canadá-México," in Mónica Verea Campos, ed., *50 años de relaciones México-Canadá: encuentros y coincidencias* (Mexico: UNAM, 1994) 15-20.
7. Meyer, *Su Majestad* 75-87.
8. For the change with Roosevelt, see David Haglund, *Latin America and the Transformation of U.S. Strategic Thought, 1936-1940* (Albuquerque NM: University of New Mexico Press, 1985).
9. Lord Palmerston was for a while convinced there was some opportunity for this kind of coalescing. But he was disabused of this view by harsh reality. See Josefina Zoraida Vázquez and Lorenzo Meyer, *México frente a Estados Unidos: un ensayo histórico, 1776-1988* (Mexico: EFE, 1989) 51-56; Enrique Krauze, *Siglo de Caudillos: biografía política de México, 1810-1910* (Mexico: Tusquets, 1994) esp. 171-72; José Valadés, *México, Santa Anna y la guerra de Texas* (Mexico: Diana, 1979) esp. 237-39.
10. The U.S. had reacted to what it saw as British (and of course Canadian) collusion with the Confederates, and to the generally poor relations between London and Washington during and after the Civil War, by cancelling the 1854 Reciprocity Treaty between the two countries in 1866. Ogelsby, *Gringos* 6.
11. John Hilliker, *Le Ministère des affaires extérieures du Canada*, Vol. 1, *Les années de formation, 1909-1946* (Quebec: Les Presses de l'Université Laval, 1990) 4; Ogelsby, *Gringos* 10-11.

12. A review of the basic terms of reference historically for Mexican foreign policy, highly useful for Canadians wishing to understand more on this complex subject, is found in the prologue by Juan María Alponte to José Navidad González Parás, ed., *La Política exterior de México en el nuevo orden mundial* (Mexico: EFE, 1993) 11-69.
13. For a brief but excellent treatment of these years, see Stephen Randall, "Sharing a Continent: Canadian-Mexican Relations since 1945," in Daudelin and Dosman, *Beyond Mexico* 15-34.
14. This question is addressed in Héctor Aguilar Camín, *Subversiones silenciosas* (Mexico: Aguilar, 1993) 42-46.
15. See Héctor Aguilar Camín and Lorenzo Meyer, *A la sombra de la revolución mexicana* (Mexico: Cal y Arena, 1993) 232-34.
16. See Jorge Alberto Lozoya, "Mexico and the Pacific Rim: Toward a Foreign and Domestic Policy Agenda," in Riordan Roett, ed., *Mexico's External Relations in the 1990s* (Boulder CO: Lynne Rienner, 1990) 123-28. For the European dimension of this matter, see in the same volume Wolf Grabendorff, "Mexico and the European Community: Toward a New Relationship?" 95-118. And for a wider view, also from the same work, see Laurence Whitehead, "Mexico and the 'Hegemony' of the United States: Past, Present and Future" 243-59.
17. Randall, "Sharing a Continent" 24-25.
18. Rochlin, *Discovering the Americas* 136-42.
19. For discussions of Mexican and Canadian handling of the Central American wars issue, there is an excellent literature, although little of a comparative nature has so far been attempted. See Luis Herrera-Lasso, "México frente a Centroamérica: emergencia de un nuevo activismo," in Christina Eguizábal, ed., *América latina y la crisis centroamericana: en busca de una solución regional* (Buenos Aires: Grupo Editor Latinoamericano, 1988) 145-68; Mario Ojeda and René Herrera, *La política exterior de México hacia Centroamérica* (Mexico: El Colegio de México, 1983); Jack Child, *The Central American Peace Process, 1983-1991* (Boulder CO: Lynne Rienner, 1992); Liisa North, ed., *Between War and Peace in Central America: Choices for Canada* (Toronto: Between the Lines, 1990).
20. For a series of views on this matter, see Ricardo Grinspun and Maxwell Cameron, eds., *The Political Economy of North American Free Trade* (Montreal: McGill-Queen's University Press, 1993).
21. Del Castillo, "Rediscovering the Neighbourhood" 40, 35-53.
22. Expo-Canada attracted some 420 Canadian firms to the city. See the introduction to Daudelin and Dosman, *Beyond Mexico* 6.
23. Dosman, "Managing Canadian-Mexican Relations" 91.
24. Jorge Castro-Valle, "México-Canadá: hacia la consolidación de una nueva relación estratégica," in Verea Campos, *50 años* 43, 38-39.
25. See the general comments on this sort of problem in Daudelin and Dosman, *Beyond Mexico* 9-10.
26. Castro-Valle, "México-Canadá" 37. On cooperation on the new technologies front, see also James Mullin, *Breaking Through Together:*

Prospects for Canada-Latin America Partnerships in Science and Technology (Ottawa: FOCAL, 1995) esp. 9-12.

27. For a recent Canadian discussion of some of these issues, see John Kirk, *Back in Business: Canada-Cuba Relations after 50 Years* (Ottawa: FOCAL, 1995) 16-17. For Mexico, see Maby González Vilaseca, "El Tratado de Libre Comercio: implicaciones para el Caribe y Cuba," in Andrés Serbín and Joseph Tulchin, eds., *El Caribe y Cuba en la posguerra fría* (Caracas: Nueva Sociedad, 1994) 171-83.
28. See the superb (if deeply troubling for Canadians) George Grant, *Lament for a Nation* (Ottawa: Carleton University Press, 1968).
29. For a wider discussion of these issues, this time in a Latin American context, see Luis Maira, "América Latina en el sistema internacional de los años noventa," in Francisco Leal Buitrago and Juan Gabriel Tokatlian, eds., *Orden mundial y seguridad: nuevos desafíos para Colombia y América Latina* (Bogotá: Tercer Mundo, 1994) 25-47, esp. 30-32.
30. This story, like most national myths, was little more than that. Most of the fighting had been done by the British, and the role of the Royal Navy was at least as important as that of the land forces. The militia's role would have been at a second, if still vital, level of importance. See Stephen Harris, *Canadian Brass: The Making of a Professional Army, 1860-1939* (Toronto: University of Toronto Press, 1988); Ronald G. Haycock, *Sam Hughes: The Public Career of a Controversial Canadian, 1885-1916* (Waterloo ON: Wilfrid Laurier University Press, 1986).
31. See Pierre Berton, *Why We Act Like Canadians* (Toronto: McClelland and Stewart, 1985).
32. Rochlin, *Discovering the Americas* 172.
33. Gilberto Castañeda Sandoval, "Actualidad y perspectivas de las relaciones Centroamérica-México-Estados Unidos," in H. Rodrigo Jauberth Rojas, ed., *La Triangulación Centroamérica-México-Estados Unidos ¿una oportunidad para el desarrollo y la paz?* (Mexico: DEI, 1991) 167-210, esp. 181-86.
34. Jorge Chabat, "México: entre el nacionalismo y la interdependencia," in Héctor Muñoz, ed., *El Desafío de los '90: anuario de políticas exteriores latinoamericanas, 1989-1990* (Caracas: Nueva Sociedad, 1990) 45-60, esp. 49-54.
35. For examples of this, see González Parás, *La Política exterior*.
36. Rafael Tovar y de Teresa, "La cultura no se negocia ni se inscribe dentro del TLC," in Carlos Arriola, ed., *Testimonios sobre el TLC* (Mexico: Porrúa, 1994) 259-65.
37. For a highly critical view of this, see Adolfo Aguilar Zinser, "Authoritarianism and North American Free Trade: The Debate in Mexico," in Grinspun and Cameron, *The Political Economy* 209-16.
38. See the two works by Victor Flores Olea: *México entre las naciones* (Mexico: Cal y Arena, 1989) esp. 73-77, and his later "México: la afirmación de la soberanía nacional," in Arriola, *Testimonios* 259-65.
39. See the concluding points of Josefina Zoraida Vázquez, *México frente* 225-32; Jorge Castañeda, *La Casa por la ventana: México y América latina después de la guerra fría* (Mexico: Cal y Arena, 1993) 245-50.

40. Judith Adler Hellman, "Mexican Perceptions of Free Trade: Support and Opposition to NAFTA," in Grinspun and Cameron, *The Political Economy* 193-204, esp. 202-03.
41. Dosman, "Managing Canadian-Mexican Relations" 85-90.
42. Castro-Valle, "México-Canadá" 40-41.
43. Quoted from Canada, Department of Foreign Affairs and International Trade, *Canada in the World* (Ottawa: Queen's Printer, 1995) 17. For a discussion of the Canadian bureaucratic context for Mexican affairs, see Dosman, "Managing Canadian-Mexican Relations" 90-94.
44. See Ricardo Grinspun and Maxwell Cameron, "The Political Economy of North American Integration: Diverse Perspectives, Converging Criticisms," in *The Political Economy* 3-25, esp. 15-17.
45. See H.P. Klepak, "Crisis y oportunidades: dos lustros en las relaciones entre Canadá y México, 1939-1944 y 1989-1994," in Verea Campos, *50 años* 53-74.
46. See the prologue by Lorenzo Meyer to Sergio Aguayo Quezada and Bruce M. Bagley, eds., *En Busca de la seguridad perdida: aproximaciones a la seguridad nacional mexicana* (Mexico: Siglo XXI, 1990) 11-16.
47. This author does not suggest that concern is spurious. See Frederick M. Nunn, *The Time of the Generals: Latin American Professional Militarism in World Perspective* (Lincoln: University of Nebraska Press, 1992) 229-30.
48. These issues, with others connecting the two countries at a more general level, are discussed in H.P. Klepak, *What's in it for us? Canada's Relationship with Latin America* (Ottawa: FOCAL, 1994) esp. 15-17.
49. On this issue, see this author's (1994) "Medidas de confianza mutua y reacercamiento entre Cuba y los Estados Unidos," *Estudios Internacionales* 27(107): 605-17.
50. For Mexico, see Maria Celia Toro, "México y Estados Unidos: el narcotráfico como amenaza a la seguridad nacional," in Aguayo Quezada and Bagley, *En Busca* 367-87. For Canada, there is H.P. Klepak (1994) "The Impact of the International Narcotics Trade on Canada's Foreign and Security Policy," *International Journal* 49(1): 66-92.
51. Clark W. Reynolds and Stephen J. Wager, "Integración económica de México y Estados Unidos: implicaciones para la seguridad de ambos países," in Aguayo Quezada and Bagley, *En Busca* 207-30. See also Adolfo Aguilar Zinser, "El Tratado de Libre Comercio, dimensión política," in Bárbara Driscoll de Alvarado and Mónica Gambrill, eds., *El Tratado de Libre Comercio: entre el viejo y el nuevo orden* (Mexico: UNAM, 1992) 159-72, esp. 164.
52. See the three articles in Aguayo Quezada and Bagley, *En Busca*: Diana Liverman, "Seguridad y medio ambiente en México" 233-63; Richard Nuccio and Angelina Ornelas, "El Medio ambiente en México: seguridad para el futuro" 264-92; Jorge Bustamante, "México-Estados Unidos: migración indocumentada y seguridad nacional" 340-66.
53. Rochlin, *Discovering the Americas* 15-20.

2

NATIONAL SECURITY IN AND OF CANADA, 1775-1989, WITH SOME THOUGHTS ON THE CURRENT CONTEXT

LA SÉCURITÉ NATIONALE DU CANADA, 1775-1989, ET QUELQUES RÉFLEXIONS SUR LE CONTEXTE ACTUEL

H.P. Klepak

Abstract: Canada's security has evolved greatly over the years. While security seemed assured in 1759 when most of the North American continent was under British control, geopolitical reality changed in 1775 with the advent of a republican state independent of Great Britain. The main threat to Canadian security was thenceforth to come from the south, forcing Britain to reinforce its position in the north. After the War of 1812, the situation became stable, if tense, for close to a half-century. With the advent of the Civil War in the U.S., four British North American colonies joined in a Confederation to form the Dominion of Canada, since a united Canada seemed the best defence against the American giant's expansionist tendencies. But Canada's transition from a "colony" to a "dominion" also meant that it would have to assume more responsibility for its own defence.

The perception of the United States as a potential military threat to Canada declined as the two countries fought as allies in two world wars. This alliance between Washington and Ottawa was strengthened during the first two decades of the Cold War. And until the end of the Cold War in 1989, Canada cooperated, although sometimes reluctantly, in U.S.-led initiatives in the security area.

Great changes in the world geopolitical context since 1989 mean that Canada must now reevaluate threats to its security. Equally important, it must develop ways of ensuring that security, through collective or cooperative, bilateral or multilateral, regional or global, means.

Sommaire : La sécurité du Canada a grandement évolué au fil des ans. Celle-ci semblait assurée dès 1759 puisque la majeure partie du continent nord-américain était sous contrôle britannique. Toutefois, la donne géopolitique nord-américaine changea en 1775 lorsque fut institué un état républicain, indépendant de la Grande-Bretagne. La principale menace à la sécurité du Canada allait donc venir du sud; la Grande-Bretagne dût conséquemment renforcer ses assises au nord. Après la Guerre de 1812, la situation s'avéra à la fois stable et tendue pour près d'un demi-siècle. L'avènement de la Guerre civile aux États-Unis incita les quatres provinces britanniques à s'unir pour former le Dominion du Canada; un Canada uni semblait être la seule solution face à un géant aux tendances expansionnistes. Mais, le passage du Canada du statut de « colonie » à celui de « dominion » signifia que ce dernier allait dorénavant devoir assumer une plus grande part de sa propre défense.

La participation du Canada aux deux grands conflits mondiaux, aux côtés des États-Unis, effaça rapidement la perception de menace qui fut longtemps entretenue face au voisin du sud. Washington devint en fait un allié du Canada, spécialement durant les deux premières décennies de la Guerre froide. Ensuite, et jusqu'à la fin de la Guerre froide en 1989, le Canada coopéra avec les États-Unis, parfois avec réticence, dans le domaine de la sécurité.

Le contexte géopolitique global ayant grandement changé depuis 1989, le Canada doit dorénavant redéfinir les menaces à sa sécurité. Mais, il doit du même coup s'assurer des moyens lui permettant d'assurer cette sécurité, qu'elle soit collective ou coopérative, bilatérale ou muiltilatérale, régionale ou globale.

NATURAL ALLIES?

THE MERE ATTEMPT to address issues of national security over a period of more than two centuries, especially in a relatively short chapter in a single volume, requires some justification or at least background explanation. The question of the utility of such a chapter must be addressed in the context of dates. Why 1775? Why 1989?

In the spring of 1775, the disgruntlement of many of King George III's subjects in the Thirteen Colonies of southern North America grew to levels of violent protest and more than mere incipient separatist feelings. Reactions to taxation, and even to rule from London, grew increasingly intense at the same time as the strategic reasons for maintaining the link with Great Britain declined as a result of the elimination of French power in North America in the exceptionally victorious efforts of the Seven Years' War of 1756-1763.

The skirmishes at Lexington and Concord in the spring of 1775 added organized violence to the movement for reform and galvanized public opinion around the idea of outright independence. Loyalists in these colonies were soon on the defensive, both because they were less organized and energetic than the opposition and because of a tendency in the early years of the war to leave matters to the British regular armed forces which were, after all, expected to deal with violent dissension.[1]

This led to the decisive formative event in the history of modern Canada—the invasion of Quebec by pro-independence forces from the south who were bent on incorporating that colony, and by extension no doubt Newfoundland, Nova Scotia, and the Hudson's Bay Company territories of the far north, into the new political entity being formed. The rejection of both the army of invasion and the idea of belonging to the new grouping gave birth to the new British North America that would evolve into the Canada we know today. It also gave birth to the context of security planning for British North America, and then Canada, that has been with us ever since, although with enormous changes from the 1930s onward.

Why then 1989? This date was chosen as another, at least probable, watershed in the history of Canada. It was in this year that the long Cold War ended, changing dramatically the context of Canadian security planning and the country's sense of threat. It was also the year after Canada agreed to a free trade area with the United States, reversing well over a century of a National Policy that rejected any such connection as dangerous to the survival of the state and indeed of Canadian society *tout court*. Finally, it was the year when the decision was taken to join the OAS and thus end many decades of turning a deaf ear to the call to consider Canada a nation of the Americas, thereby reducing the Eurocentric vision of the country's nature and means for survival.

This chapter will attempt to give an overview of the ways in which "national" security issues related to Canada were addressed over the two centuries in question. This will involve an analysis of imperial thinking and action to ensure the defence of the evolving British North American, and then Canadian, political grouping, as well as a look at the home-grown elements of more truly national defence undertaken by Canadians themselves, first within an imperial arrangement, then in a Commonwealth context, and finally, somewhat more independently, from a North Atlantic Treaty Organization (NATO) and North American defence perspective.

THE WEIGHT OF THE PAST

To do this, it will be useful to take a quick look at the regime prevailing until 1759 and the brief essentially all-British, North American security scene of 1763-1775. The geopolitical context of Canada was clear almost from the moment the first permanent French colony was set up in 1608. New France was to be a sparsely populated series of settlements hugging the southern part of the northern half of the continent. It was based upon, and its crucial communications ran along, the St. Lawrence River, a vast *fleuve* stretching deep into the continent.

The massive hinterland of the colony was little developed, allowing for British trading, fishing, and settlement in the far northern Hudson's Bay and in Newfoundland. Defence against the resistance of native peoples was added to the need for defence against other European nations, especially the Dutch and British.[2] As settlement in the English colonies to the south grew in the 17th and 18th centuries, the French colony was completely outnumbered. Its vulnerability inspired desperate remedies.

A system of conscription was set up which called on all men from teenagers to 60-year-olds to help in colonial defence. By the time the colony actually fell to superior British (largely New England) besiegers in 1759-60, this system could provide almost

15,000 defenders out of a population of only slightly over 60,000. Until that date, climate and distance, as well as at times quite serious naval efforts on the part of Versailles, had kept most of New France safe if vulnerable.[3]

Such vulnerability called for a strategy tailored to the special needs of this truly far-flung outpost of empire. The answer was the *petite guerre,* in some ways the forerunner of later Canadian defence strategies, but more so perhaps a taste of future guerrilla warfare. In the face of overwhelming numerical superiority resting permanently with the English colonies, New France used what might be termed spoiling attacks to sow fear among the English colonists, especially those on the frontier, and make them demand defensive measures to stop such raids rather than push for offensive operations that would be almost impossible for the French to counter if they were pressed seriously and consistently. The use by the French of indigenous auxiliaries merely added to the terror that such raids spread among the English.

These were the elements of *Canadian* strategy that were evident in these early days. And, rather surprisingly, they tended to be the result of the thinking of Canadians rather than of metropolitan regular officers sent to Canada. The colony produced a number of first-rate soldiers, such as Le Moyne d'Iberville, and also contributed some limited but real strategic thought.

Carried out in winter as well as summer, these tactics became the key element in a strategy for survival that served French Canada well. Enormous efforts were made to ensure the defence of the colonies in the south against the threat from a vastly inferior power to the north. Indeed, for most of the colonial period, the population of the Thirteen Colonies outnumbered that of New France in a ratio of 20-40 to 1. Yet only overwhelming British sea power and the energy of a man like Pitt were able to prevail over the French in the Seven Years' War and deliver the colony to Britain.[4]

THE BRITISH REGIME

Overnight, the strategic picture for British North America was transformed. With no potential threat from the north or even the west, the English colonies felt secure in a way never before known. Meanwhile, relatively benign British rule, culminating in the exceptionally forward-thinking and liberal Quebec Act of 1774, secured a surprising degree of loyalty from the new French-speaking and Catholic subjects of King George acquired under the Treaty of Paris in 1763.

Fortifications that formerly marked the frontier zones were left abandoned or virtually so. Garrisons were withdrawn from most colonies. Britain's attention was turned elsewhere, largely away from defence concerns in general. But with the main issue in colonial-metropolitan relations being how to pay for the recent war, the stage was set for the rebellions of the mid-1770s.

In 1775, the very first international military moves of the rebelling colonies were directed at Canada. Stealing into Fort Ticonderoga, the famous "key to the continent," rebel forces seized the fortress and were able to use it as a base for operations which surprised the tiny garrisons and militia forces in Canada. Quebec was largely overrun in the campaign but the capital held firm, and key elements of the population were largely unimpressed by rebel propaganda calling on them to join in the war against the British and "free" themselves.[5] Indeed, on the arrival of British reinforcements in 1776, resistance found its feet, stiffened, and the rebels fled southward.

Canadian loyalty was not put to the test, despite Britain's increasing difficulties in suppressing the rebellion and in dealing with the worldwide dimensions of the war caused by the entrance of France, Spain, and the Netherlands on the revolutionary side. Revolutionary victory, and the subsequent organization of the United States as an independent country, essentially created the basis from which Canada would grow. There was now a British North America and an independent, republican North America.

The colonies in the north were to be at least as threatened under these circumstances as had been their French-speaking predecessors. Loyalists fleeing northward dramatically marked the political development of the northern colonies and brought them their first real draft of English-speaking settlers. The United States proved unable and unwilling to forget the dream of a united North America under their flag. Thus, the stage was set for difficult relations between future Canadians and Americans, tensions that were exacerbated by yet others between London and Washington.

While outright war did not break out again until 1812, crises were not infrequent and armed clashes were far from unknown.

Many of these related to British support for the Indians now living in the United States.[6] The British turned also to conscription, but it proved much less efficient than that organized by the French a half-century earlier. The war of 1812 showed that many elements of the *petite guerre* had survived, however. The superb British general, Isaac Brock, organized the seemingly hopeless defence of what is now central Canada and adopted anything but a defensive posture. His offensives not only shocked the Americans but threw them off guard and delayed the inevitable attacks of this neighbour who still boasted a population many times that of the British colonies.[7]

Through a combination of determination, sea power, climate, and distance—joined to almost incredible U.S. military incompetence—the colonies survived invasion after invasion. The Royal Navy played its part, obliging the U.S. military to look to the defence of their ports and coastal cities instead of concentrating exclusively on conquest northward. Then, starting in the summer of 1814, the defeat of Napoleon freed serious British forces to assist the colonies, and the Canadians joined the general British offensive.

The Treaty of Ghent which ended the war in 1814 re-established the status quo. From a Canadian point of view, however, victory had once again been achieved against vastly superior odds, helping to create a number of the sustaining myths of Canadian nationhood that survive to this day. The Rush-Bagot Treaty of 1817, which went some way to demilitarizing frontier relations, proved merely a cover for a vast program of British fortification of key points in the colonies and for U.S. attempts to outflank the Canadian settlements altogether while preparing for more favourable times.

Thus, relations remained, to say the least, strained. Border incidents continued and significant British garrisons remained in the colonies as they developed. The growth of Manifest Destiny as a fundamental tenet of U.S. thinking on the future of the continent augured ill for those relations, although victory in the War of 1812, combined with the exceptional explosion of British power worldwide in the early years of the *Pax Britannica*, tended to make Americans think first of targets further south rather than to the north.[8]

The settlement of the Oregon boundary issue in 1846, U.S. troubles, and then war with Mexico reduced the heat of Anglo-American controversies, although some felt a great opportunity had been missed in not bringing about an Anglo-Mexican coalition. This was not to be, however, largely as a result of Mexican political conditions.[9]

Canada's "breather" was not to last long. The U.S. Civil War of 1861-65 put enormous strains on Anglo-American relations. British trade with the secessionist South was only part of the problem, as Confederate activities based in Canada were seen by Washington as having the tacit support of both London and the Canadians.

The decline in relations would not have been as serious had it not been for the wartime establishment of a huge Federal army south of the border. Thus, a hostile government in the U.S. controlled vast armed forces, more than capable of dealing with the Canadian militia and the small, albeit greatly reinforced, British garrison in the North American colonies.

This dark context had an unexpected result. Under prodding from London, and under direct threat like none seen since 1814, the four British North American colonies (today's Ontario, Quebec, Nova Scotia, and New Brunswick) joined in a Confederation in 1867 under the highly original name of the "Dominion of Canada." A direct result of shared perceptions of military and wider threat from the south, the new country was to have vast responsibilities—in many ways virtually those of an independent state—although the new Dominion remained part of the British Empire.

While defence was to be one of these responsibilities, no one was long under any illusions about the extent to which the new country could provide fully for its own security. Canada was, it is often forgotten, the only part of the vast Empire that shared a land frontier with a great power. For a seafaring Empire, this was of huge import as it meant that the country was more vulnerable to attack than perhaps any other part of the political grouping that united nearly a quarter of the globe.[10]

British garrisons rather reluctantly remained in central Canada for another four years after Confederation, and indeed stayed on well into the 20th century in the important imperial naval harbours of Halifax, Nova Scotia and Esquimalt, British Columbia. The Canadian Army grew very slowly, based primarily on its militia experience (indeed, even the permanent force was termed "Militia"), and was vitally dependent on Britain. Indeed, this dependence probably grew as the force was obliged to become more serious when British regulars were withdrawn. But the process was long and fraught with problems, as budgetary and command and control obstacles hamstrung serious progress at every turn.[11]

It must also be said that Canadian strategic thinking, held back logically enough under imperial circumstances by colonial status, improved only slightly in the first decades of the Dominion. While Canadian defence issues were occasionally debated in specialized militia publications and one or two keen and incisive writers emerged, discussions generally remained at a very basic level and materials published tended to be mostly copies of imperial or foreign articles. The tiny size of the Permanent Militia, its continuing essentially colonial links with the metropolis, and the anti-intellectual biases of such a small force were important influences in stymieing the development of such thinking.[12] Indeed, even in the purportedly academic and elite halls of the Royal Military College, subjects such as military history, strategy, or international relations had little place.[13]

Canadians seemed to understand instinctively that the only real and immediate threat to their existence as a new nation came from the United States. Although a brief war scare with Russia blew up in 1877, more serious threats arose with the United States over the Fenian Raids in the late 1860s and early 1870s. A particularly close call occurred with the Venezuela Crisis of 1895. Flare-ups over the boundaries of British Columbia and Yukon also coloured relations at century's end. While imperial membership could help bring these crises closer to Canada, that same membership was the only possible guarantee of survival.

Despite the traditions of the *petite guerre* and the myths of militia dominance in the war of 1812, few serious observers felt the Canadians had a chance on their own if war came with the United States when that country reached true world power status at the end of the century. Modern warfare seemed to offer little hope for national defence, and it was fortunate for Canada that U.S. Congressional pressures kept the strength of the army and navy well below what the burgeoning wealth and population of the United States could now afford.

Membership in the Empire, however, meant that the still-overwhelming strength of the Royal Navy would be available for Canada's defence in case of war and that raiding of American ports would still be feasible as a way of keeping U.S. forces tied down at home. Equally, the growth of the Empire, and particularly of its Indian and white colonial military forces, meant that, in a future war, Canada might be able to look to the support of significant land forces from Australia, New Zealand, South Africa, Newfoundland, India, and perhaps others, in addition to those from the mother country. Little wonder then that Canadian defence planning assumed that, during the first months of any war, the militia would attempt to hold on until major forces could be organized and dispatched from other parts of the Empire.

Conservatives, usually more loyal to the Empire than Liberals, found all this most reassuring. But even less ardent imperialists, such as the Liberals, usually understood that the national defence of a country like Canada could rest on no other basis. When war came in South Africa in 1899, even as staunch an autonomist as Prime Minister Sir Wilfrid Laurier knew that Canada would have to do something for the Empire's war effort if it wished to have the favour returned in a more serious future war with the United States.[14] Even if this was more lip-service than deep conviction, public pressure to help out in what many saw as the Empire's defence was great and irresistible; almost inevitably the strategic argument supporting it was the need to pay one's dues if one wished to have the benefits of imperial membership and support in time of crisis.

In the years between the end of the Boer War in 1902 and the outbreak of World War I in 1914, improvements in the militia were many. At the same time, Canadian defence arrangements were increasingly based on the fundamental requirement to send an expeditionary force to Europe to fight alongside the British in time of war.

In the midst of great controversy, a Royal Canadian Navy (RCN) was created. It was opposed by imperialist sentiment which considered it to be a foolish and hurtful division of the essential pillar of the defence of the whole Empire—the Navy—and by isolationists who saw it as an expensive move that brought Canada closer to European entanglements and potential conflicts.[15] For the government it was certainly a way to profit from Canadian nationalist sentiment while making a more visible contribution to imperial defence.

Strategic thinking was then very much part of an imperial whole in which separate Canadian thinking was essentially sidelined. During these years, military publications multiplied and their subscriptions increased dramatically, but the number of articles by Canadians on purely Canadian defence subjects did not. Canada would fight, and think about its defence, in imperial terms.

War in 1914 confirmed this. The Dominion's contribution to the Allied cause was out of all proportion to its population. Some 60,000 Canadians fell in action and ten times that number were mobilized. With few exceptions, these personnel were recruited through voluntary enrolment, although conscription was brought to bear in 1917 in order to replace the appalling casualties suffered.

At the same time, this contribution to the Empire spawned the growth of Canadian nationalism and, given the nature of warfare on the Western Front, fed a growing questioning of British leadership of the Empire. The great battle of Vimy Ridge, fought at Easter 1917, has been called, in this context, the coming of age of the Dominion. The Canadians fought essentially alone in this battle, following their own plan and with little support from anyone. The nature of the victory, at a place where both British and French arms had failed before, ensured an explosion of national pride that was to prove long lasting.

Thus, the inter-war years were marked by a general distancing of Canadian defence from the imperial context. And while other prime ministers did not share his zeal in this area, the governments of William Lyon Mackenzie King, which dominated the two decades of peace, felt that defence and international relations in general were far from serious concerns and could be definitely placed on a back burner. The militia atrophied, the RCN came close to total disbandment, and the new Royal Canadian Air Force (RCAF) was kept alive largely because it could find other useful things to do in peacetime, such as mapping the North. And while the Depression did not help Canadian defence, government distrust and indifference were mainly responsible for destroying the work done during World War I to build Canadian armed forces of great value.

During the inter-war years, the perception of the United States as a potential military threat to Canada also declined. The two countries had been allies in the last part of World War I, and new rail and road links were bringing the two closer within North America. And while British trade and investment remained more important than American to Canada, the United States loomed ever larger as both a trading partner and a source of capital for the Dominion.

Oddly, these difficult times saw the growth of greater Canadian strategic and tactical thinking than had been the case perhaps for centuries. Debates in the letters and articles of the *Canadian Defence Quarterly* were often first-class. And headquarters in Ottawa held on to quite original—if sometimes seemingly foolhardy—ideas as the bases of plans that were, if nothing else, distinctly Canadian and that owed little or nothing to British models.[16]

Canada held aloof from anything like firm commitments both to Britain and to the League of Nations. Its policies were close to isolationist, and the blood loss of World War I reinforced the rampant pacifism of the time by providing votes for parties trying to outbid themselves to cut defence budgets and engagements overseas. Indeed, British policies of appeasement of the dictators were fully backed, not to say loudly applauded, by King and his crucial adviser O.D. Skelton during the crucial years of the mid-1930s.[17]

By the last years of the peace, however, King seemed to be having second thoughts about pinning his hopes on distance as a means of keeping Canada out of a war. Like the armed forces staffs, he was well aware that, in the event of a major conflict, Canadian public opinion would not tolerate the United Kingdom being in danger while Canada did nothing to help. Thus, reluctantly, Canadian planning and preparations in concert with the Commonwealth began in the context of yet another war.[18]

The war saw many elements of the Commonwealth relationship strengthened. The long stay of much of the Canadian Army in Britain led to a direct connection at many levels.[19] Yet the elements of fundamental change were there for all to see. The blow to British power and influence provided by the war was immense and decisive. The country, and its Empire and Commonwealth, would come out of the war weakened beyond recuperation, and the long decline of British strength would quicken.

The RCN, a bastion of British influence in the Canadian armed forces, was obliged by the nature of the war, British losses, and relative strength compared to the Americans, as well as by geography, to work ever more closely with the United States Navy. The RCAF began to work with its infinitely more powerful U.S. counterpart in North American air defence and cooperation. The Canadian Army, while in some ways immune to such influences and more closely tied into Commonwealth arrangements, could see the writing on the wall when the decision was made for the national contribution to the final campaign against Japan to be essentially under U.S. command, to the point that many U.S. procedures and even some elements of uniforms, armament, and equipment were adopted.[20]

All this cooperation stemmed from a total change in Canadian thinking about the United States, one already visible but that moved into high gear as war approached, especially when the fall of France, the Low Countries, Norway, and Denmark in the spring of 1940 brought about a need for a common approach to the defence of North America. The fear that Britain itself might actually surrender, or at least be invaded, also played a role. In 1938, the first meetings of Canadian and American chiefs of staff occurred. In August of that year, President Roosevelt spoke at Queen's University in Kingston, Ontario and promised that his country "would not stand idly by if domination of Canadian soil is threatened by any other empire." This occurred in the same year as Canadian military studies were being carried out to find ways of avoiding acquisition by the American empire.[21]

When the president and the prime minister met at Ogdensburg, New York in August 1940, during the darkest period of Britain's "finest hour," bilateral agreements proliferated. A Permanent Joint Board on Defence was set up and, in a definitive act of linkage with its former long-standing enemy, Canada acknowledged its North American status where security was concerned. Only U.S. concerns about British sensibilities to a divided imperial effort in the war kept this linkage from being even stronger.

Thus, despite the exceptional Canadian war effort and participation in many subsequent campaigns alongside the British, the writing was on the wall. When the war ended, Britain was a world power only *par courtoisie* and was faced immediately with the beginnings of the decolonization period which was to see it shorn first of the jewel of the Empire—India—and then of the rest. The Commonwealth increasingly became merely a club of countries with a limited common history. And while attachment to the Crown remained strong and many in the armed services fought to stem the tide of Americanization, the ability to convert that sentiment into security cooperation proved slight.[22]

Canada, fresh from this second great conflict of the century and anxious to avoid another, threw itself heart and soul into the development of the UN, perhaps remembering that its role in the League had opened rather than closed the door to war. Mackenzie King, seconded by Louis St. Laurent and his deputy minister Norman Robertson at the Department of External Affairs, was by now a champion of internationalism, an evolution helped by changes in French Canada's mood over commitments overseas.

The Soviet veto and the beginnings of the Cold War meant, however, that despite Ottawa's preferences for the global organization, other arrangements would have to be made if collective security was to work. The North Atlantic Treaty offered Canada both a way out of the seeming impasse of U.S. domination and a means of contributing to block what was seen as the expansionist policies of the Soviet Union. An alliance in which multilateralism and democracy were the rule, in which both mother countries were members as well as the United States, seemed tailor-made for a country such as Canada, anxious to cooperate in defence matters with the United States but also worried about being completely swamped in the evolving if asymmetrical relationship.

Thus, NATO was initiated as a means to deter Soviet adventurism in Europe. But "hot war" was to co-exist with cold as the Korean War broke out in 1950. Canada was to send a brigade to the conflict and to dispatch another to reinforce Allied deployments in Europe in case of attack there. This was only possible because, in line with its new status acquired during the World War II, Canada had begun in 1947 to establish a serious military posture, no longer based on the militia but on a regular force of professional sailors, airmen, and soldiers. With Britain no longer willing or able to defend Canada, it was obvious to all parties that a major effort was necessary if Canada was to be taken seriously by the world, and particularly by its all-powerful neighbour.

The RCN thus became a significant peacetime blue-water force, specializing in the escort role. The RCAF took on interceptor and air transport duties in keeping with its roles in Europe and its increasing links with the United States Air Force (USAF) in continental air defence. And the Canadian Army became largely full-time, with significant armour, artillery, and infantry capabilities available at all times. All three armed services learned from Korea, however, that although they fought alongside the British once again, the Americans were now running the show; this would simply have to be accepted.

For Canada, the long Cold War was divided into distinct periods for security affairs. In the 1950s and 1960s, there was broad agreement on the need for a major contribution to NATO and Western defence in keeping with Canada's status in the world and its geopolitical situation. With the advent of Pierre Trudeau as prime minister in 1968, however, that context began to change. The new head of government was far from convinced of the reality of the Soviet threat. He also felt that Ottawa should be paying more attention to domestic than to foreign affairs. Lastly, he felt that Europe was rich enough to defend itself without Canadian help.

The result was a massive slashing of the Canadian Forces, a move that rapidly followed the disastrous 1968 unification of the three armed services. Morale within the Forces hit rock bottom, affected no doubt as much by the issue of a common uniform—of undistinguished cut, to say the least—as by an actual decline in the forces' strength. Attempts to hold onto personnel mainly took the form of major increases in pay, but even then, almost all observers agreed, many of the best simply gave up and left the service.

The Canadian Forces in Europe, which arguably provided the heaviest and best brigade group in the British Army of the Rhine, as well as six air squadrons to the support of NATO's Central Front, were cut in half, and the land elements were moved from the much exposed and key north to a reserve position in the south. Several famous regiments were disbanded, the country's only aircraft carrier was sold for scrap, and a wide range of military specializations were abandoned. The defence budget was subsequently slashed further; when added to the salary increases of all ranks, this meant that there was virtually nothing left for equipment sorely needed to keep up in the rapidly evolving conventional arms field.

This situation prevailed until the late 1970s, when other factors began to impinge on Mr. Trudeau's policy. As a nationalist, the prime minister wished to distance the country from the United States which, he felt, played far too great a role in Canadian life and was threatening national sovereignty. A number of measures were taken to reduce this dependence, including visits to the Soviet Union, a closer connection with Cuba, more vocal opposition to the Vietnam War, and the setting up of a review board to oversee foreign takeovers of Canadian industries. More dramatic still, the government declared its intention of achieving a Third Option for Canada. Taking further integration with the United States as one option and a laissez-faire approach as the second, Mr. Trudeau suggested that Canada should aim at a third option: a diversification of all kinds of links, principally trade, away from the United States and toward the European Community, Japan, and Latin America.

An attempt was made to obtain a "contractual link" with the European Economic Community (EEC) and negotiations were taken seriously. But Canadian unwillingness to shoulder more of the defence burden of NATO proved a serious stumbling block to progress. The Germans, in particular, felt that Canadian claims to special status with the Community should be backed up by a greater willingness to help in Western defence than the Trudeau government had shown to date. This, added to U.S. and U.K. pressures in the same vein, resulted in slightly increased defence spending by the end of the decade.

The election of Brian Mulroney's Conservatives in 1984 took place in the context of heavy criticism of the Liberals for starving the Forces and not favouring NATO. After the "Shamrock Summit" between U.S. President Ronald Reagan and Prime Minister Mulroney later that year, the Mulroney government seemed set on major efforts in the defence area. The 1987 White Paper by Defence Minister Perrin Beatty seemed to prove this. But economic reality soon set in, and the government was forced into major austerity measures that hit defence plans hard. Few of the major programs survived, and plans for a nuclear powered submarine force, able finally to project Canadian naval power into the country's cold Arctic seas, were among the first to go. At the same time, Mulroney abandoned any dreams of a Third Option, moving quickly to negotiate a free trade area with the United States, announcing in late 1989 his intention of joining the OAS, and soon thereafter negotiating with the United States and Mexico the expansion of the Canadian-U.S. free trade area to include Mexico.

Thus, the end of the 1980s saw a reversal of a number of the main tenets of Canadian strategic thought dating back to Confederation and indeed beyond. Free trade would largely erase the measures in existence for many decades that aimed at countering the effects of geography and making Canadian commerce (and interest) flow east-west rather than north-south. Joining the OAS would mean deserting the Eurocentric counterpoise to U.S. power that had served as the bedrock of Canadian policy for centuries and accepting once and for all that Canada was, in fact, a fully North American nation. It is no accident that these events occurred while the Cold War was ending and as the nature of the international strategic context was once again changing dramatically.

THE NEW STRATEGIC CONTEXT FOR CANADA

Students of international relations are rightly skeptical when the subject of massive change in world politics is touted. Change is the stuff of international affairs—as indeed of politics in general—and the argument is too often made that, somehow, all has changed and that the world is transformed. Nonetheless, there is general agreement that there are moments in history when there is such a transformation. The fall of Rome in 476 A.D., the capture of Constantinople by the Turks in 1453, the French Revolution of 1789, the end of the old order in 1914, the end of a truly multipolar world in 1945-47—few would disagree that these are key points in world history. Debate would rage, however, over events such as the arrival of Columbus in 1492, the end of Hapsburg hegemony at Rocroi in 1659, German unification in 1871, and the Russian Revolution of 1917.

For these reasons, one is obliged to be cautious when suggesting that the end of the Cold War was a decisive moment that dramatically changed the nature of international relations as known in recent decades. As is only too obvious, the end of bipolar rivalry has not ushered in the period of peace so long dreamt of in the West. Indeed, a "new world order" promising peace and prosperity has so far seemed to be able to provide only increased conflict and economic depression. Notwithstanding many transnational trends, the state remains the principal and essential pillar of the international system. And despite suggestions to the contrary, national interest still rules supreme in foreign policy considerations. Power remains the key to influence in other capitals even if economic rather than either military or ideological punch seems more visible at the moment. There are still only two truly massive nuclear powers and the future of the weaker of the two is far from certain. Thus, it is clear that not everything has changed in international relations; many crucial constants remain.

This being said, it is nonetheless true that the post-Cold War era is marked by truly vast changes on the international scene, some of which seem critical for Canada.

Given the country's geostrategic situation, the most significant change is, of course, the massive shift in relative power to the United States. While there is great debate as to whether the present period is a unipolar *moment* or a unipolar *era,* and while there is obviously much need for nuance about the degree to which the United States is the key, or even a major, influence in the various regions of the world, there is much less need for discussion about the fact that the present is dominated by one state.[23]

The defeat and then disappearance of the Soviet Union and the Warsaw Pact mark the first time since the destruction of Carthage in 146 B.C. that something like a bipolar era has ended with the absolute victory of one side in its struggle with the other and the elimination of the loser from *world* power status—indeed, its elimination altogether as the state it formerly was.[24] From worldwide competition at the political, economic, ideological, and military levels the United States and its allies have emerged victorious and unchallenged. That victory leaves the United States as the only nation capable of power projection around the globe. Equally, it leaves the United States as the only nation that, despite severe economic and social problems, can be and usually is a key player in all the aspects of international relations—political, economic, military, cultural, and ideological.

This is not to suggest that there are no potential competitors for first place in international relations. The critical importance of economic considerations in these troubled times makes two giant economic powers obvious possible aspirants to such a position. Both Japan and the new united Germany have arguably stronger economies than the United States, despite the fact that the latter is still the largest single economy in the world. Tokyo and Bonn/Berlin offer real scope for future competition for world leadership, especially if Germany becomes the effective leader of a European bloc of immense power and potential. But neither of these countries is in any real way tempted at present by world leadership or the sacrifices a bid for such status would require. Both, for sound historical, cultural, political, and even economic reasons, eschew a strong policy thrust aimed at world power status. While enjoying the benefits of vast economic clout, neither seems interested in engaging in the political effort, the financial cost, or especially the military effort needed to transform it into such an international power. This is especially true as their priorities are so firmly viewed as, in the one case, Central and Eastern European, and in the other, Asian.[25]

This situation may not last long, however, suggesting that the unipolar period will be short. But to date, Tokyo's and Bonn's disinclination, coupled with Washington's extremely smooth handling of issues of vital concern to those two capitals, has served to dampen any calls for major change in the world political-military balance. Thorny trade and other issues may eventually change this state of affairs, of course, and thus the dynamics of the relationship are crucial to the future of international relations.

For the present, then, and rather to its surprise, the United States finds itself the key country of the international system, sought after by virtually all, crucial in the design of the post-Cold War order, the only real military pillar of any structure that is likely to result because of its unique ability to project vast military power anywhere in the world, and a cultural influence *sans pareil*. Many in the United States may not like this new status, and the current debate over the welcome Americans should reserve for it is real and important, but the reality of the situation can scarcely be questioned.[26]

The next enormous change in international relations of special interest to Canada, and one closely related to the first, is the drive for a new international security order based on some kind of loosely defined collective security regime. During the past half-decade, the "system" has had as its base the Charter of the UN, since that organization has in recent years regained the confidence of the dominant Western powers and most importantly of the United States.

The UN is undertaking many more operations classified by the public, if not by skeptical academics and military officers, as "peacekeeping." These activities are not merely larger, more numerous, more complicated, and more costly than those in the past, but they also tend to be much more intrusive. This is because former restrictions on the use of international military force within the borders of countries whose situations do not clearly threaten international peace and stability now seem to be open to greater questioning, while insistence on the absolute sovereignty of states seem to have weakened. This could be due either to humanitarian concerns or to a propensity to consider nations in which intervention is being contemplated as having ceased to exist as functioning political entities.

The collective security situation that this implies cannot be discussed in detail here. Suffice it to say that, given the position of the United States and the West after the end of the Cold War and the increasingly intrusive nature of such "peacekeeping," much of the Third World views the new collective security arrangements as little more than a smoke screen for a new imperialism.[27]

A further dramatic trend in the post-Cold War world has been the acceleration of the creation of economic blocs, some aiming at free trade among their members, some at common markets, all at some kind of greater community in the difficult economic times through which most countries are passing. While the General Agreement on Tariffs and Trade (GATT) and the new World Trade Organization (WTO) have valiantly attempted to keep these regional and other arrangements from derailing the drive for truly international free trade—and have had some considerable successes to their credit—the reality is that states have tended to see inclusion in a free trade area as a minimum step to protect themselves from such areas organized elsewhere. Even for a country as powerful as the United States, such moves have appeared advisable. For smaller states such as Canada and Mexico, they have seemed vital for survival.[28]

IMPLICATIONS OF THESE TRENDS FOR CANADA

These trends have already had an enormous and varied impact on Canada. While much of it predates the end of the Cold War, it has been intensified since 1989. Inextricably linked, these trends constitute, in the view of the author, the most dramatic challenges for peacetime survival and prosperity that Canada has ever known. Something other than merely budget-driven analysis is required to address them.

As previously mentioned, their most direct impact must be the massive shift in relative power to the United States in the wake of Soviet collapse. It would be foolish to speak of Moscow as having played for Canada the role of counterpoise to the United States in the Cold War years. While "red scares" were rarely taken very seriously on this side of the border, it is nonetheless true that Canadians did consistently support governments that viewed the Soviet threat (at least of miscalculation) as serious and requiring a collective response. Canadians cooperated with Americans in setting up an integrated defence system for North America (especially in the air), and on many issues they came to share virtually common perceptions of threat with their southern neighbours.

It was nonetheless true that the Soviet threat generated an almost tailor-made alliance for Canada in the form of NATO, which allowed defence relations with the United States to be placed largely in the context of the greatly favoured multilateral approach to foreign policy. In that sense, the almost terrifying asymmetries of North American bilateralism were avoided for decades although, in the wake of U.S. triumphalism and British decline in the mid-1940s, they had appeared to be all too near. NATO provided an almost ideal table at which many issues could be discussed without being put on a rightfully much-feared bilateral basis where power differentials could hardly fail to crown the efforts of the stronger party.

However dangerous and uncomfortable the Cold War was for Canada, these elements of its security context were remarkably reassuring. That easy world has disappeared. Instead, Canada, perhaps forgetting that it was not in NATO so much to help the Europeans as to help itself, has allowed its defence links with the old continent (and the "old countries") to decline dramatically. To all intents and purposes out of Europe except for temporary UN-sponsored operations in the former Yugoslavia, the Canadian Forces have received a major blow to both their French and British military connections in the form of the end of the Canadian deployment in Germany.[29] And since the bulk of Canada's Commonwealth military linkages have for decades been with Britain through NATO, the withdrawal will almost certainly have a massive "continentalizing" effect on the Canadian Forces once the current level of international peacekeeping tasks has been reduced.[30]

This is not to suggest that there were not strong, perhaps all-powerful, economic reasons for the withdrawal, but to emphasize that the importance of this move—a massive one in terms of the sustainability of "multilateralized" defence relations with the United States—must not be downplayed and that its impact must be assessed in order for its disadvantages to be overcome.

The counterpoise provided by NATO, considered virtually essential for the country in the wake of British decline, can no longer be regarded as viable. The substantive security links with the Europeans are simply too minor for this to be a cohesive policy priority. While there is every possibility of keeping formal links through the North Atlantic Cooperation Council (NACC), the Organization on Security and Cooperation in Europe (OSCE), and through NATO itself, they can hardly be seen as "defining" Canada's multilateral security arrangements as they did in the past. Thus, in this sense, the shattering effect of the arrival of the United States as a superpower in the mid-1940s and Britain's steady disappearance as a power on the world stage can no longer be avoided by this country.[31] For the first time in Canadian history, there does not appear to be any obvious or effective counterpoise, or even a multilateral cadre, into which to fit national defence thought and activity.

This lack is occurring at a moment of great national self-questioning which, while not new in Canada's history, is nonetheless more powerful and more portentous than ever before. Few would disagree with Renan's suggestion that countries exist because they are different from one another. And Canadians have for long understood that they would be paying higher taxes and making all sorts of other sacrifices to sustain and develop those differences in the face of enormous cultural pressure from south of the border.

These differences were traditionally those of monarchy, system of government, language (for part of the population), religion, and a common rejection of the "pale copy" prospect so worrying to former Prime Minister Lester B. Pearson. Reinforcing measures were considered to be national (and for a long time, imperial) protective tariffs, a magnificent system of railways linking most of the country, a broadcasting service whose raison d'être was cultural defence, and a self-assured if divided education system sustaining Canadian unity. One does not have to be a prophet of doom to notice that little of this structure of national difference or cultural defence is still in place and capable of facing what may be the most powerful unifying and globalizing cultural influence since Rome—the United States.[32] Nor is national unity a given. Instead, cleavages of all kinds strike at the very survival of the state.

The new UN-oriented and vaguely "collective" security system now developing also has great potential for impact on Canada, as has already been seen in the unprecedented deployment of the Canadian Forces on related missions in recent years. The system is strongly related to U.S. power in two ways. First, U.S. influence in the United Nations, and especially in the Security Council, is currently quite extraordinary, no doubt reflecting the special circumstances discussed above. Indeed, for many, the organization has become simply a branch of Washington's foreign policy. Second, the overwhelming military power of the United States, combined with the relative decline of other major powers, makes major interventions dependent on U.S. logistical, and often stronger, support. Only Washington can provide these vital elements for large-scale interventions, for three reasons: the reduction in French and British strategic airlift, sealift, and amphibious forces, strike aircraft, and easily deployable "bayonet" strength; Germany's and Japan's unwillingness to involve themselves substantively in international military operations; and the end of Russia's pretensions to worldwide power.

Little wonder then that, whether in Haiti, Iraq, Somalia, Libya, North Korea, or even the Balkans, the world now looks to the United States for military, and usually also for political, leadership in almost all crises. The Americans have the capability to replace words with action in a way that is truly unique in today's world, even though they may decide not to do so when they consider that it will not serve their best interests. More surprising still is the willingness with which former great powers stand by and let the United States take the lead. Future historians may well consider the expectation that U.S. forces would do the real fighting in Somalia, while others attended to garrisoning duties, a breathtaking change in national self-perception among other significant powers. In other cases, "token" representation seems to have replaced real burden-sharing, a condition that will in future surely be fraught with problems.[33]

Canada, despite its exceptional efforts in support of the new "peacekeeping" initiatives, has been ill placed to do much of what it might have wished. With only six normally-constituted regular battalions and redistributed elements of the former Airborne Regiment (plus armour and artillery) available for duty, and with the normal need for rotation, Ottawa has been hamstrung in its ability to answer UN (or other) requests for bayonet strength. Instead, National Defence Headquarters have been reduced to accepting mostly requests for specialist forces (engineers, signallers, logistics) which, while enormously useful, are not always quite the same thing. Equally, strike capabilities in the air force and naval platforms have not always been ready to go, although current fleet improvements are quite impressive.

Perhaps most telling is Canadian dependence on others, particularly the United States, for airlift, that element of military power so essential in operations for deployment and withdrawal. While Canada is far from alone in this, its deficiency is all too often apparent because of the country's high level of involvement in these operations.[34]

The political elements of this new context are also potentially embarrassing. The legitimacy Canada brings to UN operations in the Third World (Central America, Iraq, Haiti, Western Sahara) comes from its being both the most "internationally linked" country in the world (alone a member of *la Francophonie,* the Commonwealth, the G-7, NATO, NORAD, the OAS, etc.) and a country concerned with the establishment of justice as the best means to address the problem of peace and war in the modern world. The combined problems of "continentalization" of Ottawa's linkages and of its defence priorities, as well as the increasing Third World perception of the UN as a cover for U.S. or Western objectives worldwide, threaten not only the Canadian role in such operations, but also the very legitimacy that Canada, sometimes almost alone, confers on such activities.

Finally, for Canada, there is the vexing problem of "blocism." One of the difficulties in coming to grips with what is happening on the world scene today is the seeming concurrent unipolarity of many political and military contexts and the obvious economic trends toward multipolarity. Three main trade blocs seem to be developing despite the WTO and GATT. They are, of course, NAFTA (perhaps to be expanded to a WHFTA—a Western Hemisphere Free Trade Area), centred around the U.S. economic giant; Asian arrangements centred around the Japanese economic powerhouse; and the European Union (EU), represented most forcefully by Germany, but much less dominated by it than Asia is by Japan or North America by the United States.

Ottawa has done everything possible to halt the development of these blocs, for reasons deeply grounded in Canadian history. Ever since Macdonald, the Canadian nightmare has been that of being forced to choose between European cultural and political linkages and those of the Americas. This has, in academic terms, been the well-known theme of John Holmes, James Eayrs, and Rod Byers in the field of strategic studies. Canadian support for GATT, and the decision to find a Third Option to North American integration in increased links with Europe, Latin America and Asia, have been the main thrusts of economic policy aimed at avoiding the nightmare choice.

The FTA with the United States must be seen within this national experience. The failure of the Third Option initiative, combined with the less than steady progress of GATT, provided stark evidence of the increasing unlikelihood of avoiding unpleasant choices. Inexorably, the United States' portion of total Canadian trade increased.[35] The decision to move toward an FTA meant the acceptance of the option of further integration with the United States as the only way to avoid U.S. protectionist dangers and find a bloc that Canada could join in a world seemingly determined to move in the direction of such groupings.

The dynamism of the Asian "new tigers" has meant that what might have been even greater U.S. domination of Canadian trading patterns has been avoided. And Latin America, especially in the context of NAFTA and perhaps a WHFTA, offers great hope for further diversification. But the realities of Canada's dependence on the United States can no longer be avoided. Even with both Mexico and Canada in NAFTA, they represent only 12 percent of the bloc's gross economic product.[36] Washington's position in the bloc is thus exceptional in terms of relative power and dwarfs that of either Tokyo in Asia or Bonn/Berlin in Europe.

Here, there is some, if little, hope for counterpoise useful to Ottawa. Asian countries have made painfully clear their lack of interest in Canadian political and security linkages where, rhetoric notwithstanding, what sense of community there is does not really include Canada. The Americas, no doubt uniquely, offer a community in which Canada is both welcome and felt (by Latin America and the United States, although less often by Canadians) to belong automatically as a result of geography, history, and culture. *Faute de mieux,* this may end up being the only community that Canada can join—politically, economically, and culturally. But the difficulties should not be underestimated. Canada naturally prefers potential counterpoises that are strong, not weak; not only is Latin America weak, but the Americas include the very country to which Canada seeks a counterpoise. This is little comfort after a tradition of Bourbon France, the

British Empire, or even NATO. In addition, although Latin America is the only area where Canadian non-extractive exports are growing relative to extractive (a much sought-after situation that is far from the case in Asia, Europe or the United States), the fact remains that trade with this region has so far shown less increase in real growth than in potential.[37] Canadian investment in the area is no doubt considerable, and immigration from the region in recent years has established an undoubted linkage, but it is easy to exaggerate the extent to which Canada feels itself "American".[38]

All this may be far away. The links with Europe have not disappeared, although they seem to be slipping at a very rapid rate as a result of policies on both sides of the Atlantic. Some, particularly in Western Canada, continue to hope that a more community-based concept will eventually predominate in relations with Asia. Still others see this hemisphere as the only conceivable bloc allowing Canada to find a real political, economic, cultural, and security community, and indeed the only one interested in even discussing this.[39] These trends are too new to offer much certainty about the way things will eventually move. They are, however, disquieting and clamour for more serious consideration of the pros and cons of the various options that may offer themselves.

This is surely where Mexico comes in from a Canadian point of view. Mexico is, as Ambassador Castro-Valle has so strongly argued, as natural an ally for Canada as Canada is for Mexico. In the present context, they may offer each other more than either has been inclined to consider.

NOTES

1. For a discussion of the Loyalist cause during the American Revolution, see Mary Beth Norton, *The British-Americans* (Boston: Little Brown, 1972).
2. For the wars with indigenous peoples, see George F. Stanley, *Canada's Soldiers: The Military History of an Unmilitary People* (Toronto: Macmillan, 1960) 4-20.
3. Desmond Morton, *A Military History of Canada* (Edmonton: Hurtig, 1990) 18-25. See also W.J. Eccles, *France in America* (New York: Praeger, 1972).
4. Gerald Graham, *The Empire of the North Atlantic: The Maritime Struggle for North America* (Toronto: University of Toronto Press, 1958).
5. See the excellent handling of this subject by Gustave Lanctôt, *Le Canada et la Révolution américaine* (Montreal: Beauchemin, 1965).

6. For Indian-British relations over this period, see the excellent work of Robert S. Allen, *His Majesty's Indian Allies: British Indian Policy in the Defence of Canada, 1774-1815* (Toronto: Dundurn, 1992).
7. Stanley, *Canada's Soldiers* 148-77.
8. J. Mackay Hitsman, *Safeguarding Canada, 1763-1871* (Toronto: University of Toronto Press, 1968).
9. Josefina Zoraida Vázquez and Lorenzo Meyer, *México frente a Estados Unidos: un ensayo histórico, 1776-1988* (Mexico: EFE, 1989) 54-57. See also Enrique Krauze, *Siglo de Caudillos: biografía política de México, 1810-1910* (Mexico: Tusquets, 1994) 170-72; and for interesting background, see Angela Moyano Pahissa, *La Resistencia de las Californias a la invasión norteamericana, 1846-1848* (Mexico: Consejo Nacional para la Cultura y las Artes, 1992).
10. See, for example, Vaughn Cornish, *A Geography of Imperial Defence* (London: Sifton, 1922); and C.P. Stacey, *The Military Problems of Canada* (Toronto: Ryerson, 1940).
11. See Desmond Morton, *Ministers and Generals: Politics and the Canadian Militia, 1868-1904* (Toronto: University of Toronto Press, 1970); and Richard A. Preston, *The Defence of the Undefended Border: Planning for War in North America, 1867-1939* (Durham NC: Duke University Press, 1967).
12. For an excellent description of the officer corps and its problems in the early decades of the Dominion's history, see Stephen Harris, *Canadian Brass: The Making of a Professional Army, 1860-1939* (Toronto: University of Toronto Press, 1988).
13. J.L. Granatstein, *The Generals: The Canadian Army's Senior Commanders in the Second World War* (Toronto: Stoddart, 1993).
14. Stacey, *The Military Problems* 278.
15. Barry Morton Gough, "The End of Pax Britannica and the Origins of the Royal Canadian Navy: Shifting Strategic Demands of an Empire at Sea," in Barry Hunt and Ronald Haycock, eds., *Canada's Defence: Perspectives on Policy in the Twentieth Century* (Toronto: Copp Clark Pitman, 1993) 19-30.
16. The most famous of these dealt with a Canadian war with the United States, which called for a return to spoiling attacks against northern states as part of a strategy of gaining time for friendly forces to be amassed to defend the Dominion. This plan was finally shelved only in the 1930s. See Preston, *Defence*. Also see Norman Hillmer, "Defence and Ideology: The Anglo-Canadian Military 'Alliance' in the 1930s," in Hunt and Haycock, *Canada's Defence* 82-97.
17. John Hilliker, *Le Ministère des affaires extérieures du Canada*, Vol. 1, *Les années de formation, 1909-1946* (Quebec: Les Presses de l'Université Laval, 1990) 206-08, 229-30, and 236-47.
18. Hilliker, *Le Ministère* 244; and Adrian Preston, "Canada and the Higher Direction of the Second World War, 1939-1945," in Hunt and Haycock, *Canada's Defence* 98-118, esp. 99-102.
19. See Charles P. Stacey and Barbara Wilson, *The Half Million: The Canadians in Britain, 1939-1946* (Toronto: University of Toronto Press, 1987).

20. J.L. Granatstein, "The American Influence on the Canadian Military, 1939-1945," in Hunt and Haycock, *Canada's Defence* 129-39. See also his *Ties that Bind: Canadian-American Relations in Wartime from the Great War to the Cold War* (Toronto: Hakkert, 1977).
21. See Morton, *A Military History* 176-84; Granatstein, "The American Influence," 130; and James Eayrs, *In Defence of Canada*, Vol. II, *Appeasement and Rearmament* (Toronto: University of Toronto Press, 1965).
22. See George Kitching, *Mud and Green Fields* (St. Catharines ON: Vanwell, 1992); and Dominick Graham, *The Price of Command: A Biography of General Guy Simonds* (Toronto: Stoddart, 1993) 245.
23. For the arguments in this debate, see Joseph S. Nye, *Bound to Lead: The Changing Nature of American Power* (New York: Basic Books, 1990); Paul Kennedy, *The Rise and Fall of the Great Powers* (London: Fontana, 1988); Marcel Merle, *Le nouvel ordre international et la guerre du Golfe* (Paris: Economica, 1991); and even R.O. Keohane and J.S. Nye, *Power and Interdependence* (Boston: Little Brown, 1977).
24. See William V. Harris, *War and Imperialism in Republican Rome, 327-70 B.C.* (Oxford: Clarendon Press, 1985) esp. 237-40.
25. For Germany, see Charles F. Doran, "*Quo Vadis?* The United States' Cycle of Power and its Role in a Transforming World," in David Dewitt et al., eds., *Building a New Global Order: Emerging Trends in International Security* (Toronto: Oxford University Press, 1993) 12-39, esp. 27-30. For Japan, see Takashi Inoguchi (1992), "Japan's Role in International Affairs," *Survival* 34(2): 71-87.
26. Interesting elements of this debate are found in Norman J. Ornstein (1992), "Foreign Policy and the 1992 Election," *Foreign Affairs* 71(3): 1-16.
27. For an excellent discussion of these matters, see Jean-François Guilhaudis, "La sécurité collective dans le nouveau contexte international," in S.J. Kirschbaum, ed., *La sécurité collective au XXIe siècle* (Quebec: Centre québécois de relations internationales, 1994) 29-47.
28. See Riordan Roett, ed., *Mexico's External Relations in the 1990s* (Boulder CO: Lynne Rienner, 1990); Scott Sinclair, "NAFTA and U.S. Trade Policy: Implications for Canada and Mexico," in Rod Dobell and Michael Neufeld, *Beyond NAFTA: The Western Hemisphere Interface* (Lantzville BC: Oolichan Books, 1993) 219-26; James Rochlin, *Discovering the Americas: The Evolution of Canadian Foreign Policy towards Latin America* (Vancouver: University of British Columbia Press, 1994) 166-80.
29. It is astonishing to note, for example, that whereas a couple of decades ago, courses and postings in the U.K. were still about half of those in the U.S., the ratio is now almost eight to one.
30. This argument is made in more detail in this author's (1992) "Canada's Pull-Out May Mean More than Losing a Brigade," *Jane's Defence Weekly* 16(15): 614.
31. See Jack Granatstein, *How Britain's Weakness Forced Canada into the Arms of the U.S.* (Toronto: University of Toronto Press, 1989); James Eayrs, *Growing*

Up Allied (Toronto: University of Toronto Press, 1980); and Granatstein, *Ties that Bind*.

32. See the excellent work of David V.J. Bell, "Global Communications, Culture and Values: Implications for Global Security," in Dewitt et al., *Building* 159-84.

33. For U.S. views on this, see Joel J. Sokolsky (1995), "Great Ideals and Uneasy Compromises: The United States Approach to Peacekeeping," *International Journal* 50(2): 266-93.

34. For a look at recent trends in Canadian attitudes to peacekeeping, its evolution, and new challenges, see Pierre Martin and Michel Fortmann (1995), "Canadian Public Opinion and Peacekeeping in a Turbulent World," in *International Journal* 50(2): 370-400.

35. The same process was occurring in Mexico where, despite enormous attempts at trade diversification, the United States' percentage of total Mexican imports and exports grew steadily and decisively. The result was Mexico's own decision to opt for a free trade area with the United States which would eventually be expanded to include Canada. See Roett, *Mexico's External Relations*.

36. See the Mexican and Canadian chapters of Ricardo Grinspun and Maxwell Cameron, eds., *The Political Economy of North American Free Trade* (Montreal: McGill-Queen's University Press, 1993).

37. This, it must be admitted, is changing rapidly in several cases, most notably that of our NAFTA partner, Mexico. There, trade has jumped some 430 percent in three years.

38. John Holmes was far from being in a minority in suggesting that Canadians "have not taken very seriously the idea that they have special links with peoples of vastly different political traditions merely because they happen to be linked by an almost intraversable neck of land." See his *The Better Part of Valour: Essays on Canadian Diplomacy* (Toronto: McClelland and Stewart, 1970) 11.

39. See, for example, this author's *What's in it for us? Canada's Relationship with Latin America* (Ottawa: FOCAL, 1994).

SOVEREIGNTY, FOREIGN POLICY AND NATIONAL SECURITY IN MEXICO, 1821-1989

SOUVERAINETÉ, POLITIQUE ÉTRANGÈRE ET SÉCURITÉ NATIONALE AU MEXIQUE, 1821-1989

Raúl Benítez Manaut

Abstract: Mexican foreign policy, based on the twin doctrines of sovereignty and non-intervention, is the result of a constant evolution of Mexico's concept of national security. Today, this is defined much more broadly than in the past.

The Mexican concept of national security is rooted in the country's history. Successive wars with the United States and then France; U.S. intervention in Veracruz; then the Second World War and the conflicts of the ensuing Cold War—all enabled Mexico to develop a distinct international personality. The establishment of the nation was accompanied by a constant evolution in foreign policy: as national institutions ensured national cohesiveness and the development of Mexican nationalism, the federal government broadened Mexico's involvement in international affairs.

Mexico's foreign policies under each of its leaders since the country's creation in 1821 have proven complementary, passing from a policy narrowly focused on the defence of its territory and on international recognition to one oriented toward the defence of broader Mexican interests and international activism. One can attribute to Juarez the consolidation of the Mexican nation-state; to Díaz, international recognition; and to Carranza and Estrada, the will to self-determination. There followed the nationalization of the oil industry under Cárdenas; Mexican activism in developing countries under Echeverría, within the Western Hemisphere under López Portillo and de la Madrid, and within the world economy under Salinas de Gortari.

Sommaire : La politique étrangère du Mexique repose de nos jours sur une doctrine à deux volets: d'une part, la question de souveraineté et, d'autre part, la question de la non-intervention. Cette orientation de la politique étrangère découle d'une évolution constante de la vision mexicaine du concept de sécurité nationale. Ce dernier se veut beaucoup plus étendu qu'une définition traditionnelle le permettrait.

Des jalons importants de l'histoire du Mexique expliquent le développement d'une telle vision de la sécurité nationale. Successivement, les guerres contre les Etats-Unis puis contre la France, l'intervention américaine de Veracruz, la Seconde Guerre mondiale puis la Guerre froide ont permis au Mexique de développer une personnalité internationale propre. L'établissement de la nation fut accompagné d'une évolution constante de sa politique étrangère: à mesure que des institutions nationales assuraient la cohésion nationale et le développement d'un nationalisme mexicain, le gouvernement fédéral élargissait la présence mexicaine sur la scène internationale.

Les politiques étrangères du Mexique de chacun des présidents en poste depuis la création du pays, en 1821, se sont avérées complémentaires. Elles sont passées d'une politique étrangère essentiellement axée sur la défense du territoire et sur la reconnaissance internationale à une politique étrangère axée sur la défense d'intérêts mexicains élargis et sur l'activisme international. On associe à Juarez la consolidation de l'état-nation mexicain; à Díaz, la reconnaissance internationale; et à Carranza et Estrada, la volonté d'auto-détermination. On assiste ensuite à la nationalisation de l'industrie pétrolière, sous Cárdenas; à l'activisme mexicain au sein des pays en développement, sous Echeverría, au sein de l'hémisphère occidental, sous López Portillo et de la Madrid et au sein de l'économie mondiale, sous Salinas de Gortari.

NATURAL ALLIES?

THIS CHAPTER PRESENTS a historical account of Mexican foreign policy and national security from the birth of the nation to the beginning of the government of Carlos Salinas de Gortari. As with any historical summary, many events have had to be omitted, but an attempt has been made to cover the most significant periods. The main proposition here is that Mexico's difficulties in constituting itself as a nation-state during the 19th century enabled the great powers, such as the United States and France, to entertain territorial ambitions at its expense. Mexican foreign policy, based as it is on the twin doctrines of sovereignty and non-intervention, has its historical roots in the war with the United States (1846-48); the long French intervention of 1861; the shorter U.S. intervention in Veracruz at the time of the Revolution; the attempts of other powers to involve Mexico as a pawn in the geopolitical chess game of that time; the nationalization of the oil industry (1938); World War II; and the conflicts of the Cold War era when Mexico had to adopt its own position.

An analysis is offered of the way in which Mexican governments since the Revolution have gone about building a new concept of national security based on an ideology of nationalism and the defence of Mexico's national sovereignty, its territory, and its natural resources.

The chapter concludes with the debate on national security during the 1980s, involving Mexico's geopolitical approach to Central America and the Caribbean, payment of the external debt, the changing role of the state in relation to the economy, and relations with the United States.

THE FOUNDING OF THE NATION

The idea of breaking away from Spain had its origins among the rural land-holding elite and clergy, and gathered momentum in the second half of the 18th century. The economic and political crisis in the mother country meant that by the time of the Bourbon reign from 1760 on, the viceroyalty of Mexico had to pay for its own army.[1] Thus, the *criollos* [those of European ancestry] came to constitute an elite led by the lower Catholic clergy and top military brass, and inspired by the political ideas of the Enlightenment.[2]

At its birth in 1821, Mexico was torn by many and varying concepts of nationhood. The decline of Spain, the republican and liberal ideals of the United States and France, and the pressures exerted by the greatest power of the time, Great Britain, to gain access for its products in the new Ibero-American markets, meant that the new nation had no firm bases on which to develop, but was at the mercy of empire-building ambitions. Mexico's territory was without communications, depopulated, and fraught with separatist tendencies. In the underpopulated north, inhabited by nomadic tribes, the only Mexican presence was the small colonies of missionaries, mainly in California and Texas. In the south, in what had been the *Capitanía* of Guatemala, riven with rivalries between monarchist-conservative-centralist tendencies and liberal-federalist ambitions, there was widespread separatist sentiment.

The original land area of Mexico in 1821 included the present territories of Guatemala, El Salvador, Honduras, Nicaragua, and Costa Rica. Central America split off from Mexico definitively in 1825. In 1848, in the wake of the war with the United States, the latter country took over California, New Mexico, Arizona, and Texas. The national territory was thus reduced to its present frontiers.

The inability to deflect centrifugal tendencies in the south and north was indeed the first characteristic of the new nation. In 1823, the Federation of Central American States was formed as an entity, which lasted until 1838 when it broke into five countries, while in 1824 the northern part of Central America, Chiapas and the Soconusco, decided to join Mexico. Border conflicts with Guatemala continued until 1882, when a frontier treaty was signed between the two countries.

In its first years of independence, the prime foreign policy efforts of Mexico's government were directed at securing its recognition as a nation. These efforts focused basically on the United States, Spain, France, and Great Britain. The United States recognized the new nation de jure, but not de facto, in 1822, and sent an "observer," Mr. Joel Poinsett.[3] Recognition from Great Britain was obtained in 1826, from France in 1831, and from the Vatican and Spain in 1836.[4] Despite this, Spain still harboured intentions of recovering its viceroyalty. France and the United States maintained an attitude which included territorial ambitions.

The declaration in 1823 by President James Monroe of his doctrine of Manifest Destiny, or "America for the Americans"[5] helped to inspire the independence-minded colonists of Texas, and subsequently led to consolidation of U.S. gains in the southwest with the war of 1846-48. In 1848, the Treaty of Guadalupe Hidalgo was signed, whereby Mexico lost more than half its territory.[6]

Throughout the 19th century, Mexico's main challenge was to achieve a single, common definition of its territory, its population, its culture, and its identity. In political terms, the divisions between conservatives and liberals made it impossible to establish a functioning state. The weakness of state and nation was reflected in an alarming statistic: between 1829 and 1855, there were 48 changes in the presidency, or almost two per year.

The conflict between liberals and conservatives continued until the liberals gained the ascendancy in 1857 with the proclamation of the second liberal constitution. This was followed, however, by the French intervention of 1861,[7] stimulated in part by the Civil War in the United States. The key to liberal reforms was the expropriation of church property, which represented the continuing power of colonial Spain. This expropriation meant that, for the first time, the Mexican state was able to triumph over one of the most important manifestations of Spanish domination. Subsequently, between 1863 and 1867,[8] a conservative-monarchist counter-reform occurred.

THE FIRST NATION-STATE: LIBERALISM AND *PORFIRISMO*

The victory of Mexican arms against French forces in 1862 was a turning point in the history of Mexico. There was no repetition this time of what had happened in the war with the United States. Military victory over France gave a signal that this nation could defend itself with its own resources and need no longer be hostage to the geopolitical balance between Europe and the United States. Nevertheless, between 1862 and 1867, the conservatives once again controlled the government and called upon a European emperor, Maximilian of Habsburg, to rule the country. This led to civil war and the return of the liberals to power—and of Benito Juarez to the presidency. This was the period known as the "Restoration of the Republic."

In July 1867, Juarez declared the fundamental principles of Mexico's foreign policy: "The people and their government must respect the rights of all. Between individuals, as between nations, peace means respect for the rights of others."[9] This first statement of foreign policy, the Juarez Doctrine, was thus an expression of—the foreign policy principles of a nation-state that was beginning to consolidate—a policy based on what we now call national security, cast in a defensive context.

In 1867, the state was finally consolidated with the definitive triumph of the liberals. Porfirio Díaz governed for the first time between 1877 and 1881, and subsequently headed the government from 1884 to 1910. This made it possible to build a nation-state. The cost, though, was that political power became centralized and personalized. The country's external relations were normalized, and massive amounts of investment flowed in to modernize its manufacturing industry, its mining, and its communications. Mexico was unified by the railway. The Díaz government succeeded in gaining recognition for Mexico from the major countries of the world, and diplomatic relations were even established with Japan and China.

At the beginning of the 20th century, petroleum began to replace the use of coal for energy. The first oil company was set up in 1901.[10] Thus, the country's resources came to be seen as an essential element in defining the state's operational foundations. New factors were being added to what is called nation-building: territory, recognition, unification of political power, and national sovereignty over strategic resources.

THE MEXICAN REVOLUTION

With the collapse of the Díaz government in 1910 began that political and military crisis known to history as the Mexican Revolution. Its greatest exponent of foreign policy principles was Venustiano Carranza, who wrote them into the 1917 Constitution. Yet it was President Francisco Madero who, in 1913, reaffirmed the principle of "the legal equality of nations," keeping in mind the imbalance of power vis-à-vis the United States. "I shall try," he said, "to maintain not only friendly but fraternal relations with our powerful neighbour the United States, if they so desire, but these relations must always be based on respect for the sovereignty, the integrity and the dignity of the Mexican Republic."[11]

The researcher Friedrich Katz points out that Mexico had been a focus of world geopolitics during the decade from 1810 to 1820, and that the Mexican revolutionaries, for their part, were now determined to take advantage of hostilities. Katz suggests that the causes of the Revolution are to be found in three processes that occurred at the same time:

The expropriation of the communal lands of peasant communities in the centre and south of Mexico; the transformation of the nomadic Indian frontier into a border with the United States, with the consequent political and economic integration of this area into the rest of the country, and into the U.S. sphere of influence; and the emergence of Mexico as the main stage for European and U.S. rivalry in Latin America.[12]

Madero was overthrown in 1913 by a *coup d'état* led by Victoriano Huerta. This launched the most intense phase of the struggle between revolutionary factions.[13] At the same time, the United States sent its forces to occupy Veracruz in 1914, justifying this action as "re-establishing order," and Germany attempted to use Mexico as a geopolitical bargaining chip during World War I by promising to restore to it the territories annexed by the United States in the war of 1846-48. "We offer Mexico an alliance based on the following principles: joint conduct of the war, a mutual peace treaty, full financial support, and our concurrence that Mexico should recover its former territories in Texas, New Mexico, and Arizona."[14]

THE CARRANZA DOCTRINE AND THE 1917 CONSTITUTION

The Carranza Doctrine was considered one of the key pillars of Mexico's foreign policy principles, and thus of its national security. It was founded on non-intervention and the self-determination of peoples and nations. This doctrine was outlined for the first time when the United States occupied the port of Veracruz: "I speak for the feelings of the great majority of the Mexican people, who are as jealous of their own rights as they are respectful of the rights of others, when I urge you to suspend the hostile actions already initiated, and to order your forces to withdraw from those places that they now occupy in the port of Veracruz."[15]

Later in 1917, Article 27 was written into the Constitution, declaring that strategic natural resources were the property of the nation, with particular reference to oil. Nevertheless, the governments of Carranza and Alvaro Obregón made no attempt to interfere with U.S. or British interests, since their main goal was to bring to a close the military phase of the Revolution and to launch a period of economic reconstruction. The key question with regard to land reform problems and foreign interests was the legislation referring to rural land-holdings, which were at the root of most of the struggles in the countryside,[16] and to ownership of subsoil resources: minerals and oil. A major part of the "nationalist" ideology of governments during the Revolution derived from Mexico's determination to defend this Article 27.

MEXICO-UNITED STATES: THE *RAPPROCHEMENT* OF 1923

General Alvaro Obregón, the leader [*caudillo*] of the victorious revolutionary forces, postulated a realistic foundation for establishing good relations with the United States. In 1920, he said: "With close cooperation from United States industrial capital, Mexico's natural wealth, its inexhaustible supply of industrial raw materials, could soon represent an incalculable source of supply for the major markets of the world."[17]

The nation began to rebuild itself during the 1920s. On the foreign policy front, priority was given to securing U.S. recognition of the new government. Oil was the key factor in these bilateral relations, since at that time Mexico produced more than 20 percent of the world's petroleum.[18] For this reason, the oil companies were the main obstacle to Washington's recognition of the new Mexican government. They wanted to have Article 27 of the Constitution abolished.

The Bucareli Agreements were signed in March 1923. These had three key features: settlement of the external debt; attention to U.S. property claims; and non-enforcement of Article 27 against the oil companies. The Mexican government feared that the United States would provide support to counter-revolutionary movements that were stirring in the country, or even that it might launch a military invasion.[19] These fears were well founded: shortly afterward, a religious counter-revolutionary movement, known as the *Guerra Cristera*, broke out, in which the Catholic Church openly opposed the revolutionary government between 1926 and 1929. This war ended with the victory of the revolutionary armies and the consolidation of the Mexican state.[20]

THE ESTRADA DOCTRINE

Obregón was assassinated in 1928 by a Catholic fanatic. He was replaced by Plutarco Elias Calles. Calles proceeded to end the *Guerra*

Cristera and, with the country pacified, he founded the *Partido Nacional Revolucionario* (PNR) [National Revolutionary Party] in 1929.²¹ Now that the country was unified in political terms, representatives of the new state continued to lay the foundations for Mexico's relations with other countries. The so-called Estrada Doctrine deserves special mention. This was based on a rejection of the policy of "recognizing governments," as practised by the major powers. It maintained that any government that arises with the express support of its people should be recognized, whatever its ideological positions and regardless of economic or geopolitical interests. Genaro Estrada, Minister of External Relations, stated in 1931:

It is a well-known fact that Mexico has suffered, as few other countries have suffered in recent years, under the consequences of the doctrine that leaves it to foreign governments to pronounce themselves arbitrarily on the legitimacy or not of another regime, thus producing situations where the legal capacity and national leadership of governments and authorities are subordinated to the opinions of foreigners.²²

MILITARY HISTORY OF THE REVOLUTION, 1917-34

The Mexican Revolution was the most important military event of this century in Latin America. Mexico's population dropped from 15,160,400 in 1910 to 14,334,800 in 1921.²³ The Revolution cost the lives of almost a million people, or nearly 10 percent of the population. The only other military event of such proportions in Latin America was the War of the Triple Alliance in Paraguay during the 1860s.

Following the armed phase of the Revolution (1911-16), the holding of the Constituent Congress that drafted the 1917 Constitution represented an "alliance" between all the factions that had taken part in the struggle. In military terms, the Revolution had differing impacts, depending on the region of the country.²⁴ The military strongmen [*caudillos*] from the north of the country, led by Alvaro Obregón, gained control of the new state. But with the lack of political institutions, the rise of such strongmen meant that the struggle between them would be a struggle to the death. Carranza, Zapata, and Obregón were all assassinated. At the beginning of the 1930s, Calles avoided assassination, but was expelled to the United States by Cárdenas.

The 1920s were marked by two military events: the building of a national army to overcome regional *caudillismo*, and the waging of the counter-revolutionary *Guerra Cristera*. The success of the revolutionaries in the *Cristera* War in 1929 led to the strengthening of the national army. In parallel with the creation of political institutions, the armed forces were beginning to become professionalized.

The army of the 1920s was the only real state institution in the country. Calles' idea of consolidating the state by building political institutions, following Obregón's assassination in 1928, served also to deal with the problem of *caudillismo*, which was fundamentally individualistic in nature and a potential catalyst for national disintegration. The key event was the creation in 1929 of the PNR, sponsored by the army.[25] In these years, besides consolidating the revolution against conservative forces, the army fulfilled a very significant role as "promoter of development." It was also the only institution that could guarantee enforcement of the new laws, which gave it a social function of the first order.[26] And, of course, it was the only player that could achieve political "conciliation" in the country.

In budgetary terms, the army absorbed a large percentage of available resources: "The national armed forces received 79 million of the 320 million pesos in the federal budget of 1926; 90 of the 284 in 1927; 100 of the 286 in 1928—that is, 20 to 40 percent of state expenditures."[27] In other words, despite the social import of the Revolution, the new Mexican state was completely militarized, and the budget was one of the main mechanisms for achieving unity among the political and military leadership.

Efforts to professionalize and unify the armed forces began in 1925 through the military colleges. The most important of these was the new *Escuela Superior de Guerra* [War College], founded in 1932. There, officers could obtain the degree of *Diplomado de Estado Mayor* (DEM) [Senior Staff Graduate]. The goal was to replace promotion through "war merit points" gained in the Revolution and the religious war by a regular institutional and professional system of promotion that recognized discipline, military career history, and education.[28]

By the beginning of the 1930s, the transition from *caudillismo* to a "government of institutions" had been achieved. The country still faced dangers, but the institutionalization of the Revolution via a strong state structure had succeeded in avoiding tendencies toward disintegration.

CARDENISMO AND THE NATIONALIZATION OF OIL

There were two factors that drove President Lázaro Cárdenas to nationalize the oil industry on March 18, 1939. The first was that, internally, the Revolution was over and the obstacles to consolidation as a nation-state had been overcome. The second was that there was a favourable international environment in which Mexico was becoming important for the major powers in geopolitical terms, just as it had been in World War I—but with the difference that, this time, the country had come through a civil war intact and was in a position to negotiate.[29]

With the rearming of Germany and its failure to comply with the Treaties of Versailles, the outbreak of World War II was imminent. The United States and Britain were thus obliged to focus their attention on Europe, and they could do no more than erect a commercial and financial wall around Mexico. U.S. President Franklin Roosevelt, who was promoting a "good neighbour" policy toward Latin America, declared:

> The sharpest test of our good neighbour policy has come from Mexico, where the radical nationalist government of Cárdenas has expropriated lands belonging to American citizens, and has seized huge American and English oil properties, in a grand gesture of self-determination. Some Americans have been pressing the government to intervene with force in Mexico—the oil companies want the government of that country to pay full value, not only for their investments in Mexico, but also broad and far-reaching compensation for their unexploited subsoil rights. The Administration is resisting both demands.[30]

President Roosevelt was acting in the national security interest of his country since, had he supported the oil companies, he would have created a likely enemy on his southern flank, and Germany and the Axis powers would have had a new ally. The fact that the U.S. government had maintained good relations with Mexico, and had sacrificed the private interests of some large corporations to the national interest, made it possible for those relations to remain in good shape during World War II. Britain did not have the same sensitivity and thus had no diplomatic relations with Mexico between 1939 and 1942.

The oil nationalization in 1939 marked the consolidation in Mexico of a security doctrine that was closely linked to the foreign policy of the Revolution: that raw materials and energy resources were for the use of the nation, under the direction of the state, so that the nation would not be economically and socially vulnerable. Oil became in this way the very crux of national security. This debate was heard many times during World War II and reappeared in the 1970s.

WORLD WAR II

Mexico declared war on the Axis powers in 1942, in response to the sinking of the oil tankers *Potrero del Llano* and *Faja de Oro* by German submarines.[31] President Manuel Avila Camacho phrased his declaration in terms of "legitimate defence":

> Our determination stems from the necessities of Legitimate Defence. We know the limits of our fighting resources, and we know that, given the massive size of the international warring forces, our role in the present conflict cannot involve military action beyond this continent, for which we are unprepared. Our forces therefore will not be dispersed. We shall however respond to any aggressive intents of our adversaries, and shall at all times defend our country's integrity and cooperate actively for the safety of the American continent, within the limits of our abilities, our security and the coordination of hemispheric defence procedures.[32]

Mexico's cooperation was important in World War II, but it was not decisive for the Allied cause. In military terms, relations were at their best during the war years, though they did not continue so for long afterward. In 1940, the Joint Mexican-U.S. Defence Commission was established. Following the Japanese attack on Pearl Harbor, the United States wanted Mexico's total support. In December 1941, the Mexican Senate authorized full use of ports and airports by the United States. Radar installations were set up, principally in Baja California, to detect Japanese ships and submarines. Transit airports were built for military aircraft flying toward the Panama Canal, and Mexico contributed in a symbolic way with an air squadron in the Philippines. Food and minerals needed to supply the armies and produce armaments were also provided.[33]

Efforts to build a bilateral defence system were part of the broader need to establish hemispheric cooperation. Mexico supported plans for hemispheric security. The only Latin American country that supported the Axis was Argentina.

These activities served to draw the two countries closer, although for different reasons: the United States needed a secure border and Mexico needed the U.S. government's support in negotiating its debts with the oil companies arising from nationalization. Both countries gained advantages. For Mexico, taking part in World War II brought great benefits, since in effect it represented the establishment of "normal" relations with the United States.

MEXICAN NATIONAL SECURITY IN THE COLD WAR

When the war was over, Mexico continued to abide by its foreign policy principles. The Juarez, Carranza, and Estrada doctrines, together with the doctrine of "non-offensive" defence (Legitimate Defence), formed the basis for Mexico's assumption of its place in the new, bipolar international system. Mexico supported the creation of the UN from its outset in 1945.

The United States then began promoting the signing of regional security treaties around the world. The first of these, in fact, was the Inter-American Treaty of Reciprocal Assistance (the Rio Treaty), signed in Rio de Janeiro in December 1947. The key point of this treaty was collective defence in the face of an "external" threat, which was identified with communism. For Mexico, there has always been some confusion between external threats and the struggle against communism, since communism finds some internal political expression in Latin American countries. This is thus an ideological and political question, rather than one of defence doctrine.

Subsequently, Mexico has maintained an international position that is "Defensive and Based on Law."[34] This means, with respect to the Rio Treaty, that Mexico considers it a mistake to invoke the treaty as an excuse to intervene in internal affairs: "If ... the Inter-American Treaty of Reciprocal Assistance were to be used contrary to its purposes, to intervene in the internal affairs of any State of the

Americas, Mexico would have to give serious consideration to denouncing the Treaty, and withdrawing from its commitments under it."[35]

During the Cold War era, under the governments of Miguel Alemán (1946-52), Adolfo Ruíz Cortines (1952-58), Adolfo López Mateos (1958-64), and Gustavo Díaz Ordaz (1964-70), the "Mexican Political System" was consolidated.[36] The economy performed at high and sustained growth rates, a communications system was put in place, and an important industrial infrastructure grew up. Mexico went from being a predominantly rural country to an urban one.

In terms of the key features of its national security, the war and the post-war period saw the strengthening of Mexico's foreign policy, its national defence doctrine, internal political stability, and social development, all of which reinforced each other during the years of economic reconstruction in the 1950s and 1960s.

The country managed to implement a political system in which the military was kept separate from direct management of the state apparatus and experienced a rapid process of professionalization, which was helpful in political, social, and economic terms. The military share of the budget diminished gradually, while social and development expenditures rose. This was the basis that made it possible to promote political stability, improve social conditions for the masses, and promote economic growth.

The following table shows how the budget for the armed forces has declined as a share of total government expenditure:

MILITARY SPENDING AS A PERCENTAGE
OF TOTAL GOVERNMENT SPENDING*

1936-40	Lázaro Cárdenas	22.03%
1940-46	Avila Camacho	17.85
1946-52	Miguel Alemán	10.08
1952-58	Adolfo Ruíz Cortines	7.87
1958-64	Adolfo López Mateos	6.92
1964-70	Gustavo Díaz Ordaz	2.63
1970-73	Luis Echeverría	1.86

*Average expenditure for the six-year period. For Echeverría, only the first three years of his government are included.[37]

On the international scene, the principles cited above were strengthened and reinforced. During the Cold War, Mexico's international position clashed on many occasions with that of the United States at the diplomatic level. Differences appeared in 1954, when the OAS was called on to pass judgment on the Guatemalan government of Jacobo Arbenz[38] for supposed nationalist tendencies and links with socialist countries of the Eastern Bloc. Mexico invoked the principle of non-intervention, and refused to qualify the existence of a nationalist government as "communist."[39]

Subsequently, the Cuban situation became the focus of attention for Mexican diplomacy and the occasion for reasserting its principles in the face of the insistent efforts of U.S. foreign policy to overthrow the government of Fidel Castro. Mexico refused to accept the exclusion of Cuba from the OAS in 1961, and rejected the 1964 trade embargo. Nevertheless, when the missile crisis broke out in October 1962, Mexico supported the United States unconditionally.[40] In the same vein, Mexico did not approve of the military invasion of the Dominican Republic in April 1965, and it opposed both the formula and the justification for the occupation army, the Inter-American Peace Force:

My country absolutely repudiates these interventionist practices, which we believed had been set aside for good, and wishes to help preserve the full validity of the basic principles embodied in the OAS Charter.... We urge the government of the United States to withdraw the armed forces that it has sent to the Dominican Republic.[41]

With respect to nuclear weapons, Mexico promoted the Treaty of Tlatelolco which was finally signed in 1967. There are several interpretations of this creation of a nuclear-free zone in the Americas.[42] Some authors maintain that the denuclearization of Latin America was of strategic advantage to the United States, since it would thereby have no competition on this continent in the nuclear arms race.[43]

On the internal political scene, political control and the stability of the Revolution and its institutions were assured primarily by the PNR (transformed into the PRM in 1938, and into the PRI in 1946) and its "corporations."[44] Political opposition was never able to challenge the PRI's power via the electoral process. A "hybrid" political system was thus created—a mixture of authoritarianism and corporatism cloaked in public support—that allowed enough margin for individual liberties to ensure political acceptance by the citizenry.[45]

This political system was based on co-opting and neutralizing political opposition. Only under exceptional circumstances did state force (police or military) have to be used to deal with protests.

The Mexican political system fell into a period of decline and rigidity during the 1970s. Rural guerrilla groups sprang up in the state of Guerrero, and simmering urban protest broke out in the student movement of 1968. The armed forces had to be used repressively to contain this uprising. The outcome was an untold number of dead and wounded, political prisoners, and the closing of the National University for four months. The last three years of the Díaz Ordaz government (1968-70) are looked on as the most repressive period in Mexico's modern history. In effect, the Díaz Ordaz government shared the strategy promoted by the United States for combatting communism, one that was based on use of the armed forces to overcome internal political opposition.[46]

The official historical interpretation of the events of 1968 cites the need to "avoid chaos and anarchy," since "the Mexican army has the solemn task of maintaining internal peace and order, under the rule of the Constitution."[47] Roderic Ai Camp, in his book *Generals in the Palacio*,[48] and the researcher Michael Dziedzic[49] both maintain that it was the *regente* [governor] of Mexico City, with the agreement of the minister of defence, who took the decision to act, and not the president.

The events of 1968 cast serious doubt on the regime's legitimacy and its political stability. The change of government in 1970 thus represented a recasting of the political system.

NATIONAL SECURITY IN THE 1970s: "THIRD WORLDISM" AND OIL

Luis Echeverría assumed the presidency in December 1970. The country was still living the political trauma of the repression unleashed against the students. To overcome this, the new president declared a political amnesty for those imprisoned because of the student movement, and proposed the need to undertake a profound political reform that would legalize political opposition, essentially on the Left.[50] At the same time, because of the repression—and because of the conditions prevailing in some parts of the country—rural guerrilla movements arose, mainly in Guerrero, as well as some urban ones. Various movements also emerged in support of workers' and peasants' rights.

Echeverría dealt with these protests using the traditional mechanisms of the political system: co-option, corruption, mediation, and neutralization. Only in exceptional circumstances, such as in anti-guerrilla campaigns in the state of Guerrero, did he resort to the armed forces.[51] The effectiveness of Echeverría's reforms was such that, in the presidential election for change of government in 1976, the political opposition was unable to mount an alternative candidacy.[52]

The Echeverría government rebuilt the political system on the basis of social policies that raised the real income of workers, nationalized several companies, and revitalized the system's weakened "corporatist" features. This was considered a "populist," "statist," "nationalist" government, and it went on to formulate an active foreign policy based on Third World solidarity.[53] Echeverría had several major confrontations with the business sector and with the United States government. The country's external debt grew significantly, and the president handed his successor, José López Portillo, a huge economic crisis.

López Portillo (1976-82) promoted export development of the oil industry as a means of pulling the country out of its crisis. This was the heart of his security policy. The fact that oil was once more the basis for development meant that the whole debate of the 1930s was reopened. Once again, oil was front and centre in Mexico-U.S. relations, and there was talk of its vital strategic importance for the economic functioning of the developed countries.[54] From this moment on, and parallel to the debate of the 1970s over the existence of newly industrialized countries and their ability to influence the global alignment of forces, there was much talk of how Mexico could now influence many aspects of its economic and foreign policy with a significant degree of independence from the United States.[55] There arose the idea of a new sub-regional strategy, based on Mexico's own interests, for which new foreign policy tools would have to be designed.

With regard to national security, the political elite in Mexico abstained from using this term during the 1970s, because it was so widely employed in South America. The so-called "National Security Doctrine," in its various manifestations in Peru, Brazil, Argentina, Chile, and Uruguay, was being used to justify militarization of the state, political repression, the declaration of states of siege, and suspension of laws defending citizens' human and political rights.[56]

NATIONAL SECURITY IN THE 1980s: CAUGHT BETWEEN CENTRAL AMERICA, THE DEBT, THE DRUG TRADE, THE UNITED STATES, AND DEMOCRATIZATION OF THE POLITICAL SYSTEM

López Portillo used oil to revive Mexico's economy.[57] Mexico came to see itself as a middle power with the capacity to entertain its own ideas of security. Thus, Mexico's policy toward the Caribbean and Central America differed radically from that of the United States. López Portillo strengthened the already good relations with the Cuban government. He promoted unprecedented Latin American moves to achieve negotiation of the new Panama Canal Treaties, which were signed in 1977 and entered into force in 1979.[58] In a joint diplomatic operation with Costa Rica, he broke relations with the Somoza government in Nicaragua, thus accelerating its downfall, and offered heavy economic and political support to the *Frente Sandinista de Liberación Nacional* (FSLN) [Sandinista National Liberation Front], first in its war against the Nicaraguan dictatorship (1978-79), and then in the country's economic reconstruction (1979-82).[59]

López Portillo characterized these bursts of activism as follows:

> I speak with a mandate from all of Latin America.... As of today this Canal belongs solely to Panama.... We rejoice at the end of this humiliating nonsense that separated Middle America. Let the rightful flag now fly over the Canal—Panama's flag!... We will never be neocolonies, nor subjects for foreign domination. No one can assume the right to look out for our sovereignty.... Either we unite and put our house in order, or order will be imposed through the tortuous routes of economic and political domination, by military and financial powers that have no rightful place in our history. We can no longer wait to overcome injustice and underdevelopment, unless we want to see our continent burst into flames of revolt.... It will do us no good to fight off external intervention and pressures if we allow disunity, repression, poverty and inequality to persist in our own countries.[60]

At the same time, the taboo against speaking of "national security" was broken. In the *Plan Global de Desarrollo* [Comprehensive Development Plan], which was the final guiding document of López Portillo, there is a section entitled "National Security," in which is found the following:

This direct subordination of the armed forces is intended to reaffirm and consolidate Mexico's viability as an independent country. Within our own vision and understanding of Mexican conditions, the defence of our nation's integrity, its independence and its sovereignty translates into the maintenance of constitutional normality and the strengthening of Mexico's political institutions.[61]

This view came to be known as the "comprehensive concept" of national security. On this basis, the military education system was reformed and the National Defence College was founded, under the National Defence Ministry.[62] The National Defence College thus became the highest teaching institute in the military system. There, the doctrine of Mexico's national security to the end of the century was developed.[63]

The Mexican army's defence plans were reaffirmed on the basis of this comprehensive doctrine.[64] These plans fell under three headings:

- DN1 was a defence plan for confronting an external aggressor by building links between the armed forces and the civilian population. It covered only Mexico's own territory and excluded any involvement of Mexican forces in military missions abroad.
- DN2 was intended to deal with serious internal threats to social peace and stability. This was the plan activated during the student uprising of 1968 and used to justify the use of the armed forces against the drug trade.[65] DN2 is the most controversial defence plan in political terms: it has been used to justify the existence of the *Guardias Rurales* [Rural Guards]; it has been the basis for use of the armed forces against drug traffickers since World War II; and currently—it is not known if the armed forces support this aspect—it allows the armed forces to become, in effect, part of the electoral process through their deployment in monitoring and surveillance work. This has unleashed a heated debate over whether the armed forces should, in fact, have a political role at election time.

- DN3 dealt with the organization of the army and navy for civil defence in times of natural disasters. This is the most widely accepted plan: it is seen as drawing the armed forces closer to the people, and confirms the theory about the social function of the forces in supporting public welfare, especially for the marginalized groups.

The final two years of the López Portillo administration (1981 and 1982) were a decisive time for national security. Whereas the country had been experiencing a boom time that allowed it to purchase high-tech weaponry such as F-5 supersonic fighters[66] and to devote resources to an active Central American policy, Mexico was now plunged into an economic crisis that began with the August 1982 devaluation of the peso, and produced an economic recession that lasted until 1989. External debt became the key factor in Mexico's relations with developed countries, especially the United States. Ideas of Mexico's emergence as a regional "middle power" that had been entertained between 1977 and 1982 were cast into doubt by the debt crisis.[67] This led to conflicting interpretations in the United States of a certain contradiction perceived in Mexican policy—Mexico had to negotiate with the United States, but at the same time it was trying to develop policies that were distinct from those of the United States.[68]

The most significant difference was over how to handle the crisis in Central America. The deepening of this crisis in 1981 and 1982 was seen by the Mexican government as a national security issue, and an active diplomatic campaign was mounted to defuse the situation:

[We seek] to stabilize the area through a defence policy of détente, while the policy of the United States is to stabilize the area through deterrence and containment. While our goals may be the same, the means we are employing are different, and this is producing sometimes violent disagreements, arguments and opposition.[69]

Because Mexico was opposed to the policy of "containing communism" through military means, as practised by Central American governments with the encouragement of the United States,[70] its position was another factor of geopolitical polarization in the region. Mexico rejected the idea of trying to eliminate movements through counter-insurgency strategies and instead took the side of those countries that insisted on a diplomatic approach. This was based on recognition of the Sandinista government[71] and on including the guerillas of El Salvador and Guatemala in the process of democratization to wean them from military action and convert them into a political force. Mexico's two most important moves on the diplomatic front were to forestall military action in Nicaragua in 1979, when attempts were being made to use the mechanisms of the Inter-American System (OAS-Rio Pact), and to recognize the *Frente Democrático Revolucionario-Frente Martí de Liberación Nacional* political alliance in El Salvador.[72]

There were several national security reasons for Mexico's preoccupation with Central America. In the first place, the flow of Central American emigration was growing. Even though much of it was headed for the United States, it aroused fears in Mexico because of the country's high unemployment and the economic crisis it was experiencing in the 1980s. In fact, a large group of migrants took refuge along the Mexican border with Guatemala. These refugees were essentially indigenous peoples who were fleeing the counter-insurgency attacks of the Guatemalan army.[73] In the second place, Mexico's southern border was threatened with destabilization in two respects: problems with the Guatemalan army;[74] and the danger that the "domino theory" postulated by the United States might be true and that the revolution in Central America might "cross the border" into areas of Mexico where similar economic and social conditions prevailed. In the third place, there was the risk that differences with the United States might lead to problems in other areas of the bilateral relationship, such as the debt, the drug trade, and the U.S. attitude to Mexico's own political problems.

The main point of tension with the United States was the latter's insistence on the "domino theory," whereby Central American guerrilla activity might spill over into Mexico and from there to the United States itself, thus posing a risk of destabilization and a threat to national security.[75] The conflict between the two governments was essentially over Mexico's refusal to support U.S. military strategy, Mexico's diplomatic and economic support of Nicaragua's government, and its insistence on granting residency rights in Mexico to members of the Salvadorean opposition.[76]

An important change was noted in Mexico's diplomatic policy toward Central America, coinciding with the change of government in Mexico. (López Portillo handed over the presidency to Miguel de la Madrid in December 1982.) In January 1983, the "Contadora Group" was formed by Mexico, Venezuela, Panama, and Colombia as a reflection of their national concerns. The Contadora Group was the only forum for dialogue within the region between 1983 and 1986 and was accorded support by the EEC, Canada, Japan, and other major countries. The main opponent of the Group was the United States: Washington was still seeking the overthrow of the Sandinista regime in Nicaragua and the crushing of guerrilla activity in El Salvador, while the Contadora Group favoured a negotiated solution both to the regional conflict and to the various internal conflicts in Nicaragua, El Salvador, and Guatemala.

In the end, the Central American crisis was resolved through political means—internal democratization, elections, and negotiations between governments and insurgents. From the first meeting in Esquipulas in May 1986, and especially after the signing of the peace accord of Esquipulas [*Acta de Paz de Esquipulas*] in August 1987, the process of détente accelerated and those favouring a military solution were increasingly isolated. Participation by the UN from 1988 onward marked a period of very active multilateral diplomatic activity in which Mexico was a key player. Indeed, Mexico was the decisive element in the negotiations over El Salvador.[77]

Of the four fundamentals of Mexican national security policy that have been cited, the most sensitive has been that concerning the country's political stability. In the 1980s, it became a point of friction with the United States.[78] Three problems became the critical points in Mexico's bilateral relations with the United States in the middle of the decade: the economic crisis; the expansion of the drug trade; and the emergence of political opposition, with the United States initially taking a favourable view of the creation of the PAN party.[79] Each of them was seen, in both countries, as an issue of national security, but it was the manner of dealing with them that was contentious. Mexico insisted that they were internal issues, while Washington insisted on interventionist attempts to impose solutions on Mexico.[80]

Under the weight of its foreign debt and the pressures coming from the financial community, Mexico was forced to undertake profound economic reforms: opening its borders to trade (Mexico joined the GATT in 1986); reduction of state activity, mainly in the "social expenditure" field; privatization of most state enterprises, and so on. The Mexican economy went through periods of recession, which had repercussions in the political arena as the opposition gained strength.[81]

Mexico believed that it had the drug trafficking problem under control. Yet, with the surge in the demand for cocaine in the United States during the 1980s, the problem took on new proportions. The United States was insistent that Mexico prevent narcotics from reaching the U.S. border[82] by using its navy for maritime surveillance, sending its army to destroy crops, and engaging its law enforcement system [*Procuraduría de la República*] to control the major cartels.[83] There was, however, much disagreement over antidrug strategies.

The Mexican political situation in the 1980s was characterized by a gradual process of democratization, with the opposition parties offering increasing competition to the ruling PRI party—in stark contrast to the process being witnessed in South America. The critical moments were the presidential election of July 6, 1988, and the change of government on December 1 that same year.

The relationship between democracy, political stability, and national security has become a focus of the debate that was launched in 1988. Democracy must provide a sufficiently solid basis on which to build a replacement for the dominant-party system, without provoking a political crisis. If it can do this, it will provide a solid basis for national security as well. On the other hand, if democracy provokes political instability, that will also have an effect on national security. This dilemma has been the crux of the problem with the United States. The United States makes a principle of encouraging democratic political processes all over the world—and Mexico is right on its southern flank. So which will take priority: democracy or national security? Sergio Aguayo Quezada puts forward the proposition that democracy is a challenge to national security;[84] he combines the two processes into an analytical unit for understanding Mexico's political transition.

The change of government on December 1, 1988, when Salinas de Gortari took office, was traumatic. The Mexican government faced a crisis of legitimacy and credibility, which it set out to overcome through a new economic policy launched in 1989. At the outset of his administration, Salinas de Gortari created a National

Security Cabinet as a new institutional attempt to coordinate the various activity centres of the executive branch.[85] The presidency of Salinas (1988-94) sought to achieve national security by reviving the economy, and the chosen route for accomplishing this was NAFTA.

SOME CLOSING THOUGHTS: MEXICO-U.S. RELATIONS AND A COMPREHENSIVE CONCEPT OF NATIONAL SECURITY

National security has been a topic of open debate since the early 1980s. The academic world has taken the principles of foreign policy as its point of departure.[86] In military circles, a concept distinct from that prevalent in South America has been developed, one in which the army is subordinate to the civilian authorities and to the rules set by the Constitution.[87] Within the presidency itself, the three development plans (those of the administrations of Lopez Portillo, Miguel de la Madrid, and Carlos Salinas de Gortari) have subscribed to a "comprehensive concept" of national security, one that focuses on the interaction between economic and social considerations, political democracy, defence policy, and foreign policy.[88]

In academic circles, the main theme of national security has been identified since the mid-1980s as the need for political democracy.[89] One author defines this link as follows:

Whether there is a greater or a lesser degree of democracy has a decisive influence on national security. In a society where the majority are discontented because of a continuous deterioration in their standard of living, and where despite a theoretically democratic regime there is no real room for popular participation, the level of public support and solidarity with the actions of the state will in all likelihood show a descending curve.[90]

The notion of national security that is held in the United States is very different from that in Mexico. Except during World War II, the two countries have never seen eye to eye on their strategic interests. Thus, for example, the bilateral treaty on military cooperation has never been ratified, because Mexico has opposed the perception of national security that prevailed during the Cold War—a perception that was based on the struggle against communism.[91] In Mexico's case, day-to-day items on the bilateral relations agenda often turn into national security issues. This is what happened with the Central American crisis of the 1980s, the problem of migrating Mexican workers, trade-related issues, and, since the end of the 1980s, the question of Mexico's political stability.[92]

With the fall of the communist regimes around the world, the United States is now transforming its national security doctrine. For the first time, internal issues are coming to dominate its agenda: governance, violence, drug use, economic productivity, racial integration, linguistic and cultural minorities, environmental stewardship, and others. A more comprehensive doctrine is being created which adds additional elements to the foreign and military policy considerations that were the focus of national security during the Cold War.[93] In this sense, the national security agendas of the two countries have had many more points in common since the end of the Cold War.

The new economic configuration of the world has meant that, since the beginning of this decade, free trade and the creation of integrated economic zones have become factors of real importance. Mexico, the United States, and Canada thus now pursue many common policies. A question arises here: are economic integration proposals going to lead in future to political and military integration or alliances?

Mexico is faced with the task of completing its political transition to democracy while assuring new mechanisms for internal stability, new relations between the civilian and military spheres, a new relationship between state and society, a new economic system, and new international relationships. Only by doing so can Mexico ensure its national security as the century draws to a close.

NOTES

1. Christon I. Archer, *The Army in Bourbon Mexico,* 1760-1810 (Albuquerque NM: University of New Mexico Press, 1977).
2. Maria del Carmen Velázquez, *El estado de guerra en Nueva España, 1760-1808* (Mexico: El Colegio de México, 1950).
3. Mexico, *Política exterior de México: 175 años de historia,* Vol. 1 (Mexico: SRE, 1985) 68.
4. Mexico, *Política exterior* 119-27.
5. President Monroe's actual words were part of his annual message to the U.S. Congress, December 2, 1823. The key line reads: "the American continents,

by the free and independent condition which they have assumed and maintain, are henceforth not to be considered as subject for future colonization by any European power." Richard Morris, *Documentos fundamentales de la historia de los Estados Unidos de América* (Mexico: Libreros Mexicanos Unidos, 1962).

6. "Treaty of Peace, Friendship and Boundaries of 2 February 1848, between the United Mexican States and the United States of America," *Política exterior* 189-207.
7. France's justification for intervening in Mexico was based on President Benito Juárez's cancellation of the Mexican debts owing to France in July 1861. France was counting on support from Spain and Great Britain. The intent was to obtain payment of the debt by force. Spain and Great Britain withdrew in April 1862, as France sent its armies into the state of Veracruz. The Battle of Puebla, in which Mexico was victorious, occurred on May 5.
8. Patricia Galeana de Valadés, *Las Relaciones Iglesia-Estados durante el Segundo Imperio* (Mexico: UNAM, 1991).
9. Benito Juárez, "Manifesto a la Nación," July 15, 1867, in Boris Rosen, ed., *México y la paz. Testimonios 1810-1896.* Vol. 1, *El Estado* (Mexico: Centro de Investigación Científica Jorge L. Tamayo, 1986).
10. Lorenzo Meyer, *México y Estados Unidos en el conflicto petrolero, 1917-1942* (Mexico: PEMEX, 1988) 23.
11. *Madero y su obra. Documentos inéditos publicados con motivo del XXV aniversario de la grandiosa Revolución Mexicana, 1910-1934* (Mexico: Talleres Gráficos de la Nación, 1934) 17.
12. Friedrich Katz, *La Guerra secreta en México*, Vol. 1 (Mexico: ERA, 1982) 23.
13. See Miguel Angel Sanchez, *Historia militar de la Revolución Mexicana en la época maderista* (Mexico: INEHRM, 1976).
14. This is a portion of the famous Zimmerman telegram of January 1918. See Katz, *La Guerra secreta*, Vol. 2, 41.
15. "Letter from President Carranza to the State Department, April 22, 1914," in *Política exterior* 239.
16. For more on these aspects, see David Bradging, ed., *Caudillo and Peasant in the Mexican Revolution* (Cambridge: Cambridge University Press, 1980); and Daniel Nugent, ed., *Rural Revolt in Mexico and U.S. Intervention* (San Diego: Center for U.S.-Mexican Studies, 1988). The agrarian-inspired Zapatistas were the most radical faction in the Revolution; they mounted armed insurgencies in the states of Morelos and Guerrero, and had a significant influence in the capital. See John Womack, Jr., *Zapata y la Revolución Mexicana* (Mexico: SEP-Siglo XXI, 1985).
17. "From President Alvaro Obregón's cable to the *Chicago Commercial Herald and Examiner,* September 22, 1920," in Rosen, *México y la paz* 130.
18. Lorenzo Meyer, *Historia de la Revolución Mexicana. Período 1928-1934. El conflicto social y los gobiernos del maximato,* Vol. 13 (Mexico: El Colegio de México, 1978).
19. Meyer, *Historia* 118-28.

20. Jean Meyer, *La révolution mexicaine, 1910-1940* (Paris: Calmann-Lévy, 1973) 161-92.
21. Meyer, *Historia*.
22. Genaro Estrada, *Obras Completas* (Mexico: Siglo XXI, 1988) 144.
23. Mexico, *México demográfico. Breviario, 1980-81* (Mexico: Consejo Nacional de Población, 1982) 11.
24. The only region of the country that was untouched by military action was the southeast. The Revolution reached as far as the state of Tabasco, but no combat was recorded in the Yucatan Peninsula or Chiapas. This meant that the rural land-holding oligarchy was unaffected by it. See Octavio Gordillo, *La revolución en el Estado de Chiapas* (Mexico: INEHRM, 1986).
25. More on the history of the Mexican army during the 1920s and 1930s may be found in the following books: Guillermo Boils, *Los militares y la política en México: 1915-1974* (Mexico: El Caballito, 1975); Mexico, *El ejército mexicano. Historia de los orígenes hasta nuestros días* (Mexico: Ministry of National Defence, 1979); José Luis Piñeyro, *Ejército y sociedad en México: pasado y presente* (Mexico: UAP-UAM.A, 1985); Roderic Ai Camp, *Generals in the Palacio: The Military in Modern Mexico* (New York/Oxford: Oxford University Press, 1992); Edwin Lieuwen, *Mexican Militarism: The Political Rise and Fall of the Revolutionary Army, 1910-1940* (Albuquerque NM: University of New Mexico Press, 1968).
26. Claude Heller, ed., *El ejército como agente de cambio social* (Mexico: FCE, 1980). One historian ascribes a significant social role to the army in the countryside: see Hans-Werner Tobler (1971), "Las paradojas del ejército revolucionario: su papel social en la reforma agraria mexicana, 1920-1935," *Historia Mexicana* 21(1): 38-79.
27. Jean Meyer et al., *Historia de la Revolución Mexicana. Período 1924-1928. Estado y sociedad con Calles*, Vol. 11 (Mexico: El Colegio de México, 1977) 60.
28. A detailed analysis is found in Ai Camp, *Generals* 154-62.
29. A detailed analysis of this point is offered in Raúl Benítez Manaut, "México 1920-1945: la expropiación petrolera y la reinserción de México al sistema internacional," in *México a cincuenta años de la expropiación petrolera* (Mexico: CIIH-UNAM, 1988).
30. Franklin D. Roosevelt, *The Roosevelt Reader: Press Conferences and Letters of Franklin D. Roosevelt, 1882-1945* (New York: Rinehart, 1957) 195.
31. Cesar de Windt Lavandier, *La segunda guerra mundial y los submarinos alemanes en el Caribe* (Santo Domingo: Universidad Central del Este, 1982) 283.
32. "Message read before the Congreso de la Unión by President Manuel Avila Camacho, on May 28, 1942," in Mexico, *Memoria de la Secretaría de Relaciones Exteriores*, September 1941-August 1942 (Mexico: SRE, 1942) 101-02.
33. Stetson Conn et al., *The United States Army in World War II: The Western Hemisphere. Guarding the United States and Its Out-posts* (Washington: Office of the Chief of Military History, 1964). See Chapter 13, "The United States and Mexico: Solidarity and Security" 331-63.

34. See Jorge Castañeda, *México y el orden internacional* (Mexico: El Colegio de México, 1981).
35. Castañeda, *México* 205.
36. Luis Medina, *Historia de la Revolución Mexicana. Período 1940-1952. Civilismo y modernización del autoritarismo*, Vol. 20 (Mexico: El Colegio de México, 1979); Olga Pellicer and José Luis Reyna, *Historia de la Revolución Mexicana. Período 1952-1960. El afianzamiento de la estabilidad política*, Vol. 22 (Mexico: El Colegio de México, 1978).
37. Boils, *Los militares* 103.
38. The OAS was founded in Bogotá in April 1948. It is regarded as the key institution of inter-American diplomacy. Its headquarters are in Washington.
39. Luis Padilla Nervo, Minister of Foreign Relations, "México en la X^a Conferencia interamericana," in Rosen, *México y la paz* 12.
40. Olga Pellicer (1965-66), "México en la OEA," *Foro internacional* 6 (2-3).
41. "Declaration of the special representative of the Ministry of Foreign Relations, Rafael de la Colina, at the 10th Consultative Meeting of American States, May 4, 1965," in Rosen, *México y la paz* 390-91.
42. *Vigésimo Aniversario del Tratado de Tlatelolco* (Mexico: OPANAL, 1987).
43. For a detailed analysis of this point, see Luis Herrera-Lasso et al., *México y la seguridad hemisférica* (Mexico: Centro Latinoamericano de Estudios Estratégicos, 1990).
44. PRM = *Partido de la Revolución Mexicana;* PRI = *Partido Revolucionario Institucional.*
45. The most comprehensive analysis of the Mexican political system and its mechanisms for control, legitimacy, exercise of power and mediation, and co-opting of the opposition is found in Pablo Gonzalez Casanova's *La Democracia en México* (Mexico: ERA, 1965).
46. The fullest analysis of the student movement of 1968 is that of Sergio Zermeno in his *México: una democracia utópica. El movimiento estudiantil del 68* (Mexico: Siglo XXI, 1985).
47. Gral Luis Garfias, "El ejército mexicano actual," Mexico, *El ejército mexicano* 533.
48. Ai Camp, *Generals.*
49. Michael J. Dziedzic, *The Essence of Decision in a Hegemonic Regime: The Case of Mexico's Acquisition of a Supersonic Fighter* (Austin TX: Ph.D. dissertation, University of Texas, 1984).
50. The Mexican Left in those years was divided between the militant Left, organized into armed guerrilla groups, and a Left that was also outlawed, but that did not support the strategy of armed struggle. The latter faction's most important organization was the Communist Party. The government finally legalized the non-armed Left as a means of channelling opposition movements into the electoral competition process.
51. For more on the structure and organization of the Mexican army's campaign against the guerrillas, see Piñeyro, *Ejército y sociedad.*
52. Américo Saldivar, *Ideología y política del Estado Mexicano, 1970-1976* (Mexico: Siglo XXI, 1980).

53. For an analysis of the shift from a defensive and legalistic foreign policy to an active external policy, see Mario Ojeda, *Alcances y límites de la política exterior de México* (Mexico: El Colegio de México, 1980).
54. John Saxe-Fernandez, *Petróleo y estrategia. México y Estados Unidos en el contexto de la política global* (Mexico: Siglo XXI, 1980).
55. Guadalupe González, "Incertidumbre de una potencia media regional: las nuevas dimensiones de la política exterior Mexicana," in Olga Pellicer, ed., *La Política exterior de México: desafíos en los ochenta* (Mexico: CIDE, 1983).
56. For basic reference works on contemporary Latin American militarism, see Antonio Cavalla, *Geopolítica y seguridad nacional en América* (Mexico: UNAM, 1983); Pablo Gonzalez Casanova, *Los militares y la política en América Latina* (Mexico: Oceano, 1988); D. Kruij and Edelberto Torres, eds., *América Latina: militares y sociedad* (San José: FLACSO, 1991); Alain Rouquié, *El estado militar en América Latina* (Mexico: Siglo XXI, 1984); and Augusto Varas, ed., *La Autonomía militar en América Latina* (Caracas: Nueva Sociedad, 1988).
57. A U.S. Congressional analyst maintains that a reassessment of the strategic value of Mexican oil had led to the revival of a plan for the United States army to occupy the oil wells. See Clyde Mark, "México en el proyecto de Estados Unidos para la ocupación militar de pozos petroleros," in *El Día*, "Testimonios y Documentos," Mexico, April 9, 1981. See also David Ronfeldt et al., *Mexico's Petroleum and U.S. Policy: Implications for the 1980s* (Santa Monica CA: RAND Corporation, 1980).
58. To show support for the Panamanian government of Omar Torrijos during negotiations over the Panama Canal between 1973 and 1976, a coalition of countries headed by Mexico, Colombia, and Venezuela was formed. This coalition led subsequently to the Contadora Group (1983) and the current Group of Three. The United States government viewed this as a diplomatic Odyssey, according to William Jorden, *Panama Odyssey* (Austin TX: University of Texas Press, 1984).
59. For a detailed analysis of this point, see Raúl Benítez Manaut and Ricardo Cordova Macias, eds., *México en Centroamérica. Expedientes de documentos fundamentales, 1979-1986* (Mexico: CIIH-UNAM, 1989).
60. "Address by President José López Portillo, speaking on behalf of Latin American leaders, during the ceremony marking transfer of sovereignty over the Panama Canal (October 1, 1979)," in *El gobierno mexicano* (Mexico: Presidencia de la República, 1979) (35) 98-102.
61. Extract from Chapter 6.3, "Seguridad Nacional," in Mexico, *Plan Global de Desarrollo, 1980-1982* (Mexico: Talleres Gráficos de la Nación, 1980) 132.
62. Gloria Fuentes, *El Ejército Mexicano* (Mexico: Grijalvo, 1983) 158.
63. General D.E.M. Gerardo Vega, *Seguridad Nacional, Concepto, Organización, Método* (Mexico: unpublished dissertation, 1988). General Vega was Director of the National Defence College of Mexico until the beginning of 1992.
64. See José Luis Piñeyro, "Fuerzas armadas mexicanas y modernización militar," in Varas, *La Autonomía* 272.

65. The researcher Stephen Wager maintains that the campaign against the drug trade, which has become permanent and extensive, is now in effect a new defence plan—DN4; see Stephen Wager, *The Mexican Military Approaches the 21st Century: Coping with a New World Order* (Washington: Strategic Studies Institute, 1993) 5.
66. For a detailed analysis of the purchase of the F-5 aircraft, see Dziedzic, *The Essence of Decision* 116-32.
67. The two forces affecting Mexico's position (its emergence as an independent actor and the realignment needed to renegotiate its debt) are analyzed by Bruce Bagley (1981), "Mexico in the 1980's: A New Regional Power," *Current History* 80(469); and his (1983), "Mexican Foreign Policy: The Decline of a Regional Power?" *Current History* 82(488): 406-10.
68. For an analysis from the U.S. perspective, see Edward Williams, "Mexico's Central America Policy: National Security Considerations," in Howard Wiarda, ed., *Rift and Revolution: The Central American Imbroglio* (Washington: The American Enterprise Institute, 1984).
69. Rear Admiral Mario Santos Caamal (1985), "México frente a Centroamérica. Un concepto estratégico nacional en acción," *Armada de México* (51).
70. Lilia Bermúdez, *Guerra de baja intensidad. Reagan contra Centroamérica* (Mexico: Siglo XXI, 1987). There is an abundance of U.S. literature on the strategy for containing communism. The first phase of this strategy is analyzed by Richard Alan White in *The Morass: United States Intervention in Central America* (New York: Harper & Row, 1984).
71. Mexican government documents show that, from the very beginning of the Central American crisis, it was recognized that to overcome the crisis the political systems there would have to be demilitarized through political negotiations. See Bernardo Sepúlveda (1986), "México y Centroamérica" (Roosevelt Conference on Central America, held in Chicago, October 28, 1985), *Revista Mexicana de Política Exterior* (10).
72. See "Statement by Secretary Jorge Castañeda at the 28th Consultative Meeting of OAS Foreign Ministers, 21 June 1979," and "Text of the Franco-Mexican Declaration on El Salvador (28 August 1981)," in Benítez Manaut and Cordova Macias, *México en Centroamérica* 35-38 and 45-46. These initiatives left Mexico isolated in the region, since El Salvador, Guatemala, Honduras, and Costa Rica, as well as the United States, believed that Mexico was openly siding with the Sandinista government of Nicaragua and with the guerrilla movements in El Salvador and Guatemala.
73. Sergio Aguayo Quezada, *El Exodo Centroamericano* (Mexico: SEPFORO 2000, 1985).
74. One researcher has compiled a record of 69 military incursions from Guatemala into Mexico up to June 1984. See Sergio Aguayo Quezada, "La seguridad nacional y la soberanía mexicana entre Estados Unidos y América Central," in Mario Ojeda, ed., *Las Relaciones de México con los Países de América Central* (Mexico: El Colegio de México, 1985) 52.
75. The Reagan government spoke of a "common manifest destiny" between the two countries, and warned of the danger to U.S. national security should

the influence of Central American guerrillas engender an armed movement in Mexico. See Regino Diaz's interview with Ronald Reagan, "What affects Mexico affects the United States: Reagan," in *Excelsior,* Mexico, August 17, 1987.

76. For an analysis of this point, see Raúl Benítez Manaut and Lilia Bermúdez, "Seguridad Nacional y Crisis en las Relaciones Mexico-Estados Unidos-Centroamérica (1979-1987)," in *Viejos Desafíos, Nuevas Perspectivas, México-Estados Unidos y América Latina* (Mexico: UNAM-Porrua, 1988).

77. See Raúl Benítez Manaut, "Civil War in El Salvador and Efforts to Achieve Peace," in Kumar Rupesinghe, ed., *Internal Conflict and Governance* (New York: St. Martin Press, 1992); and Raúl Benítez Manaut (1992), "La ONU y el proceso de paz en El Salvador," *Revista Mexicana de Política Exterior* (34).

78. Abraham Lowenthal, *Partners in Conflict: The United States and Latin America* (Baltimore MD: Johns Hopkins University Press, 1987). See Chapter 3, "The United States and Mexico: Uneasy Neighbors."

79. Brian Latel, *Mexico at the Crossroads: The Many Crises of the Mexican Political System* (San Francisco: The Hoover Institution, 1986).

80. There was strong criticism of Mexico between 1985 and 1988, including suggestions that an "Iran Syndrome" was in play. The public utterances of Senator Jesse Helms, in particular, aroused great concern in the Mexican government. There was also frequent criticism in the mass-circulation press. Carlos Rico points out that policy making in the United States was in many respects inconsistent and even contradictory; see Carlos Rico, "The Making of U.S. Policy toward Mexico: Should we expect coherence?" in Rosario Green and Peter Smith, eds., *Foreign Policy in U.S.-Mexican Relations* (San Diego CA: Center for U.S.-Mexican Studies, 1989).

81. Pablo Gonzalez Casanova, ed., *México hacia el año 2000: desafíos y opciones* (Caracas: Nueva Sociedad, 1989).

82. Maria Celia Toro, "México y Estados Unidos: el narcotráfico como amenaza a la seguridad nacional," in Sergio Aguayo Quezada and Bruce M. Bagley, eds., *En Busca de la seguridad perdida: aproximaciones a la seguridad nacional mexicana* (Mexico: Siglo XXI, 1990).

83. Steven Wisolsky, *Breaking the Impasse in the War on Drugs* (New York: Greenwood Press, 1986).

84. Sergio Aguayo Quezada, "Los usos, abusos y retos de la seguridad nacional mexicana, 1946-1990," in Aguayo Quezada and Bagley, *En Busca* 135.

85. Mexican agencies considered to have national security functions are: Ministry of National Defence, Department of the Navy, Ministry of the Interior, Ministry of Foreign Relations, and Office of the Attorney General (which coordinates anti-drug trade operations). The ministries within the "Economic Cabinet" also belong to this group.

86. Academic discussion of this topic began with publication of Olga Pellicer's essay, "La seguridad nacional de México: preocupaciones nuevas y nociones tradicionales," in Carlos Tello and Clark Reynolds, eds., *Las Relaciones México-Estados Unidos* (Mexico: FCE, 1981).

87. Vega, *Seguridad Nacional.*

88. *Plan Global de Desarrollo, 1980-1982; Plan Nacional de Desarrollo, 1983-1988* (Mexico: Secretaría de Planificación y Presupuesto, 1983); and *Plan Nacional de Desarrollo, 1989-1994* (Mexico: Secretaría de Planificación y Presupuesto, 1989).
89. Roger Bartra, "Nacionalismo Revolucionario y Seguridad Nacional en México," in Aguayo Quezada and Bagley, *En Busca*.
90. Luis Herrera-Lasso, "Democracia y seguridad nacional," in Rolando Cordera, *El Reclamo Democrático* (Mexico: Siglo XXI, 1988) 287.
91. See Howard Cline, *The United States and Mexico* (New York: Atheneum, 1971); and also the section entitled "La realidad geopolítica de México," in Ojeda, *Las Relaciones* 87-94.
92. For a compilation of the most important aspects of Mexico-U.S. relations during the 1980s, see Riordan Roett, ed., *México y Estados Unidos: el manejo de la relación* (Mexico: Siglo XXI, 1989).
93. Sam Sarkesian and John Mead Flanagin, eds., *U.S. Domestic and National Security Agendas* (London: Greenwood Press, 1993).

II

CURRENT PERSPECTIVES ON INTERNATIONAL SECURITY ISSUES

4

CANADA'S LONG-TERM STRATEGIC SITUATION: IMPLICATIONS FOR CANADIAN INTERNATIONAL SECURITY POLICIES

LA SITUATION STRATÉGIQUE À LONG TERME DU CANADA ET SES IMPLICATIONS POUR LES POLITIQUES CANADIENNES EN MATIÈRE DE SÉCURITÉ INTERNATIONALE

Paul Buteux

Abstract: Canada's security policy, like the world geopolitical situation, has evolved greatly since the end of World War II. However, six elements of this policy have remained constant.

The first of these "invariants" is Canada's geographical situation which dictates that Canada enter into a "natural" alliance with the United States when faced with an intercontinental threat. The second is a shared interest in security questions, as Canadian and American strategic visions are largely complementary. The third is a situation of complex interdependence, deriving from Canada-U.S. interaction at many levels and in many fields. The fourth is the dominating influence of American policies on those of Canada, which serves to limit Canada's options. The fifth is the absence of a real U.S. threat. And the sixth invariant is the impact of international changes on Canada's security policy.

The changes that have occurred in the international system since the end of World War II—and more so since the end of the Cold War—have not altered these invariants in Canada's long-term strategic situation. What has changed, however, is their political and military significance. Gone is the need for urgency in continental defence cooperation, international security is no longer collective but cooperative; Canada no longer holds the same geostrategic importance for the U.S.; and Canada's zone of influence and intervention has shifted somewhat from Europe toward Asia-Pacific and Latin America.

Thus, new security policy options present themselves to Canada. But it should be clearly understood that the promotion of these security interests requires adequate military means.

Sommaire : La politique de sécurité du Canada, comme la situation géopolitique mondiale, a grandement évolué depuis la fin du Second Conflit mondial. Néanmoins, certains éléments de cette politique de sécurité, au nombre de six, sont demeurés les mêmes durant cette période.

Le premier de ces invariants est la situation géographique du Canada qui, en cas de menace inter-continentale, incite à une alliance naturelle avec les États-Unis. Le second consiste en un intérêt partagé pour les questions de sécurité, les visions stratégiques du Canada et des États-Unis étant pour l'essentiel complémentaires. Le troisième est une situation d'interdépendance complexe, découlant d'une interaction Canada-États-Unis se situant à plusieurs niveaux et dans plusieurs domaines. Le quatrième est l'influence dominante des politiques américaines sur les politiques canadiennes, limitant le nombre d'options offertes au Canada. Le cinquième est l'absence de menace en provenance des États-Unis. Le sixième est l'impact qu'ont les changements internationaux sur la politique de sécurité du Canada.

Les changements survenus depuis la fin du Second Conflit mondial, et surtout depuis la fin de la Guerre froide, n'ont en rien modifié ces invariants. Seule leur signification politique et militaire a changé. Ainsi, l'urgence de la coopération continentale en matière de défense s'est effacée; la sécurité internationale ne se veut plus nécessairement collective mais plutôt coopérative; le Canada n'a plus la même importance géostratégique pour des États-Unis; et la zone d'influence et d'intervention du Canada n'est plus l'Europe mais bien l'Asie-Pacifique et l'Amérique latine.

En somme, des choix nouveaux s'offrent dorénavant au Canada en matière de politique de sécurité. Toutefois, il doit être compris que les intérêts en matière de sécurité devront se traduire par des investissements militaires adéquats.

NATURAL ALLIES?

ANY ATTEMPT TO DISCUSS Canada's strategic situation in broad terms and to draw out of the discussion some implications for Canadian policies concerning international security involves acknowledgment of R.J. Sutherland's seminal 1962 article on the subject.[1] The analytical framework that he provided and the insights that he displayed have stood the test of time remarkably well. Nonetheless, the political context and policy implications of Canada's strategic situation are in many important ways different from those of thirty years ago.

In one respect, however, Canada's strategic situation is unchanging, and this results from the country's location in the northern part of the North American continent. To restate the obvious: Canada occupies an enormous land mass that is inhabited by a highly urbanized, relatively small, and unevenly distributed population; Canada borders on three oceans, one of which is mostly covered by ice; and Canada shares a long common border with the United States. From these geographical facts it follows that policing Canadian territory and exercising surveillance over it and contiguous waters and airspace pose considerable technical and resource problems. These problems are compounded if the active defence of Canadian territory is contemplated.

THE SIX "INVARIANTS" OF CANADIAN STRATEGY

Canada's geographical position constitutes a fundamental "invariant" of Canadian strategy (to use Sutherland's term), and it ensures that there will always be a continental dimension to Canada's defence and security policies. That this continental context should entail defence cooperation with the United States has been explicitly recognized by Canadian governments since at least 1938. Following President Roosevelt's declaration in Kingston, Ontario in August 1940 that the United States "would not stand idly by" if Canada was threatened by "any other empire," Prime Minister Mackenzie King responded by recognizing that Canada had an obligation to make itself secure in such a way that "should the occasion ever arise, enemy forces would not be able to pursue their way either by land, sea or air, to the United States across Canadian territory."[2] This recognition of mutual security interests, and of the logic of continental defence cooperation that it has entailed, has remained a constant of Canadian defence policy ever since. Indeed, it may be said to constitute the second invariant of Canada's long-term strategic situation.

The emergence of this natural alliance with the United States marked a fundamental transformation in the Canada-U.S. security relationship. For most of Canadian history, the United States itself had posed the major threat to Canada's territorial integrity and national existence. Canada's security rested on its links with Britain as part of the Empire and, as a consequence, Canadian security policy was determined more by decisions made in London than in Canada. As long as London paid the bills, such a state of affairs was satisfactory to the Canadian colonies, but after Confederation it was clear that the territorial defence of Canada would have to be undertaken by Canadians themselves. The Royal Navy might maintain the strategic balance through its "command of the seas,"[3] but it would be up to Canadians to protect their border with the United States.

The response of the new government of Canada was to pursue complementary strategies of domestic consolidation and, following the model adopted by the imperial government in London, reassurance of the Americans. It was a slow process of evolution from the Rush-Bagot Treaty of 1817 to the Ogdensburg Agreement of 1940, which resulted in what, in effect, was a mutual non-aggression pact between the United States and Canada. In turn, this commitment to non-aggression was buttressed by mutual security guarantees. The result was not only the undefended border, but from 1940 onward an expanding program of defence cooperation and, with the Hyde Park Agreement of 1941, a substantial degree of integration of Canada's defence-industrial base with that of the United States.[4]

Literally hundreds of formal and informal agreements now bind the United States and Canada together in shared defence arrangements. The complexity of the Canadian-American defence relationship is the result of an accumulation of agreements originating during World War II, which were then modified and added to during the Cold War. Now, with the end of the Cold War, many of these arrangements will be subject to review both in Canada and in the United States. It may be surmised that not all the resulting changes will be welcome to Canada, and that the adjustment of the continental defence arrangement is likely to prove a thorny problem for Canada's policy makers.

Of course, the emergence of a continentalist context for Canadian defence and security policies was not simply the result of shared security challenges and complementary strategic visions; it also reflected the degree to which Canada had become bound to the United States economically, politically, and culturally. In the jargon of political science, the Canadian-American relationship is one of complex interdependence. Among other things, this means that many issues arise as a result of the cross-border interaction of numerous formal and informal governmental contacts, non-governmental links at the individual and corporate levels, and interactions between governmental and non-governmental actors. These issues are managed and dealt with in the same complicated manner. One very important consequence of this is that it becomes very difficult, if not impossible, for a government to exercise consistent and centralized control over these highly interdependent relationships. These issues of public policy emerge in no particular hierarchy of political salience and, in practice, the traditional distinction between "high" and "low" politics becomes blurred. Thus, military issues constitute but one class of issue-area among the many that arise in the bilateral relationship with the United States, and defence and security matters, most of the time, are treated in a routine fashion by means of standard operating procedures. As long as Canada meets the minimum requirements of the continental defence bargain it has made with the United States, there is no compelling principle that requires the subordination of other issues to the needs of national defence. In other words, under normal circumstances, national defence does not take priority over other government objectives. Complex interdependence may be said to constitute the third invariant of Canada's strategic situation.

Consequently, defence is usually dealt with as just another issue-area in Canadian-American relations, with the result that, in Canada, defence matters rarely receive consistent, high-level political attention. Occasionally, this leads to Canadian governments being caught by surprise as matters that have been handled in routine fashion suddenly become politically salient. Perhaps the classic example is the embarrassment of the Conservative government of John Diefenbaker following its signature of NORAD in 1958. It appeared after parliamentary and media scrutiny that the government had signed an agreement with the United States without being aware of what the agreement meant in terms of both the integration of Canada's air defence with those of the United States and, perhaps more importantly, the political pitfalls that it created. More recently, an example is provided by the political fall-out from the testing of American cruise missiles in Canada. Here again was an issue arising from a bilateral agreement on reciprocal access to testing and training facilities that was negotiated very much at the official level and with only nominal political input. Subsequently, when the United States requested access to Canadian testing facilities under the agreement for cruise missile trials, the requests caused Canadian governments some political embarrassment.[5] The current Liberal government of Jean Chrétien has made it clear to the United States that it will not welcome further requests of this kind, but in the process it has compromised the overall agreement and, possibly, the benefits that Canada derives from it.

To describe the Canadian-American relationship as one of complex interdependence is not to imply that the relationship is an equal one. Any index of national capabilities will illustrate the disparities of power between the two countries. Furthermore, as a superpower, the United States possesses what some have termed "structural power," which means essentially that it possesses the power to determine the rules of the game, or at least to exercise major influence on their determination. More specifically, structural power refers to the ability to determine the social and institutional structures that provide the context within which, to paraphrase Harold Lasswell, who gets what, when, and how is determined.[6] This prerogative, historically associated with great powers, is not available to Canada. Nonetheless, Canada is not powerless in its relations with the United States. What Canada does possess is "relational power," which is understood as the capacity to bargain successfully for outcomes that, in the absence of relational power, would not be forthcoming.[7]

Given that bargaining usually involves both the carrot and the stick, both the offer of rewards and the threat of sanctions, relational power is issue-area-specific. Thus, on some issues—those having to do with the international trade in primary resources, for example—Canada possesses significant relational power based on the international importance of its resource base; on others, such as international monetary policy, Canada possesses far less leverage given the limited international role of the Canadian dollar. With specific respect to continental defence arrangements, given the size and geostrategic location of its territory, for most of the Cold War period Canada possessed an asset absolutely crucial to American security.

Nonetheless, even where capabilities are limited, the opportunity to exercise relational power often still exists. This is because, under conditions of complex interdependence, most of the issues that arise are rule-governed in some way. In other words, they fall within the framework of an international regime, and the ability to exploit the institutional arrangements and manipulate the rules of the regime constitutes a form of relational power. Moreover, Canada is at times able to exploit the fact that issues that are important to Canada are not necessarily of equal importance to the United States, with the result that the United States may be prepared to give way on what for itself are rather minor points and that involve relatively minor costs.[8] Within the context of the Canadian security relationship with the United States, there is plenty of evidence that the elaborate structure of collaboration that has been built up over a fifty-year period has provided Canada with influence and leverage on the United States beyond what a simple comparison of their respective military capabilities would suggest.[9]

In matters of international security, it is quite clear that the United States has structural power, and the end of the Cold War has not diminished American capabilities in this respect. The fact that the United States also possesses structural power with respect to the regimes governing such vitally important areas as international trade and finance simply underlines the unique position of hegemony that the United States has enjoyed since 1945. Even if, as some argue, the United States is a declining *hegemon*, it will be many years before Washington ceases to be the single most powerful political influence on the main security and economic structures of the international system. This state of affairs is intensified for Canada given its geographical propinquity to the United States and the high degree of social, economic, and cultural integration that has occurred. Thus, along with geostrategic location, the dominant influence of American policy on the determination of the Canadian security agenda and the constraints this places on Canada's policy choices must be considered a fourth "invariant" of Canada's strategic situation.

Taken in combination, the context of complex interdependence and the dominant influence of American policies on the determination of Canada's agenda of security issues have meant that Canada's most important security relationships are with a neighbour vastly more powerful than itself. Thus, the United States is a security problem for Canada. This is not new, but what was once at times a direct threat to the territorial integrity of Canada has been transformed into a close Canadian-American alliance. This creates problems of a different kind, and many in Canada today would argue that the very closeness of the Canadian-American relationship constitutes a threat to the political, economic, and cultural autonomy of Canada. Very few would suggest, however, that the United States any longer represents a military threat to its sovereign independence. Nonetheless, the fact that Canada cannot unilaterally balance the United States has led to what some have seen as a policy of "counterweights."[10]

With the exception of the Empire, Canada has never had the opportunity to pursue a Kautilyan strategy of organizing a "circle of states" in which a neighbour is counterbalanced by alliance or alignment with that neighbour's neighbour.[11] For Canada, no counterweights to the United States have existed on the American continent and, therefore, with the decline in the effectiveness of Britain's imperial guarantee, Canada had little or no alternative but to follow a policy of security alignment with the United States. Canada has practised a strategy of bandwagoning with the regional *hegemon* rather than attempting to ally with others in order to form a "balance" against it.[12] Rather, Canada, whenever possible and whenever it has been in Canada's interest to do so, has sought to multilateralize its security relations with the United States. In other words, Canada has practised a policy of selectively managing the relationship with the United States within the framework of intra-alliance and other multilateral relationships.

Thus, NATO has proved to be a congenial security arrangement for Canada because it has provided an institutionalized and multilateral context within which Canada can form alignments with various Allied partners to influence American policy in desired directions.[13] On the other hand, politically at least, the bilateral relationship with the United States in NORAD has always caused discomfort for many Canadians. Nonetheless, depending on the issue, both the multilateral context of NATO and the wide range of bilateral defence arrangements with the United States have provided Canada with effective relational power in the service of its policies. One further point follows from this: the necessity of bilateralism and the desirability of multilateralism in Canada's security relationship with the United States rule out neutralism as a viable policy option for Canada.

The fifth invariant of Canada's strategic situation is that, once the United States no longer represented an actual or potential military threat to Canada, the only possible military threats to Canadian security were extra-continental. In the 20th century, the most serious of such threats have all emerged in Europe. Canada's membership in NATO for over forty years has been an acknowledgment of this fact. Involvement in the Cold War and in two world wars, all having their origins in Europe, amounts also to a recognition that Canada has had a fundamental interest in preventing any hostile power from dominating the European landmass. The Cold War presented a particularly direct and dangerous threat to Canada since the possibility of a central strategic nuclear exchange between the superpowers jeopardized the physical survival of Canada as well.

NATO has also been the centrepiece of policies related to what may be considered the sixth invariant of Canada's long-term strategic situation: namely, that Canada has been directly affected by the character of the overall international security environment. Canada is not immune or indifferent to the impact on it of the global security structure, which historically has done much to shape Canada territorially and constitutionally. It may be said of Canada that, like its allies, it has a general interest in global stability. At the level of public debate, global stability is non-controversial: everybody is in favour of it. What particular form of global stability is to be preferred is, however, contested internationally, and, to some degree, domestically. This is because what constitutes stability is embedded in the particular form of global order that prevails. The rules of this order are determined primarily by those possessing structural power: except for the former Soviet bloc, the post-1945 order has been dominated by the United States and its allies.

Canada has had a vested interest in this American-led international system in all its major military, economic, and political dimensions. The designation of Canadian foreign and security policies as "internationalist" has meant, in practice, active participation in Western institutions designed to facilitate the maintenance of a relatively open, pluralistic, and capitalist economic and political international system. Here again, NATO has been the key institutional expression of Canada's interest in the security dimensions of this favoured international order.

Canada's active—and at times activist—role in the UN should be seen in light of the kind of international system that Canada has favoured. The rhetoric of internationalism complements the universalism of the UN Charter, but Canada's role in the collective security and peacekeeping activities of the UN, from Korea through "Desert Storm" to Croatia and Bosnia, has generally promoted the kind of security order favoured by the West. The Western conception of international order has by no means received universal acceptance, and it should be recognized that, at times, it has been sustained only through the application of military power. Whether through collective defence arrangements, peacekeeping, or participation in combat, Canada has contributed militarily to sustaining this order. It has done so because it has been determined that Canadian strategic interests are served thereby, but, more specifically, Canada has made a military contribution in order to remain an ally in good standing of countries that are militarily, politically, and economically important to it.

Within the framework of this preferred global order, it should be recognized that Canadian policy has always treated the security of some regions as more important than that of others. Clearly, North America on the one side and Western Europe on the other, linked politically and militarily by the Atlantic Alliance, have constituted the regions of greatest security concern to Canada. Even though Canadian armed forces have not been in combat since 1945 except outside the North Atlantic region,[14] it is possible to argue that the strategic rationale for these "out-of-area" interventions was directly linked to the security of this area of vital geopolitical interest. In this respect, it is noteworthy that, despite growing Canadian economic and political interest in the Asia-Pacific region and in Latin America, no Canadian government has so far been willing to contemplate security commitments in these regions that are at all comparable to those in the North Atlantic area.

NATURAL ALLIES?

REDEFINING CANADIAN SECURITY POLICIES

The rapid and revolutionary changes that have occurred in the international system in recent years, even when coupled with a number of long-term structural developments of an economic, social, and technological nature, have not altered these invariants of Canada's long-term strategic situation. What has changed, however, is their political and military significance.

With the end of the Cold War, Canada no longer confronts any direct extra-territorial military threat to its territorial and political integrity, there is no hostile potential *hegemon* threatening the Eurasian landmass, and, consequently, there is no longer any need for urgency in continental defence cooperation. When these changes are coupled with a revised agenda of issues that are perceived as affecting security—the impact of social and economic change on national well-being, the purported globalization of the international economy, and threats of ecological damage, for example—it is possible to draw the conclusion that Canada has an opportunity to make choices about its defence policy and its international military commitments unhampered by decisions made forty years ago and conditioned by historical circumstances that no longer exist.

This has led to the view being expressed in Canada that, beyond the surveillance and policing of national territory, all the military roles and commitments that might be undertaken, particularly those having a bearing on international security, are discretionary.[15] Canada, it would seem, has again become—in Senator Dandurand's famous phrase—"a fire-proof house far from inflammable materials." Thus, a posture of what Sutherland called "minimum defence" is possible. However, whatever choices a Canadian government might make will inevitably involve opportunity costs. These costs, in general terms, will be a function of the interaction of the invariants of Canada's strategic situation and domestic political decisions about the nature of Canada's interests. Given Canada's geostrategic location and the nature of Canada's current entanglements in the wider world, it is doubtful whether Canada will have the freedom to pick and choose its international security commitments to the extent that some fondly imagine to be the case.

Conceptually, the range of policy choice is bounded by two poles, which may be characterized either as policies of *engagement* or as policies of *isolation*. Clearly, in contrast to the inter-war period when Canada in fact adopted a posture of minimum defence, Canadian international security policy since 1945 fits the engagement model. Indeed, in the 1940s, those in Ottawa who formulated the "functional principle" did so in conscious rejection of the policies of the inter-war period in which Canada had sought to eschew international security obligations, whether within an imperial or a League of Nations context.[16] Now it was in Canada's strategic interest to participate actively in the determination of Western security policy. The foundations of Canada's post-war international security policy that were laid down at this time survived substantially intact until the close of the Cold War. This attests to both the strength of the grand strategy they were designed to serve and their appeal to important domestic needs and constituencies. They were also in tune with Canada's long-term strategic situation.

Undoubtedly, with the end of any direct military threat to Canada and the absence of any emerging threat, the way is clear to redefine Canadian security policies. Official use of the term "cooperative security" reflects the appreciation that many issues that threaten the well-being of Canadians and others can be resolved, if at all, only through cooperative action. Moreover, there is a strong perception that many of these problems—be they economic, environmental, or whatever—are not susceptible to military solutions because the threat and use of armed force are simply irrelevant as a response. Nonetheless, the notion of cooperative security, at least as articulated in Canada,[17] gives recognition to the fact that armed force remains an important currency of international politics. Whatever the range of choices available to Canadian governments, their international security policies necessarily must take into account the possibility of the use of force as the *ultima ratio* of international politics.

Canada has choices, but those that involve doing less in the way of defence will incur costs in terms of Canada's international security objectives. These costs lie primarily in their impact on Canada's relational power with respect to the United States and with others whose actions might affect Canadian security, however narrowly or broadly that security might be defined. Here, particularly, the second and third invariants of Canada's strategic situation are relevant, namely those having to do with continental defence cooperation and with the character of complex interdependence. It is not that these strategic invariants operate in a deterministic fashion, but that policy that runs counter to them is likely to prove ineffectual and may result in consequences counter to the objectives sought. The results of Canadian security policies in the inter-war period provide salutary examples.

Given the crucial impact of the United States on all aspects of Canadian security and given that, even in present circumstances, Canada and the United States share mutual and complementary security interests, Canada still needs defence capabilities that will provide relational power with respect to the United States. Not least, Canada requires the military wherewithal to practise defence cooperation with the United States on terms that are not overwhelmingly determined by Washington. Though this is a point that any Canadian government would find difficult to accept in present circumstances, the impact of the end of the Cold War on Canada's strategic situation may require Canada to do somewhat more in the way of defence rather than less.

The explanation of this apparent paradox lies in the interaction of Canada's strategic situation with the nature of its relational power in the security field. For most of the Cold War, Canada's geostrategic location between the superpowers, and the active support of Canadian governments for the continental defence arrangements that this entailed, meant that Canada could exercise relational power in Washington on the basis of modest defence expenditures. (Since 1965, these have been 3 percent or less of gross domestic product, and currently are less than 2 percent of GDP.) Though Washington urged Canada to do more, from its point of view Canada kept up its end of the defence bargain by not making the defence of the United States more difficult than it needed to be. Now, of course, the absence of an extra-continental threat has reduced both the geostrategic importance of Canada to the United States and the urgency and priority of continental defence in American strategic thinking. If Canada does not wish to be a complete supplicant to Washington on matters of defence and security, it needs forces capable of supporting its own international security policies and, more directly, of protecting specific Canadian interests from the fall-out of what otherwise might be unilateral American decisions. This cannot be done on the basis of a posture of minimum defence.[18]

Much the same kind of argument applies to the Canadian role in NATO. It can be argued that, particularly after 1969, when Canada halved and redeployed its forces in Europe, Canadian military deployments there served primarily symbolic purposes. For example, Canadian forces in Europe represented a tangible symbol of Canada's interest in and commitment to the security of its Western European allies. Nonetheless, the symbolic value of Canada's forces to its allies depended on their serving a militarily useful purpose. From the middle of the 1970s onward, Canadian governments sought to repair the damage caused by the 1969 decision by upgrading Canada's remaining forces. Symbolic they may have been, but they were never merely token.

Even though Canadian forces in Europe have now been withdrawn (with the exception of Canadians serving in the multinational Airborne Warning and Control System [AWACS] force), Canada has indicated that European security is still a major interest. In the aftermath of the Cold War, NATO is now the dominant military element in the new European security architecture. The Conference on Security and Cooperation in Europe (CSCE) has neither collective defence nor collective security functions, and does not possess any military capabilities. It is noteworthy that, at the 1992 Helsinki summit meeting of the CSCE, it was agreed that NATO's resources could be called upon in support of its peacekeeping functions. Moreover, NATO, through such arrangements as the NACC and the Partnership for Peace, has been creating a network of military cooperation with its former adversaries in Central and Eastern Europe. Whatever the long-term effectiveness of these arrangements, the alliance is at present the only institution available that can sponsor such a program of pan-European military cooperation.

Canada is a member of both the CSCE and NATO, and such membership conforms to Canada's long-standing interest in the politics of European security. However, it has been made clear by Canada's NATO allies in many ways and on many occasions that the price of the pursuit of Canadian security interests in Europe includes credible, but not necessarily substantial, military commitments. For Canada to support its strategic interests in regions important to it, access to and credibility in those multilateral institutions that have a security mandate are required. By the same token, when Canada does make the commitments that warrant a say in the policies of those institutions, it is up to Canadian diplomacy to exploit the opportunity. For example, the substantial role played by Canada in the UN peacekeeping operations in what was formerly Yugoslavia does not seem to have been utilized as well as it might have been in the service of Canada's longer-term political and strategic goals. Perhaps this is because these goals have still to be defined authoritatively.

One consequence for Canada of the end of the Cold War is that, as Canadian military commitments in Europe run down, other regions of the world assume greater security importance. In this respect, as Canadian political and economic interests in Latin America grow (membership in the OAS and NAFTA may be seen as a tangible indication of this), Canada's security interests in the Americas are likely to increase as well. And indeed, Canada's growing military commitment in the region is already manifested through its peacekeeping activities in Central America and its involvement in the internal politics of Haiti. There are indications that the institutional basis of Latin American security arrangements is likely to undergo fundamental change, and Canada is already involved in this process. Like Mexico and a number of other Latin American states, Canada rejects American notions of hemispheric security, but its ability to influence American policies in this respect will require assets that can support Canadian diplomatic efforts. This does not necessarily mean specific military commitments, but it does require some ability to project military power in the region, under whatever auspices this might take place.

In a similar vein, Canada's economic and political interests in the Pacific Rim have been growing steadily. The fact that Canada sponsored a North Pacific Cooperative Security Dialogue in 1991 may be interpreted as a recognition that the growing importance of the region to Canada entails security interests as well. It would be wishful thinking to believe that, if Canada does define security interests in the region, there will be no military implications. As Canada recognized with its security interests in North America and Europe, there were no military free rides. It is difficult to see why there should be any reason to think it is any different in Asia or Latin America.

Canada's international security policies are affected not only by the invariants of its strategic situation, but also by its larger foreign policy goals. Since the end of World War II, Canada, in accordance with the functional principle, has sought to play an important role in world politics. This has involved not only the acceptance of significant international security commitments, but also participation in most of the major economic and political institutions of the developed world. Canadian membership in the Group of Seven (G-7) perhaps indicates best the standing that successive Canadian governments have considered Canada's due. The effectiveness of Canadian participation in these various instruments of multilateral diplomacy has depended on Canada's ability to exploit relational power. Though a distinctive feature of the politics of complex interdependence is that relational power tends to be issue-area-specific, it is also affected by linkages across issue-areas. Reputation in one area can have payoffs in another.

It is not only in its international security environment that Canada faces dramatic change; it is also the case that major transformations in many other areas of the post-war international system are taking place. Thus, for example, at the Naples meeting of the G-7 in July 1994, Russia became a member of its political arm, which will now be known as the G-8. In addition, the summit called for a fresh look at the Bretton Woods financial institutions and a revitalized UN. In short, there was agreement that many features of the world economic and political order should be systematically reviewed. If Canada wishes to be an effective actor in this process, it must take into account the fact that whatever post-Cold War international order emerges will still depend in important ways on the existence of military power. It would be a dramatic step indeed if the present Canadian government turned its back on a fifty-year heritage of Canadian foreign policy and sought refuge in a new isolationism that would be the concomitant of a posture of "minimum defence." Were this to occur, the political and economic costs to Canada would be high indeed. Seen in this light, defence expenditures that are currently less than 2 percent of GDP do not appear to be an undue burden.

NOTES

1. R.J. Sutherland (1962), "Canada's Long Term Strategic Situation," *International Journal* 17(3): 199-223.
2. It is noteworthy, and typical of Mackenzie King's caution, that the Canadian response to what amounted to a unilateral American security guarantee to Canada (even though it could be interpreted simply as a restatement of the

Monroe Doctrine) was in effect no more than a statement of the obligations of a non-belligerent state under international law. It is also relevant to note, however, that such a response implied an obligation on the part of Canada that it should possess the means to defend itself.

3. A concept and phrase popularized by an American, Alfred Thayer Mahan. See *The Influence of Sea Power upon History, 1660-1783* (1890), and *The Influence of Sea Power upon the French Revolution and Empire, 1793-1812* (1892). Both works can be found in Alfred Thayer Mahan, *The Influence of Sea Power upon History* (Englewood Cliffs NJ: Prentice-Hall, 1980).

4. The essential documents on the background to both the Ogdensburg and Hyde Park Agreements may be found in David R. Murray, ed., *Documents on Canadian External Relations, 1939-1941: Part II*, Vol. 8 (Ottawa: Department of External Affairs, 1976).

5. "The Canada-U.S. Test and Evaluation Program" was initially signed in February 1983. It has subsequently been renewed.

6. Harold Lasswell, *Politics: Who Gets What, When, How* (New York: McGraw-Hill, 1936).

7. A number of authors have developed the distinction between structural and relational power. My usage here draws directly on the distinction as made by Susan Strange. See *States and Markets* (London: Pinter, 1988) 24-32.

8. Aspects of the Defence Development and Defence Production Sharing Arrangements reflect this. However, with the rapid decline in the American defence budget in the aftermath of the Cold War, a reevaluation of the value of the present agreements is taking place in the United States.

9. Evidence of this is provided, *inter alia*, by Joseph S. Nye (1974), "Transnational Relations and Interstate Conflicts: An Empirical Analysis," *International Organization* 28(4): 961-96. More generally on bargaining between unequals, see William Mark Habeeb, *Power and Tactics in International Negotiation* (Baltimore MD: Johns Hopkins University Press, 1988).

10. A clear restatement of this thesis can be found in Stéphane Roussel et al. (1994), "Le Canada et la sécurité européenne, 1943-1952: à la recherche de l'équilibre des puissances," *Canadian Defence Quarterly* 23(4): 23-27.

11. L.N. Rangarajan, ed., *Kautilya, The Arthashastra* (New Delhi: Penguin, 1987) 555-63. Kautilya was a 4th-century BC Indian scholar and statesman, and the text ascribed to him is a classic of early Hindu literature.

12. For a formal definition of "balancing" and "bandwagoning," see Stephen M. Walt, *The Origins of Alliances* (Ithaca NY: Cornell University Press, 1987) 17-49.

13. This is an under-researched aspect of Canada's involvement in NATO. However, it is clear that on various issues and at various times Canadian policy objectives have been greatly facilitated by close cooperation, particularly with Britain and the Federal Republic of Germany.

14. Korea, and the Gulf during "Desert Storm."

15. This view has been expressed in a number of contributions to the 1994 parliamentary review of Canadian defence and foreign policy. Representative

of this line of thought is the report produced by the Canada 21 Group: *Canada and Common Security in the Twenty-First Century* (Toronto: Centre for International Studies, University of Toronto 1994).

16. Functionalism, as first publicly formulated in a speech to Parliament by Mackenzie King in 1943, referred to the principle that effective representation in the councils that would determine the shape of the post-war international order should be based on the contribution that a country could make "to the particular object in question." Canada had played virtually no part in the diplomacy that preceded the outbreak of war in Europe in 1939, and despite Canada's considerable military efforts during that war, Canada had very little say in the determination of Allied grand strategy. Ottawa was determined that this would not be the case in the future and accepted that Canadian interests would require active engagement in post-war security arrangements.

17. A succinct discussion of the concept of cooperative security from a Canadian perspective can be found in David Dewitt (1994), "Cooperative Security: A Canadian Approach to the Promotion of Peace and Security in the Post-Cold War Era," *Canadian Defence Quarterly* 23(3): 11-18.

18. The argument has been made that Canada has been a "free-rider," meaning Canada has done less in acquiring military capabilities than it has potentially had the capacity to do because it had the benefit of security provided by others. What this argument fails to take into account is that Canada has contributed to its own defence and has invested in military capabilities designed to secure its wider security objectives, including retaining influence with its allies. On the other hand, Canada has spent no more than absolutely needed, but in this respect is no different from any of its allies. Rather, the problem is that Canada has taken on a range of commitments that have strained the military resources available to meet them; hence the so-called "gap" between capabilities and commitments.

5

NATIONAL SECURITY AND THE COLD WAR: SOME CONCEPTUAL INTERPRETATIONS

LA SÉCURITÉ NATIONALE ET LA GUERRE FROIDE: QUELQUES RÉFLEXIONS CONCEPTUELLES

Jorge Chen Charpentier

Abstract: The end of the Cold War has brought about fundamental changes in many countries' concept of national security and led to a reassessment of the threats they face. Today, three main types of threat confront them: external, internal, and those related to underdevelopment.

Because external threats arise outside the borders of the state, national security is closely related to international security: it also poses questions of survival, defence, and the promotion of the state's own interests. With the end of confrontation between the superpowers the main external threats disappeared, only to be replaced by new, more diffuse transnational threats.

Internal threats are posed by the "enemy within," those "agents" or "local emissaries" of foreign powers who dare to challenge the established order. The fight against these 'subversive elements' provided justification for one group to maintain its political dominance over others. The end of the Cold War, however, has removed a key part of the ideological justification for combatting internal enemies, thus leading to a growing intolerance of human rights abuses.

Threats arising from the development process are related to the degree of liberty states enjoy in implementing development programs to meet their needs. For many states, liberty, peace, and social justice cannot be attained simply by liberalizing trade: market forces by themselves will not build infrastructures in the South.

Sommaire : La fin de la Guerre froide a grandement modifié la conception de sécurité nationale qu'entretenaient plusieurs états. On assiste ainsi à une redéfinition de la défense nationale suivant une redéfinition des menaces auxquelles font face les états. On peut dorénavant identifier trois types de menace: les menaces externes, les menaces internes, et les menaces découlant du sous-développement.

Les menaces externes sont celles qui tirent leurs origines à l'extérieur de l'état en question. La sécurité nationale est donc liée de très près à la sécurité internationale; elle est aussi une question de survie, de défense ou de promotion d'intérêts propres à l'état. Toutefois, la fin de la confrontation est-ouest a modifié la nature de ces menaces externes: diverses menaces de nature transnationale sont apparues.

Les menaces internes se rapportent plutôt au combat de l'ennemi intérieur, soit ces « agents » ou « émissaires locaux » à la solde de puissances étrangères. La lutte à des soi-disant éléments subversifs aura permis à un groupe de maintenir son emprise politique sur les autres. Cette logique s'est dissipée avec la fin de la confrontation est-ouest: l'absence d'une idéologie adverse au capitalisme ne peut dorénavant justifier la violation des droits de la personne.

Les menaces reliées au processus de développement se rapportent à la capacité des états de mettre en oeuvre des programmes de développement taillés sur mesure, par eux et pour eux. Il s'agit du niveau de liberté dont les états en développement bénéficieront. Pour bon nombre d'entre eux, atteindre la liberté, de paix ou la justice sociale ne passe pas nécessairement par la simple libéralisation des échanges. Les forces du marché à elles seules ne suffiront pas à édifier les infrastructures du sud.

NATURAL ALLIES?

THE END OF THE COLD WAR has had a significant impact on many countries' ideas about national security. The abrupt changes brought about by the disappearance of the Soviet Union have led many governments to reassess relationships with their allies and to redefine the risks or threats that might endanger the existence of the nation or state.

The political and methodological confusion of the last years has changed the meaning of international competition and cooperation and has challenged the relevancy of factors that contribute to internal stability. In recent years, we have seen some new approaches to national defence that put emphasis on preventive action. We have also seen new instruments and justifications worked out for intervening or interfering abroad. At the same time, there has been a search for alternative standards of international behaviour that may give rise to new ideas about sovereignty and national independence. The end of the Cold War has thus prompted a review of national security that has transformed the basic underpinnings of this concept. This process has raised questions about the current and future validity of the various theoretical approaches to national security and has led to a redefinition of the threats now arising in the international system and within states themselves.

The threats confronting countries today are of at least three kinds: external threats, or those that originate in other states; internal threats, or opposition movements—violent or not—that challenge prevailing legality; and threats that arise from models of development, or problems associated with underdevelopment, such as the poverty and injustice experienced by large portions of society. Concepts of national security can be classified and their evolution analyzed on the basis of the perceived source of threat.

EXTERNAL THREATS TO SECURITY

Societies that have achieved political and social integration and that have developed generally accepted rules for challenging the internal order were frequently inclined to view national security essentially as an extension of international security. To the extent that there existed a stable and predictable global society, there was less danger to individual countries. From this point of view, therefore, threats to the existence of a nation were almost always seen as coming from abroad; there was a tendency to minimize the importance of internal failings and to see new, transnational phenomena such as the drug trade as the main threats to domestic well-being or the maintenance of a certain way of life. Economic problems and shortcomings in terms of health, productivity, economic infrastructure, crime, and violence were recognized and interpreted only as incidental challenges to those countries' fitness for world leadership.[1]

The existence of a competing bloc, the spread of a different ideology, or a country's search for a new geostrategic hegemony became overriding justifications for policies of confrontation and for attempts at economic and social domination. National security in this sense meant the survival and promotion of a state's interests and attitudes and their impositon on its enemies, its competitors, or any given source of opposition. At various stages of the Cold War, this was translated by the United States into the belief that its most basic duty was to combat socialism and, by the Soviet Union into the belief that it must seek new spheres of influence.

This competition became the guiding principle of countries at the centre of world affairs (central countries) and was applied rather simplistically to those at the periphery (peripheral countries). Subsidiary players found themselves caught up in a framework of micro- and macro-political initiatives that committed them to undertakings that were quite irrelevant to their own goals, both internal and external.

The identification of international and national security as essentially the same thing meant that countries that were geographically or politically close to the superpowers had to adopt positions that were for the most part the same. Their ability to dissent was therefore severely constrained.

With the end of confrontation between the superpowers, the disappearance of the Soviet Union, and the general rejection of Marxism as an ideology, the main external threats were removed. The feeling of greater security and stability that flourished at the beginning of the 1990s in the more powerful countries was based on the false belief that the apparent and superficial sharing of democratic and free-market values would be enough to reduce the chances of confrontation, and would help to build a set of common and complementary interests. Under these conditions, it was thought, ideological or military threats would no longer exist; all that would remain would be economic and technological competition.

It is now apparent that this is unrealistic because of the emergence of two phenomena: the appearance of new, more diffuse threats that have now made their way onto the international agenda; and the growing importance of some states as sources of regional instability.

The end of the Cold War has revealed that there are, in fact, a multitude of enemies, but they are still placed in an international context. The perception that threats are more diffuse tempts some people to isolationism. With no single enemy to confront, the central powers try not to get involved in conflicts that do not appear to engage their interests directly. Furthermore, there seems to be a growing tendency to minimize the dangers inherent in international security strategies that no longer rely on the existence of clearly defined opponents and threats.[2]

Since 1989, the spontaneous reorganization of the international system has lent new importance to the north-south axis. More specifically, it has encouraged the rebuilding of links between centre and periphery that go beyond economics to include political and strategic considerations. A key feature of these new relations has been a propensity to fill the international agenda with transnational issues that are classified as threats to peace and international security: drug trafficking, immigration, pollution, and poverty, among others. "Some of the forces for renewal that we do not discern on our planet could lead to future instability and conflicts. People and governments need to rethink their old definitions of what constitutes a threat to national and international security."[3]

In this context, the problem of drug trafficking—which is more severe in the centre than at the periphery—has been transformed from a criminal matter to a national security matter that demands transnational action to combat it. Yet such a focus merely serves to downplay the importance of the demand for narcotics and puts the emphasis on their supplier. Similarly, the mass movement of people that is affecting ways of life and patterns of consumption in the more advanced societies is considered to be only marginally related to global imbalances in production factors; therefore, there is a perception that migration must be prevented at its source.

Pollution has also suddenly become a security threat, and ecological recovery a national security goal. At the same time, the great economic and developmental needs that have been of such concern to the poorer countries and that are still a concern to developed countries are accorded low priority. From this perspective, poverty that is limited geographically is not a factor of global destabilization and so does not require any urgent attention from the international community or its institutions.

Population growth and migration, pollution and environmental protection, free markets and democracy—these issues will be viewed from divergent, and even opposing, points of view, depending on a country's situation. Nevertheless, the fact that they are included on the international and multilateral agenda means that they will have various implications for national security. At the same time, other concerns have arisen, such as instability in the Third World or violent confrontations between competing nationalisms. Conflicts within states are not considered threats to global stability although, in 1993, there were a total of 52 large-scale conflicts in 42 countries, while 37 other countries experienced outbreaks of political violence. Of these 79 countries, 75 are part of the developing world.[4]

One result of the makeup of the current international agenda is that positions adopted are apparently contradictory. The development of independent military and nuclear capabilities is condemned, for instance, while no criticism or action is offered against non-tariff trade barriers. Violations of human rights may be selectively criticized while, at the same time, terms of trade for developing countries' exports have depreciated by 50 percent over the last decade, and the per capita income of the inhabitants has fallen each year independently of world economic cycles.

On the other hand, governments that do not proclaim at least formal acceptance of democracy and the free market have been isolated and declared enemies of humanity. These countries are called "pariah" states and strategies for neutralizing them and ultimately absorbing them into the community of nations committed to common values become a priority, in the hope that this will contribute to international stability.[5] The greater such countries' capacity for nuclear, chemical and bacterial, or conventional warfare, or the more flagrant their defiance of generally accepted standards, the greater the attention that is paid to them.

INTERNAL THREATS TO SECURITY

A second threat to national security is that of the "enemy within," a concept that inspired openly repressive measures in peripheral countries during the struggle against communism. Because of their political and economic structure, such countries did not need to look abroad for enemies, but found them at home among the "agents" or "local emissaries" of foreign powers. Global confrontation thus tended to find its counterpart at the domestic level, represented by specific political personalities or movements. Since there was no threat from outside the nation's borders, the need for defence was not against another country but against individuals or groups who dared to question the established order and whose actions were seen as an extension of schemes alien to the national interest.

The theory of the "enemy within" allowed international security to be used as a justification for one group to maintain its political dominance over others. In this sense, national security became one more weapon in the struggle for power within some countries where, with conveniently simplified ideology, social activists could readily be tagged as surrogate agents for the world's superpowers. This kind of absurd simplification meant that, in many cases, efforts to achieve greater democracy—a goal that is, in fact, universally accepted and promoted—were classified as destabilizing and were seen as benefiting totalitarian movements.

The struggle against the internal enemy in peripheral countries was reinforced by the interpretations of analysts and politicians in the developed world who saw social movements at the periphery as portents of some change in the global balance of power. "The anti-communist struggle produced a preference for stability and maintenance of the status quo.... Only by preserving world stability could we contain the Soviet Union from infiltrating around the world."[6] Such alarmist utterances in turn fortified the support that the governments of some central powers granted to groups at the periphery who were trying to justify the permanence of poverty and privilege in the name of national security.

The logic of the connection between internal threats and East-West competition fell apart with the end of the Cold War, and particularly with the ideological and political transformation of the Soviet Union. Today, little credibility is accorded to attempts to explain instability and armed insurgency as the result of acts or conspiracies inspired by a socialist bloc that no longer exists and whose members are, for the most part, trying to integrate themselves into the Western world.

This does not mean that the search for internal enemies is over, or that national security will no longer be used as an excuse to persecute and destroy critics and opposition forces. Nevertheless, there has been a marked reduction in internal support for actions of this kind, to the point where, on certain occasions and in certain regions, human rights violations and accompanying measures have been openly criticized and harshly censured at international and multilateral levels. It has also meant the breakdown of the broad internal consensus that had been built up in some countries to legitimize repression and the suspension of political and civil rights.

The end of the Cold War has thus removed a key element of the ideological justification for combatting the "enemy within" and has contributed to its growing disrepute as a political weapon. It must be recognized, nevertheless, that a new variant of this interpretation of national security has appeared in the last few years. Some proponents seek to hold various ethnic or minority groups responsible for a state's problems, and they propose solutions to these ills based on racial uniformity and social and geographic integration. The very definitions of pluralism, diversity, and national unity are thus being challenged. Individual or collective differences are once again becoming grounds for confrontation. Political, religious, and ethnic minorities are being branded as the new "enemy within."

DEVELOPMENT MODELS AS THREATS TO SECURITY

There is a third way of looking at threats to national security, linked to the ability to define alternative and independent models of development. This means the ability to identify and promote national interests independent of those of other countries. It is not a question of trying to institute autarchy, but of recognizing and defending the fact that differences and alternatives do exist.

Mexico has envisioned its national security in terms of its own development. According to its national strategy plans, security lies in the comprehensive development of the country as a means for maintaining conditions of freedom, peace, and social justice within a constitutional framework.[7] These plans also call for "acting with firmness and foresight so as to pre-empt any external action that might pose a threat to national security."[8] From this third perspective, the end of the superpowers' confrontation should make it possible for a country to orient its development planning in any direction it chooses, without this being seen as an attack on the basic, vital interests of the central countries.

The chance of success for alternative models depends on how the global situation evolves, and on how regional economic blocs can be integrated into the new economic landscape. These blocs are faced with contradictions arising from the fact that, while they are increasingly trying to adopt the same lifestyle, there are ever-wider gaps in living standards among their different components. The play of market forces alone will not be enough to build up the South's infrastructure nor to improve the services or guarantee prices for its products.[9]

There are no simple theoretical guidelines in the search for alternative models of development. The concept that national security means an independent route to national welfare must be tested in the efforts to meet people's needs and demands within the strict limits set by trade mechanisms or international economic arrangements.

From a broader perspective, it may be that the understanding of threats to national security—external threats, internal threats or threats derived from the model of development—will be shaped and limited by the course of regional and subregional integration.

PRIMACY OF THE CENTRAL COUNTRIES' INTERESTS

The international agenda that is now being adopted is the result of definitions of security accepted by central countries, which must also mean that their interests are broadly acknowledged by most of the international community. It would seem that there is a kind of perverse mimicry involved when each nation sets goals. This is not a new phenomenon, but it has generally gained emphasis, although in varying degrees depending on a country's geography, or its strategic or economic importance.

In most cases, the growing relationship between central countries and some peripheral ones shows similar features. For example, we will continue to hear that a new world order is a matter of common interest, and that internal political democracy is a prerequisite for both economic development and world prosperity.[10] Such concepts will form the basis for trade agreements adopted on any continent, particularly in America and, to a lesser extent, in Asia and Africa.

Regionalization is now progressing as similar economies become drawn into a complementary interrelationship. Various countries are being pulled into the orbit of central countries because they have some special feature that is of interest to the more developed economies. In this sense, privileged relationships are being granted mainly to countries that can contribute in some way to the welfare of the more powerful nations.

This means that, in the next few decades, the international scene will be marked by growing disparities. Despite differences among developing countries, the centre-periphery phenomenon has doomed large parts of the planet to continued marginalization, especially those that have no strategic value or ethnic links to the centre, those that are the source of heavy immigration flows, or those that possess raw materials of only moderate interest to developed countries.

Countries of the Third World that have some strategic or military importance will tend to adopt a notion of international security that is close to that of the dominant central countries. Those that become integrated economically will seek to ensure the uninterrupted flow of capital, even while trying, with decreasing conviction, to maintain a doctrine of national security based on the promotion of development. In this way, it is easy to see how the advanced countries will be selective as they draw closer to developing countries.

The regionalism now flourishing is reinforcing the marginalization of the greater part of the Third World. At the same time, it is increasing the community of interests shared by countries with different standards of public welfare. Thus, "mercantilism and an unhealthy isolation may be the fate of many countries of the Third and Fourth Worlds. This situation can only be improved to the extent that individual countries can use the resources of the state to make the most of the conditions of the moment while they are attempting their transformation."[11]

The adoption of new forms of international association, regardless of specific goals and objectives, will change the various participants' concepts of their national security. "One feature of the security of peripheral societies is their dependence on the political processes of societies at the centre, processes that always have an impact on those countries within the spheres of influence of the central powers, but over which it is very difficult for the periphery to have an influence."[12] In this sense, the growing trend toward regional and subregional groupings will restrict the capacity of states to take independent action and will expand the security aspects they hold in common.

The international system now emerging will be more unstable politically and militarily and will pose short-term risks for the rich regions. The ideological justification for getting rid of internal enemies will also be different in this new system. Two of the basic theories underpinning national security are thus about to disappear, or be radically changed: bipolar competition and the struggle against the "enemy within."

It is likely that, in the near future, the definitions of the new challenges to the national security of the central countries will be copied and adopted by close associates without serious questioning. This tendency will be reinforced by the fact that many of the threats to global order are interrelated and do not respect institutional or national frontiers.[13] In this context, we need to question the viability of the national security propositions that are based on defending a model of self-development. Limits to the workability of independent models will be greater as asymmetries increase. As a result, we may ask: Can a doctrine of national security that seeks comprehensive and independent development exist in a peripheral country when the central countries with which it is associated have such a different and dominating focus?

The chances for success of the ideals of independent development are surely in doubt given the growing tendency toward integration into regional and subregional blocs. We need to recognize that the prospects for such a focus of national security will improve to the extent that we can reach at a consensus for the defence of national interests and goals and can clearly establish the type of model that we choose for our country.

NOTES

1. Zbigniew Brzezinski, *Out of Control* (New York: Charles Scribner's Sons, 1993) 103-07.
2. John Roper (1990-91), "Shaping Strategy Without the Threat," Adelphi Papers 257 (London: The International Institute for Strategic Studies) 76-83.
3. Paul Kennedy, *Hacia el Siglo XXI* (Barcelona: Paz y Janés Editores, 1993) 26.
4. United Nations Development Program, *Informe sobre Desarrollo Humano, 1994* (Mexico: Fondo de Cultura Económica, 1994) 53.
5. Anthony Lake (1994), "Confronting Backlash State," *Foreign Affairs* 73(2): 45-56.
6. Eraham Fukker, *The Democracy Trap* (New York: Outlon Books, 1991) 244.
7. Sergio Aguayo Quezada and Bruce M. Bagley, eds., *En Busca de la seguridad perdida: aproximaciones a la seguridad nacional mexicana* (Mexico: Siglo XXI, 1990) 115-17.
8. Mexico, *Plan Nacional de Desarrollo, 1989-1994* (Mexico: Secretaría de Planificación y Presupuesto, 1989) 27.
9. Jacques Attali, "Lineas de Horixonte," in Luis Angeles, ed., *Los Desafíos de la globalización: economía múndial y sociedades nacionales* (Mexico: PRI, 1990) 17.
10. Charles Doran, "The Globalist-Regionalist Debate," in Peter Schrader, ed., *Intervention into the 1990s* (Boulder CO: Lynne Rienner Publishers, 1992) 69.
11. Thomas Callaghy, "Visions and Politics in the Transformation of the Global Political Economy: Lessons from the Second and Third Worlds," in Robert Slaten et al., eds., *Global Transformation and the Third World* (Boulder CO: Lynne Rienner Publishers, 1993) 247.
12. Aguayo Quezada and Bagley, *En Busca* 16.
13. Joseph Camilleri and Jim Falk, *The End of Sovereignty?* (Hants U.K.: Edward Elgar Publishing, 1992) 151.

6

RECENT DEVELOPMENTS IN THE CONCEPT OF HEMISPHERIC SECURITY

NOUVEAUX DÉVELOPPEMENTS RELATIFS AU CONCEPT DE SÉCURITÉ HÉMISPHÉRIQUE

Luis Herrera-Lasso

Abstract: The end of the Cold War made redundant the prevailing hemispheric defence system, shaped in large part by the United States, which had been in place during the East-West conflict. Until then, national security arrangements throughout the Hemisphere had incorporated the concerns of the American giant.

The security system then in place was primarily a system of defence, perceiving the major threat as strictly military and as coming from outside the Western Hemisphere. Because this threat never materialized, the system was never utilized. The end of the East-West conflict means that the very foundations of our hemispheric security system have to be reviewed and modified.

The U.S. intervention in Panama in 1989, on grounds that that country's role in drug trafficking threatened American national security, marked the beginning of a new era in Western Hemisphere security affairs.

Although a system of hemispheric security existed during the Cold War, no permanent military body was ever created to carry through joint efforts. Neither the Inter-American Defence Board nor the Organization of American States could efficiently assume this role. The United States thus came to act unilaterally throughout most of the Hemisphere.

Today, efforts are underway to redefine the nature of threats, to draw up an agenda for action, and to create an inter-American organizational structure to implement new measures. Initiated at the 1994 Summit of the Americas, these discussions are now being pursued through the OAS, the IADB, and ministerial defence meetings.

Sommaire : Le système de sécurité de l'hémisphère occidental découlait, durant la Guerre froide, de la rivalité est-ouest; les États-Unis jouèrent un rôle primordial dans l'élaboration de ce système. Les politiques nationales de sécurité observées à la grandeur de l'hémisphère étaient ainsi adaptées aux besoins du géant américain.

La fin du conflit est-ouest signifie que les fondements mêmes du système de sécurité hémisphérique doivent être revus et corrigés. Ce système prévoyait une menace tirant ses origines à l'extérieur du monde occidental. Le système de sécurité se voulait plutôt un système de défense hémisphérique. La menace, qui eût été strictement militaire, ne se concrétisa jamais.

C'est en 1989 que le système change du tout au tout. L'intervention américaine au Panama signale une redéfinition de la sécurité dans l'hémisphère : le trafic des stupéfiants représente dorénavant une menace à la sécurité des États-Unis. La sécurité hémisphérique s'est donc écartée du domaine strictement militaire.

Bien qu'un système de sécurité ait en partie existé durant la Guerre froide, aucune instance militaire permanente ne fut mise sur pied pour gérer les efforts communs. La Junte interaméricaine de défense et l'Organisation des États américains existaient mais ne pouvaient remplir ce rôle de manière efficace. Les États-Unis en sont donc venus à agir unilatéralement, pratiquement à la grandeur de l'hémisphère.

Depuis peu, on s'affaire à redéfinir les menaces, à dresser des plans pour leur faire face et à tenter de mettre sur pied un système organisationnel interaméricain qui permettra de gérer le tout. Le Sommet de Miami a permis de relancer le débat, qui se poursuit maintenant au sein de l'OEA, de la Junte interaméricaine de défense ou par l'entremise de rencontres ministérielles portant sur la défense.

NATURAL ALLIES?

THE CLOSE OF THE COLD WAR marked the end of the prevailing hemispheric defence system which had been in place during the East-West conflict. Instruments such as the Inter-American Treaty of Reciprocal Assistance (the Rio Treaty) and the charter of the IADB provided the legal framework and policy setting for a system of defence which, in the end, was never utilized.

Nevertheless, it is important to note various aspects of its history which today have special relevance for our understanding of the transition period through which the defence of the Western Hemisphere is passing.

BASIC PREMISES OF THE HEMISPHERIC SECURITY SYSTEM

The central component of the hemisphere's defence system during the Cold War was the highly ideological nature of the premises upon which security systems in the region were based.

- The East-West conflict was pre-eminent as the ideological and political framework for activities in the area of security. The principal threat was seen as coming from outside the Western Hemisphere.
- The enemy had various methods of penetration, among which ideological warfare played a major role. In this area, the conflict did not lend itself to reconciliation.
- As one of the principal protagonists in the East-West conflict, the United States needed to protect strategic areas in its own backyard. To ensure that this objective was met, it therefore had to assume active leadership in the shaping of security policy within the other countries of the hemisphere.

As a result of these premises, all major activities in the area of hemispheric defence and security had to be coordinated with the United States, which led to the adoption of national security policies throughout the hemisphere that, for the most part, incorporated the global concerns of the United States into each country's internal security arrangements. This, in turn, enabled governments to define internal threats and enemies in terms of political-ideological premises that went far beyond their national situations and that not only furthered the interests of the United States in the global arena, but also fitted in with those of particular countries of the region, many of which were governed by military regimes of a distinctly anti-democratic cut.

In many cases, this perspective on hemispheric defence and security permitted military governments to consolidate their power, delayed the restoration of democratic forms of government, and encouraged the adoption of systems of development that led to a greater concentration of wealth and helped to maintain—and, in many cases, exacerbate—social inequities.

The end of the Cold War also saw the collapse of ideological confrontation as the mainstay of global conflict. This did not mean the disappearance of ideologies or of their role in national and international conflicts. But it did signify the "re-dimensioning" of certain paradigms in the game of international politics—with consequences for most of the featured players in that game. In this context, the global power struggle has acquired other characteristics that have a not inconsiderable impact on regional policies: other components of the global power structure have been revitalized; economic variables have led to the formation of new trading blocs; and a new era has dawned in which there is greater reliance on international organizations for settling regional or domestic conflicts among states, and in which a new legitimacy is attached to the collective use of force under a renewed doctrine of humanitarian intervention.

In the Western Hemisphere, the major defence strategy and security systems have lost one of their main components due to this fundamental shift in the nature of the threat facing the region. With the collapse of communism as the great enemy to overcome, a process of redefining defence strategies and security systems has begun.

DIFFERENTIATING BETWEEN HEMISPHERIC SECURITY AND DEFENCE

The central theme of the current debate has to do with the distinction between the concepts of defence and security at the hemispheric level.

This distinction is of the greatest moment in that "defence" implies a military strategy for responding to a common enemy, whereas "security" is a broader and essentially political concept which may or may not involve military action and which represents the convergence of the not necessarily compatible interests and perceptions of security held by the various members that make up the system.

The ideological transformation brought about by the gradual disappearance of the East-West conflict has dissolved the legal framework that prevailed during the Cold War and that was designed to support defensive measures taken to protect the hemisphere. The Rio Treaty, the OAS, and the IADB provided a scaffolding for coordinated action within a plausible scenario in which the hemisphere had to be defended against possible attack from outside forces. In the event, this system was never activated since it was never necessary to confront military aggression, and with the end of the Cold War its original rationale evaporated.

During the entire period, the only event that came close to activating the system was the armed conflict between Great Britain and Argentina over the Falkland Islands or Islas Malvinas. In this case, its utilization was not a viable option since the system was designed for confronting the enemies of the Western world, not an ally of the United States. This event underscored the ideological-political content and gaps in the defensive system adopted in the hemisphere.

The idea of a hemisphere-wide defence policy had an important corollary in the region's national security systems. Indeed, no hemispheric defence policy was ever formalized since, in practice, the United States viewed national security systems in Latin America as primarily a matter of bilateral relations in the form of cooperation between the United States and those governments it considered its allies, or between the United States and other elements within each nation when the governments in power did not see eye to eye with the leader of the system.

Without prejudging United States' policy toward the hemisphere, it is certainly worth noting that that country's proposals for joint action in security matters within the OAS—such as in the case of the Dominican Republic in 1965—were supported primarily by military regimes or anti-democratic governments.

At any event, it is clear that, while the region's defence system and systems of national security followed parallel paths, they never combined to form a system of hemispheric security. This sort of scenario would hardly have been in the interests of the United States. The hemispheric defence system accepted by the majority of countries in the region provided the legal and operational framework for joint action, should this become necessary. Meanwhile, the bilateral handling of security issues proved more efficient and left more room for the United States and the majority of other regimes in the Americas to manoeuvre. Moreover, it had the advantage of excluding or quietly circumventing those governments that strayed from the basic security premises which permeated the perspective shared by the United States and its allies within the region.

In formal terms, there was a hemispheric defence policy during the Cold War but no hemisphere-wide security system. It is for this reason that, with the end of the East-West conflict, the Rio Treaty appears as an instrument whose potential application is no longer meaningful. With this, a large gap is revealed in the regional strategy which has little to offer by way of defence policy when faced with the new scenarios, a situation that does much to explain the opening of a security agenda in search of new threats to the region.

IDENTIFYING THREATS TO THE REGION

The test of any defence or security system is its response to the question: What are the threats that the system must cope with? The answer given forms the basic premise for designing the relevant strategy.

In the case of the hemispheric defence system, both the threat and the means for combatting it were very clear. The enemy was defined in terms of the East-West conflict, and the threat was to be realized through military action. As pointed out above, this threat never materialized.

The year 1989 marked the beginning of a new era in the Western Hemisphere. The United States had begun to perceive General Antonio Noriega as inimical to its interests, yet given the background of Panama's leader there was no question of linking his removal to the struggle against communism. His alleged involvement in drug trafficking provided the political rationale needed to justify military intervention, since the drug problem clearly affected the national interests of the United States. But beyond this, it is possible to speculate on the more important geopolitical and strategic reasons for the action taken—reasons that have to do with the positioning of the United States within the new scenarios.

For the purposes of this analysis, it is important to note that the government of the United States attempted to legitimize its military intervention in Panama through joint action under the OAS banner. For this reason, it helped revitalize the organization which had become virtually bankrupt in 1989—both politically and economically. In the event, the effort backfired.

Various political and other events took place in Latin America in the 1980s that prevented this consensus: the return to democracy in the majority of the region's countries, which made it more difficult than in the past to find automatic allies for military intervention; the emergence of purely Latin American systems for settling disputes within the region (as in the case of the Contadora Group) to fill the gap left by the OAS; the various political agreements reached among Latin Americans, including the Rio Group and the Ibero-American Summit, in which conflicts within the hemisphere were discussed and positions staked out.

For the subsequent phase in the region's development, it is important to point out that, even though the intervention in Panama was undertaken unilaterally as part of U.S. foreign policy without consensus being achieved first, the events were accepted by the governments of the countries in the region without undue posturing or recrimination. With the disappearance of the East-West conflict, the United States would have the opportunity to take more direct action in the Americas without worrying that this might affect its global policies.

Thus began in earnest the search for a definition of hemispheric security that encompasses two fundamental characteristics. The first is that the concept must be broader than—in fact, must transcend—that of hemispheric defence policy. Second, the threats perceived under the new scenario are more diverse, less homogeneous in nature, and without clear distinctions between security issues per se and those that hold the potential for military or other conflicts of an entirely different nature, such as combatting drugs, defending democracy, enforcing human rights, promoting democracy among the military, protecting the environment, and even stimulating socio-economic development. All of these are to be placed in the same basket without any clear distinction between the various types of threat, which inevitably creates confusion and eventually leads to a breakdown in the strategies and mechanisms for carrying out these tasks.

To this must be added the growing tendency at the global level to support and promote humanitarian intervention in internal conflicts, a trend necessarily affecting the traditional concepts of sovereignty, self-determination, and non-intervention since they broaden the scope of collective action taken by the international community. This is clearly another of the more important topics being debated at present.

MILITARIZATION OF THE HEMISPHERIC SECURITY AGENDA

The absence of any real link between the military component of the hemisphere-wide defence system and the development of a hemispheric security system after the Cold War suggests the need for a restructuring of the region's security agenda. And this in turn makes it vital that those threats—if they exist—that might be described as systemic in that they endanger the Americas as a whole, must be clearly identified. It is then necessary to clearly determine the threats that may require the use (or potential use) of a joint military component.

It is first necessary to note that, while a system for hemispheric security—including the legal framework and provisions for its implementation—existed during the Cold War, no permanent military body was ever created to carry it out.

It is likewise noteworthy that, throughout the entire Cold War period, the IADB remained a consultative body only, and that at no time were the ministers of defence convened under the OAS Charter provision covering emergency situations requiring activation of the hemispheric defence system—not even during the Cuban missile crisis of 1962.

During this period, the military cooperation provided by the United States for countries of the region was never part of the hemispheric defence system. Rather, it came through unilateral military assistance in the form of equipment, training, joint manoeuvres and, occasionally, joint operations or coordination in matters of intelligence, with the participation of U.S. international security agencies—primarily the Central Intelligence Agency (CIA) and the Drug Enforcement Administration (DEA).

The point is that there has never been an operational military presence at the regional level in this hemisphere, despite the perceived threat and a clearly enunciated defence policy. Yet, under the present circumstances when the threat is much less clearly defined, certain perceptions of the situation appear to support the need to create a permanent body with a military agenda: the need for demilitarization of certain countries in Central America; the view that we are entering a new era that requires confidence-building measures for handling or preventing outbreaks of hostility over various territorial claims in the region; the perception that the armed forces within the region need to be fully converted to democracy in order to avoid military takeovers in the countries of this hemisphere; and the view that it is necessary to reduce and control the arms race in the region in order to avoid new imbalances; and the conviction that democracy is the only acceptable form of government for the region's countries and that anything less than full democracy is a threat to the entire hemisphere.

This last point is particularly important in view of the fact that the crisis in Haiti was taken before both the OAS and the UN Security Council even though, strictly speaking, it did not endanger the stability and peace of the region as a whole and was highly unlikely to spread even to Haiti's immediate neighbour. It is also interesting in the case of Haiti that intervention in that country was authorized by the UN and the OAS. More to the point, it appears to have been successful, which ultimately underscores the stark contrast between its effectiveness and the fragile legal framework that sustained it. On the other hand, any discussion of hemispheric security systems—especially a system espoused by the United States—must sooner or later deal with the question of Cuba as a principal bone of contention.

It is important to point out at this juncture that, while the prevailing perception of hemispheric security during the Cold War was that of the United States, which was not above using various means to apply pressure, this was far different from what happened in the Soviet Union and Eastern Europe where security measures were simply imposed. Governments in this hemisphere had some leeway to negotiate and remained autonomous in their decisions. In this regard, it is surprising that Mexico and Canada, both bordering the United States, managed to retain the greatest degree of autonomy during this period: Canada by not taking out membership in the OAS, and Mexico by steadfastly refusing to participate in military stratagems and offering only the slightest cooperation with the United States in this area.

NEW QUESTIONS FOR OLD ANSWERS

Redefining a concept such as hemispheric security requires finding answers to new questions, although there are times when it appears that we are moving toward the formulation of new questions for old answers.

To begin with, it is necessary to define objectives, and the first step is to ascertain that threats in fact exist that will require a system of hemispheric security. If an attempt is made to answer this question from the traditional American perspective on regional security, it becomes an exercise consisting almost entirely of establishing the existence of threats or potential conflicts within the hemisphere and then drawing up an agenda for action—preferably joint action—to avert any that could damage its interests: governments that fail to adopt its vision of the world; control of certain networks and individuals involved in the drug trade; control over strategic defence plans and the main suppliers of arms to countries in the region; control over certain political processes to avoid unrest within the hemisphere; and any other agenda topic that may help in permanently influencing the political, military, economic, and social development of the Americas.

If this is to be the scenario, then we are indeed seeking new questions for old answers. Values such as democracy or human rights, and threats such as drug trafficking or deterioration of ecosystems, take on a transnational dimension whose solutions—under the new conception—transcend the responsibilities of the state: in the first case because of their universality, and in the second because they extend beyond international borders and require coordinated action by the international community. The concept of humanitarian intervention fits neatly into this scenario and is the basic premise for recent UN operations in Africa, Europe, and Asia. These operations, despite the enormous political and operational difficulties encountered, appear to represent a new willingness on the part of the international community to intervene in the internal affairs of states.

What are the new threats to security? Who will participate in the actions taken to defend against these threats? Which threats will be classified as internal matters and which ones will require hemispheric cooperation? Which will require military action? Where does coordination stop and joint action begin? Which bodies will be responsible for dealing with the new threats or situations of potential conflict? Should the present bodies be retained, or is it necessary to create new ones?

INSTITUTIONAL PROGRESS

Determining strategies is a political exercise that consists of defining threats and the methods for coping with them. The implementation of whatever strategy is devised will require an institutional apparatus, an organizational structure, objectives, and the assignment of specific tasks to the various bodies involved. In the case of the hemispheric defence system, there was the OAS, the Rio Treaty and the IADB to provide the institutional and organizational setting and to carry out operations in the event that it became necessary to activate the system.

Today, there is no longer a clear definition of what should go into forming the basis for a regional security system. Within the OAS studies that have been carried out to define the agenda, important decisions such as the intervention in Haiti have been assessed, and action has been taken in crisis situations, including those intended to help restore democratic order in Guatemala and Peru in 1993. The OAS has also played an active role in promoting the activity of the IADB aimed at demilitarization within Central American countries.

However, it is significant that little progress has been made toward setting the agenda for hemispheric security—in other words, in defining the threats facing the region. Even less clear are the institutional mechanisms that will be used to implement strategy in this area.

In this context, let us consider the Summit of the Americas, sponsored by the United States and held in Miami in December 1994. A total of 31 heads of state or government attended that meeting, including Canada, now fully integrated into the OAS system. Cuba was not invited.

This meeting had several important characteristics. An exhaustive review of hemispheric matters was conducted, including topics relating to security. Views were exchanged on the main problems facing the region; strategies and guidelines were proposed for dealing with specific problems. A mechanism was established for regularly monitoring the actions taken by each country in each of the sectors dealt with and for each of the tasks it agreed to carry out. Subsequent meetings were proposed on specific topics, among which the most important—for our purposes—were the ministerial meetings on money laundering and on hemispheric defence topics.

In terms of institutional structures, three important decisions were taken:
- The agenda, with the same topics and the same participants, was moved from the OAS to another forum. At the very least

this means that one, several, or all participants consider the OAS no longer adequate as a forum for discussion and resolution of hemispheric matters.
- A cooperation mechanism, similar in nature and structure to the Rio Group and the Ibero-American Summit, was created in which, for the first time, all the countries in the Western Hemisphere (except Cuba) will participate. It is hoped that this body will have greater flexibility and lower costs than the more formal organizations.
- Strategies and guidelines were put forward for attending to hemispheric problems. For the purposes of this chapter, the most notable of these is the 21st-century drug interdiction strategy, which is very advanced in its design and preparation.

Given this new situation, several important questions arise:
- In light of the new scenarios, where are the threats and strategies for hemispheric security to be defined and by whom?
- What mechanisms will be employed to establish these strategies and place them in operation?
- How will these mechanisms be monitored? Will the Coordination Office of the Summit of the Americas be responsible for this task?
- Does the activation of the Summit of the Americas represent a weakening of the OAS? Is there a new era of ostracism? Will the OAS eventually disappear?

The answers to these questions are of the utmost importance, yet they are anything but clear. The difficulty in finding answers is an indication of the transition that the hemispheric system is undergoing. However, it is possible to discern certain trends:
- At least some members of the system have expressed a clear intention to create a hemispheric security agenda to replace the earlier hemispheric defence system.
- The search for a security agenda is being broadened to include a wide range of topics.
- Special emphasis is put on topics that have military implications and on the possibility of creating the means for taking joint action in dealing with problems and crises in this area.
- There is a tendency to create new bodies for the purpose of defining, dealing with, and monitoring topics related to hemispheric security.

The member countries of the system will have to take a stand with respect to these trends. The result will be the establishment of new forms of interaction in which members will determine the degree of autonomy and independence to be permitted in security matters, and in those areas and items in which collective action will be required—in other words, the orientation and rules of the game for sharing power within the hemisphere during the coming decades of what might be termed the post-Cold War period, an era that is just beginning.

7

COOPERATIVE SECURITY AND CANADA'S ROLE IN INTER-AMERICAN SECURITY REFORM

LA SÉCURITÉ COOPÉRATIVE ET LE RÔLE DU CANADA DANS LA RÉFORME DE LA SÉCURITÉ INTERAMÉRICAINE

Brian J.R. Stevenson

Abstract: Although Canada has long participated in the development of international organizations, it delayed joining the Organization of American States until 1990. The OAS appeared to be not only totally ineffective but also dominated by the United States. Since its entry, however, Canada has played a leading role in reforming the OAS.

The end of the Cold War has profoundly changed international relations. This change had required modifying international institutions and rethinking traditional concepts. Canada considers that two of the three existing Western Hemispheric organizations, the Rio Treaty and the Bogotá Pact, are either outdated or ineffective given current trends in Latin America toward democratization, trade liberalization, and the emergence of transnational problems. The concept of national security must also likewise evolve: the model Canada is promoting is that of "cooperative security."

Those who find it difficult to explain Canada's entry into the OAS should consider that, with the end of the Cold War, Canada distanced itself from Europe while it recognized the growing importance of regionalism. Moreover, Canadians have become increasingly interested in Latin America over the past 25 years. Finally, NAFTA offers a solid anchor for a more open strategy toward the southern part of our hemisphere. Canada has truly become a country of the Americas and intends to promote peaceful and harmonious inter-American relations based on transparency and openness.

Sommaire : Le Canada participe au développement d'organisations internationales depuis longtemps. Pourtant, ce n'est qu'en 1990 qu'il s'est joint à l'Organisation des États américains. Pendant longtemps, l'OEA semblait être totalement inefficace, en plus d'apparaître contrôlée par les États-Unis. Depuis son entrée, en 1990, le Canada joue un rôle de premier ordre dans la réforme de l'OEA.

La fin de la Guerre froide signifie la modification profonde de la nature des relations internationales; il faut donc non seulement adapter les institutions internationales, mais aussi repenser les concepts qui prévalaient jadis. En ce qui concerne l'hémisphère occidental, deux des trois organisations en place, soit la Junte interaméricaine de défense et le Pacte de Bogotá, apparaissent désuètes ou inutiles aux yeux du Canada. On explique cette perception par de nouvelles tendances en Amérique latine: la démocratisation, la libéralisation des échanges et l'émergence de problèmes transnationaux. La notion de sécurité hémisphérique doit ainsi évoluer; Ottawa fait la promotion de la « sécurité coopérative ».

D'aucuns s'expliquent mal l'entrée du Canada à l'OEA. Pourtant, la fin de la Guerre froide a amené le Canada à s'étoigner de l'Europe et à réaliser l'importance croissante du régionalisme. Aussi, l'intérêt des Canadiens envers l'Amérique latine n'a cessé de croître durant les 25 dernières années. Finalement, l'ALENA représente le point d'ancrage d'une stratégie d'ouverture à la portion sud de l'hémisphère. Le Canada est bel et bien devenu un pays des Amériques et il entend faire la promotion de relations interaméricaines pacifiques et harmonieuses, axées sur l'ouverture et la transparence.

NATURAL ALLIES?

LIKE MOST COUNTRIES, Canada is grappling to understand the end of the Cold War and is searching for ways to adapt to the new order. For Canadian policy makers this is a particularly difficult task, since it was the post-war period, as well as the emergence of the Cold War itself, that made Canada come of age as an international actor. The defining characteristics of Canadian internationalism, with Canada's participation in the Atlantic military alliance led by the United States, as well as its support for multilateralism and particularly the UN system, served the purpose of augmenting its influence beyond its international standing and therefore balance its dependence on the United States.

In this manner, Canada enthusiastically participated in a wide variety of military and economic international organizations during the Cold War. Canada's membership ranged from NATO and NORAD to GATT, the Commonwealth and, later, *la Francophonie,* not to mention an active and distinguished role in the UN, including participation in nearly every UN peacekeeping operation to date.

During the Cold War, it was clear to Canadian policy makers that it was in Canada's strategic interest to play an active role in multilateralism, especially in Europe, where Canada had both commercial and security interests. This was a time for the promotion of multilateral free trade and collective security. It is interesting to note that, during this period, Canada supported, in the first instance, universal multilateral institutions such as the UN and, in the second instance, regional ones such as NATO and NORAD. Canada felt more at ease in the company of many than in partnership with a few or just one.

Indeed, it is because of this active participation in multilateral organizations that Canada has been dubbed "the Great Joiner." Curiously enough, however, this participation in multilateral organizations and military alliances did not encourage successive Canadian governments to join the OAS—the world's oldest general-purpose international organization and, most importantly, the foremost organization in Canada's own neighbourhood—until 1990. The lack of interest in both the strategic and economic life of the inter-American system is most remarkable considering that Canada was such an activist internationally.

Avoiding membership of the OAS was initially intentional, because it was seen as counter-productive to Canada's efforts to make the UN an effective instrument for peace and security and, later, because the organization was seen as ineffective. For Canada, the Cold War was a time for hope and faith in universal international institutions; regional ones were seen as counter-productive to the creation of world order, and the OAS was seen as an organization in which Canada could play only a small role due to the dominance of the United States. But the end of the Cold War brought with it a reevaluation of these universal institutions and a reassessment of regional institutions, particularly in this hemisphere.

Once Canada joined the OAS, it assumed an active role in its reform, as well as in the promotion of democratization, development, and freer trade. However, Canada refused to sign the prime instrument of collective security of the inter-American system, the Inter-American Treaty of Reciprocal Assistance (the Rio Treaty), and did not participate in either the IADB—although it contributed to it financially—or the Inter-American Defence College (IADC). Does this mean that Canada was unwilling to participate in security matters in the hemisphere? Was Canada abandoning its long-standing concerns over such issues as peacekeeping, disarmament, and arms control? Did Canada feel that it had no security interests in the hemisphere?

It is the purpose of this chapter to explore the role that Canada has played in the debate over security reform in the OAS since joining that organization in 1990, and to begin to answer these questions. Notwithstanding Canada's rejection of the Rio Treaty and its non-participation in the IADB and the IADC, it will be argued that Canada has, in fact, been a very active protagonist in the security reform of the OAS, and that the principal instrument of Canada's approach to reform has been the new and innovative concept of "cooperative security," a concept that has emanated from the Department of Foreign Affairs and International Trade and has subsequently become a central concept in the OAS debate. It will be further argued that cooperative security, as championed by Canada, is an attempt to introduce Canadian internationalist values, not normally associated with traditional security, into the vocabulary and agenda of hemispheric debate over security reform. This will lead to the conclusion that, although the concept of cooperative security projects traditional Canadian values, it is also a concept that seems especially suited to a post-Cold War period in which regionalism has become more relevant and emerging issues, such as the environment, human rights, narco-trafficking, and trade, have risen in importance and relevance in the hemisphere. However, it may be that the concept of cooperative security as it is used today is too broad to be made operational in its present form, and that a concerted effort should be made to refine this concept to make it more practical and useful.

It will be assumed in this chapter that the importance of increasing both political and commercial ties with Latin America is reflected in government policy in order to diversify Canada's relations and to begin to fill the gap increasingly left open by Europe's military, political, and commercial disengagement from Canada. This will inevitably increase Canada's strategic stake in the Western Hemisphere, as it will in Asia-Pacific, and hence Canada's interest in security reform is fundamentally important for its long-term interests.

COOPERATIVE SECURITY AND THE CHANGING NATURE OF SECURITY IN THE AMERICAS

The OAS has formally operated on three "cylinders" since the beginning of the Cold War: the Charter of the organization, the Rio Treaty, and the Pact of Bogotá.[1] All three deal with security matters, but the last two—which are supposed to be the heart of the collective security system and pacific settlement of disputes between member states—have been ineffective. While the Cold War made its presence felt, the Rio Treaty was a valuable instrument, particularly for U.S. national security against Soviet incursions in the hemisphere. But, with the end of the Cold War, the provisions of the Rio Treaty have become irrelevant and those of the Pact of Bogotá, a legalistic and cumbersome instrument, useless. The OAS, therefore, operates on only one of its three cylinders. There is no reason, however, why it cannot operate well on this one cylinder and have hemispheric security concerns dealt with according to its principles. What is odd, perhaps, is that the inter-American system has to operate on the fiction that all these instruments serve some purpose, while their existence is proof of the inability of the OAS to formulate the means to face a new era in inter-American relations. Indeed, the OAS might function better if the two obsolete instruments were eliminated, even if they were not replaced.

When focusing on security reform in the hemisphere, one must tackle at least two fundamental issues: the changing nature of hemispheric security; and the attempt to produce a new conceptual framework in order to understand security issues in a post-Cold War world and respond to them in an effective and relevant manner. As Jeffrey Stark has recently argued, security in the Americas needs rethinking.[2] Part of the rethinking must take into account the changing nature of international relations, and particularly greater interdependence among nations.

In this context, four factors have emerged as crucial.

- First, many of the nations of Latin America with long histories of military regimes have cast aside the shackles of military rule and have embarked on a long process of democratization. This process has had a profound impact on the international relations of the hemisphere's countries and on the reform process of the OAS itself. The whole notion of non-intervention has begun to erode as civilian governments realize that their best protection against military intervention is a strong inter-American system that will not accept the overthrow of civilian rule. But the process of democratization has not solved the problems of human rights abuses in the region, which are still of great concern. Both these issues have become important, not only in the relations among nations, but in the relations between peoples in the hemisphere. NGOs throughout the hemisphere have sprung up to sustain democratic regimes and condemn abuses of human rights. One need only consider the case of Haiti to understand the security implications to states that defy the democratic norms set by the international community. And although the intervention by the United States in Haiti under UN sponsorship might be an extreme case, many countries in the hemisphere have become increasingly sensitive to the importance of democratic principles and the promotion of human rights.
- Second, after suffering a decade of economic stagnation and burdening debt, most countries in the hemisphere have embarked on a slow process of economic liberalization and free trade. This process has unleashed a new potential for economic and commercial activity, but has simultaneously threatened to increase poverty among the less fortunate. The result of this

condition is increased migration, caused by both political and economic factors, and the emergence of insurgency movements, both clearly causing security problems.
- Third, the magnitude of drug trafficking has created a whole new threat in the region by challenging state sovereignty and fostering a multi-billion-dollar underground economy that is transnational in nature. Drug trafficking interferes with the process of democratization by adding to corruption and the destabilization of fragile regimes.
- Finally, environmental degradation is causing profound concern, not only with respect to the hemisphere's effect on world ecology and the long-term impact on its economies, but also with respect to its impact on the health and well-being of generations of Latin Americans.

All these issues impinge in some way on the new security concerns of the hemisphere. As a result, these themes, not traditionally regarded as security issues, are engaging policy makers throughout the hemisphere and challenging them to review and rethink the whole concept of security.[3] The security tools of the Cold War, upon which the OAS is founded, are not adequate for an interdependent world that has left the Cold War behind and must face a whole new set of problems. As Stark suggests, the fact that the "menu of possible security problems has been expanded and enriched is in some ways a positive development, but it creates a situation in which authorities lack a clear understanding of what is or is not a matter of national security, [they] are constrained by policies which are outdated or confused, and feel limited by institutional structures that are often poorly suited to the tasks at hand."[4]

It must be emphasized that it is not only the vacuum left by the end of the Cold War that poses this challenge, but also the growing interdependence of nations which is broadening and deepening the ties between them and redefining the whole concept of security beyond the confines of the state's physical sovereignty and capability for military defence. Not that military matters are of no importance—war has certainly not disappeared—but these traditional security concerns seem to be less apparent and less immediate in the hemisphere. As Stark concludes, "Perhaps the central intellectual paradox in the formulation of the concept of national security is that it must account for the gradual erosion of sovereignty characteristic of the 'post-postwar' era of interdependence."[5] The problem is that, if security involves everything, it becomes useless as a concept that helps differentiate one kind of political phenomenon from another. The task is to begin to understand what the limits are, not within the traditional concept of national security involving matters of state sovereignty and war, but within the concept of security in an interdependent world.

Given Canada's traditional aloofness from the rest of the hemisphere, it is rather puzzling that it has not only taken an interest in redefining security in the region, but has taken a leading role in this process within the OAS. In a recent article, David Dewitt has argued that cooperative security has become the Canadian approach for promoting peace and security in a post-Cold War world.[6] Dewitt argues that the outset of the Cold War was the last time there was a conceptualization of how Canadian security should be constructed. With the end of that era, Canada is embarking on a similar exercise that will guide Canadian security into the new order. But he states that "the notion currently referred to as 'cooperative security' holds out such a promise, but it has yet to be realized."[7] For Dewitt, the basic elements of cooperative security will survive changes of government in the future, as Canada needs to recast its approach to security: "We are moving into an era of the regionalization of security politics and political security. The essential elements of the notion of cooperative security offer a more appropriate way to deal with this emerging regionalization than did the security policy premises of an earlier era."[8]

If the whole notion of security in the hemisphere is evolving in order to respond to important changes and demands in the international system, a new response and a novel formulation of security are needed. At the very least, the concept of cooperative security can help to redefine what security means in light of the new challenges that are bringing countries into closer and more frequent contact and potentially into greater conflict. If this implies the security of individuals as well as of states, as cooperative security suggests, then perhaps it will involve a new framework for international politics. In any event, a new security framework must be found in an era that still has no name to identify its main characteristics.

NATURAL ALLIES?

STRUCTURAL CHANGE, REGIONALISM, AND CANADA'S EMERGING STRATEGIC INTERESTS IN THE HEMISPHERE

It would be a mistake to assume that Canada's rejection of the Rio Treaty did not involve a realization by policy makers that Canadian security interests are increasingly being tied not only to the North American continent, but also to the Western Hemisphere. Canada had traditionally been discouraged from participating in the OAS for fear of being entangled in U.S. strategic interests and conflicts in the region. But Canada also had a long-standing policy of broadening its relations with countries in the hemisphere. Indeed, in the late 1960s, the Canadian government, as well as private citizens, began the long process of establishing closer ties with the region, which were additional to the long-standing relations with the Commonwealth and Francophone Caribbean nations. This long-term policy of getting closer to the Americas, begun with the release of Pierre Trudeau's foreign policy review in 1970[9] and increasing activity by Canadian NGOs in the development of the region, set the stage for the flourishing relationship of the 1990s.[10]

In this process, three factors have combined to become a strong catalyst for greater Canadian participation in the life of the inter-American system and have set the stage for an increased stake in the security of the region.

- First, although Canada seriously considered joining the OAS and becoming an active participant in inter-American affairs several times during this century, it took a profound structural change to the very nature of the international system to make participation in the Western Hemisphere a priority.[11] It took the end of the Cold War and Canada's gradual detachment from Europe for Canadian policy makers to take the hemisphere seriously and begin to realize its present-day potential in economic, political, and security terms. The end of the Cold War has greatly diminished, if not entirely eliminated, Canada's military and political role in Europe. The increasing importance of commercial blocs, and especially the creation of the European Union, has further eroded Canada's participation in European trade.

    The emergence of trade blocs has thus forced Canada into an economic arrangement with the United States that has diminished Canada's long-standing policy of trade diversification, the so-called Third Option. The Western Hemisphere and Asia-Pacific have thus become targets of renewed Canadian trade diversification. Regionalism, therefore, is an important new element in Canadian foreign policy which supplements the traditional involvement in universal multilateral organizations. As Dewitt states: "In the Western Hemisphere, there is little doubt that with NAFTA, the changing nature of the OAS, and the effects of generational changes which are inevitable among the leadership of Caribbean states, security relations, as well as political, economic and social relations will not be a simple linear extension of this past century."[12]

- Second, as part of this structural change to the international system and the increased importance of regionalism, there has been an incremental interest by Canadians in Latin American affairs, which has translated into an unprecedented activism in what is referred to as the "Latin American constituency" in Canada—a well-organized and motivated collection of NGOs that have pressured the Canadian government on a number of foreign policy issues in the hemisphere. From the time of the Chilean coup d'état that overthrew Salvador Allende's government in September 1973 and the Central American crisis of the 1980s, to the opposition to NAFTA in the 1990s, this constituency has become increasingly vocal and influential in promoting such issues as democratization, human rights, the environment, and development assistance as part of Canadian foreign policy toward Latin America and the Caribbean. The promotion of these goals, which insert Canadian domestic values into its foreign policy ideology, has been an important element in defining Canada's relations with the region.

Canada's entry into the OAS in 1990 was the result of both greater domestic interest in the hemisphere and a broadening of Canadian foreign relations in the post-Cold War period. Most Canadian NGOs were at the time opposed to Canada's entry into the OAS on the basis that it would mean joining an organization that they believed was dominated by the United States. However, once Canada had taken the plunge, many of these NGOs took the opportunity to press their concerns through Canada's representation in the organization and to make direct requests to Canada's mission to the OAS to promote the development of human rights, democracy, and the environment.[13]

- Finally, the negotiations and ratification of NAFTA have involved Canada, for the first time, in an overarching commercial arrangement with a Latin American country, an arrangement that will have important long-term political and strategic implications. From at least the late 1960s, Canadian businesses and governments were interested in developing closer commercial ties with Latin America.[14] A number of barriers, among them protectionist economies and political instability, made trade risky in Latin America and prevented these ties from deepening. But NAFTA has provided a window of opportunity for Canadian businesses to penetrate the Latin American market. Once Canadian businesses learn to deal with Latin American business culture and overcome stereotypes and language barriers, dealing with the rest of Latin America will become less of an obstacle, particularly with the opening up of these economies and the encouragement of the Canadian government to extend NAFTA to the rest of Latin America.

Canada is now linked to the Western Hemisphere in an unprecedented manner. But, most importantly, it is developing a real stake in the security of the hemisphere. This will be especially relevant if Canada pursues trade relations with Latin America and continues to participate actively in the inter-American system. What exactly Canada's security interests are in Latin America is still being defined,[15] but a good indicator of how those interests are consolidating can be found in Canada's participation in OAS reform.

CANADA'S ROLE IN REFORMING THE INTER-AMERICAN SECURITY SYSTEM

One year after becoming a member of the OAS, Canada began to tackle the issue of security reform. In a speech, Stanley Gooch, the Assistant Under Secretary of State for Latin American and Caribbean Affairs, underscored the growing importance of hemispheric security for Canada. He argued that, "As we move into our second year of membership and expand the scope of our participation in the Inter-American system, we cannot ignore broad hemispheric concerns."[16] At the centre of Gooch's analysis of security in the OAS was a criticism of the inability of its main instruments to fulfill their intended purposes, although the argument was that the Charter itself had sufficient authority to guide member countries into more effective security arrangements. Especially important to Gooch was the fact that the security instruments of the OAS were based on peacemaking—bringing conflicting parties together—rather than peacekeeping—keeping the parties apart. The criticism centred on the fact that formal legalistic instruments such as the Rio Treaty and the Pact of Bogotá have failed, whereas informal arrangements have had greater success. In this context Gooch argued:

Based on our assessment of the past, it seems clear that first and foremost in the OAS context informal, flexible processes will continue to work best. The OAS needs to avoid any attempt to re-create any elaborate mechanisms such as the Rio Treaty and the Charter of Bogotá [sic]. In our view, the Charter of the OAS to which all hemispheric nations now adhere provides sufficient legal framework for collective and cooperative action on a full range of hemispheric issues including those related to peacemaking.[17]

In this speech, Gooch introduced the concept of cooperative security. After discussing the importance of peacemaking in the OAS, he focused on the emerging issues of importance to the hemisphere which, according to him, included "new issues such as environment, strengthening of democracy, human rights and drugs and also economic cooperation and integration."[18] This certainly reflected the myriad issues that were getting on the OAS agenda in an important period of revival, but what was significant was that Gooch was arguing that these were important security issues: "We must recognize that security is more than something to be achieved by military means alone. It is multidimensional and it is cooperative. An OAS engaged in all of these issues can make a vital contribution to cooperative security in this hemisphere."[19]

This suggests that Canada was developing a view that challenged the traditional concept of security, with its focus on military matters, and was looking at issues more in line with an inter-dependent world. By April of that year, Canada had requested the addition of a new item on the agenda of the 21st General Assembly, entitled "Cooperative Security in the Hemisphere." After discussion with the preparatory committee, the title was changed to "Cooperation for

Security in the Hemisphere," which, in fact, changed the meaning and the scope for reform. Not only was the designation of the concept of "cooperative security" changed, but the subsequent issue for discussion fell well within the traditional concept of security, and the title of the Canadian government's background paper was changed to "Curbing the Proliferation of Instruments of War and Weapons of Mass Destruction."[20] The background notes provided to the planning committee therefore dealt with traditional concerns of security rather than those outlined by Gooch.

The Canadian government seemed to have two simultaneous strategies at work, however: one dealt with traditional security themes, and in particular arms proliferation; the other attempted to introduce a whole new conceptualization under the rubric of cooperative security. The Canadian strategy combined both traditional and non-traditional concepts of security. The Canadian government believed that "Member states could contribute to peace and security by exercising restraint in their transfers of conventional arms, without prejudice to the requirements of national security."[21] Most importantly, however, as it had done with the establishment of a Unit for Democracy, the Canadian government proposed the establishment of a "mechanism of consultation among member states, in which they could consider situations where arms are being acquired beyond legitimate defence requirements and explore ways of alleviating such build-ups before they result in destabilizing arms races and/or armed conflict."[22] For the Canadian government, the most important step would be ensuring increased transparency in conventional arms transfers on a universal and non-discriminatory basis.

But, by the time the 21st General Assembly approved a resolution entitled "Cooperation for Security in the Hemisphere: Curbing the Proliferation of Instruments of War and Weapons of Mass Destruction," the OAS had begun to make the connection to a broader view of security. The resolution stated that cooperation for security in the hemisphere was of fundamental importance and that "such cooperation must address, in a positive and active manner, significant themes bearing on security, among them the encouragement of arms control and disarmament."[23] The General Assembly resolved, among other things, to support efforts that would eliminate all forms of proliferation and to request that the Permanent Council study the problems of international security. That same resolution, which dealt with traditional security concerns, stated that "a climate of enhanced peace and security, both globally and within the hemisphere, should liberate human and material resource needs for the promotion and strengthening of democracy, the furtherance of economic and social development, the protection of the environment and the safeguarding of human rights."[24]

But perhaps the most interesting development came with resolution 1123, which set out the task of reviewing the security framework of the inter-American system in view of the changing international situation. The resolution entrusted the Permanent Council with the establishment of "a working group to study and make recommendations on cooperation on the various dimensions of hemispheric security."[25] The statement was quite vague and certainly unclear about what cooperative security meant. But the work was only beginning.

By the fall of 1991, the Working Group on Cooperation for Hemispheric Security, with Hernán Patiño, the Argentine Ambassador to the OAS, as chairperson, had got under way by requesting study topics for the Working Group. At this point, the agenda could have been filled with two types of subject. On the one hand, the Working Group could have begun to tackle traditional security issues such as arms control, military-civilian relations, the reform of the IADB, and the IADC. On the other hand, there could have been a comprehensive questioning of the security instruments and institutions of the OAS. The first approach might have led simply to tinkering with some instruments of the security system, such as the IADB and the IADC, but the second approach had the potential to challenge the whole notion of security in the post-Cold War world.

Although Canada wanted to deal with traditional security issues, which is proved by the submission on arms proliferation to the OAS General Assembly, by the fall of 1991 the vision that had been expressed by Stanley Gooch at the beginning of the year was crystallizing. In its submission to the Working Group, Canada presented two official views: "Views of the Government of Canada on Curbing Weapons Proliferation"[26] and "Views of Canada on Cooperative Security."[27]

Canada's views on curbing weapons proliferation echoed the statements made in the background paper of April. The paper covered conventional weapons, nuclear weapons, chemical weapons, and biological and toxin weapons. Several important suggestions were made. First, the Canadian government, although recognizing that arms buildups could be effectively controlled only if there were global acceptance, believed that regional efforts were also important. In the second place, Canada suggested that secrecy was a major problem in discouraging arms proliferation and therefore recommended that OAS member states promote increased transparency. On the issue of nuclear weapons, the Canadian government suggested, among other things, that member states urge non-parties to the nuclear Non-Proliferation Treaty either to sign the treaty or to help bring into force the Treaty of Tlatelolco and promote an indefinite long-term extension of the Non-Proliferation Treaty in 1995.

With respect to chemical weapons, Canada proposed that member states develop the proper controls for their chemical industries in anticipation of a Chemical Weapons Convention and "undertake further confidence building measures in conjunction with other member states."[28] With respect to biological and toxin weapons, Canada proposed greater involvement by OAS members, particularly in encouraging transparency "in relation to the Biological and Toxin Weapons Convention through the annual submission to the United Nations Department of Disarmament Affairs of information and data as agreed by states parties to the Convention."[29] There was thus a recognition that UN initiatives had to be complemented by regional arrangements, in this case those of the OAS. There was also a staunch belief that regional initiatives on arms proliferation had to be coordinated at the UN level, no matter what arrangements were made regionally. This appears to be an attempt to balance global and regional benefits on an issue that needs pressure at both levels.

The second paper outlined Canada's views on substantive change to the concept of security in the hemisphere. It began by stating: "There is a growing recognition that security should no longer be defined in strictly traditional military terms ... the security equation is in fact far more complex involving such factors as: economic underdevelopment, overpopulation, migration populations and refugees, trade disputes, environmental degradation, political oppression, human rights abuses, terrorism, and the illicit trade in drugs, to mention but a few."[30] The paper argued that, although there would also be security threats from more traditional areas, the new security agenda was broader and deeper than before and thus reflected a security reality that was "multifaceted and multidimensional."

The concept of cooperative security, therefore, was designed to respond to these new challenges. A comprehensive approach was thereby promoted because the Canadian government assumed that security was both complex and indivisible, and thus any piecemeal approach to the issue would not be effective. The concept of "cooperation" was of fundamental importance. Finding a common approach and discovering common solutions was central to this novel approach to security:

Cooperative security is, in essence, the development of relationships and functional links across a broad spectrum of issues (military, political, economic and social) at all levels of interaction (official and unofficial) through regular and systematic dialogue which will permit and promote transparency and thus security—a security which is based not on military strength or fortified borders, but on openness.[31]

It was also argued in the paper that cooperative security was most effective in regional and sub-regional settings, and thus the conclusion was that the OAS provided an ideal forum to develop cooperative security. But for the Canadian government it was also important to find a permanent forum for the development of new security parameters. This was the next task. What was not entirely clear from these papers was whether traditional security matters should be dealt with primarily by the UN collective security system and non-traditional issues primarily by the inter-American system.

By the beginning of 1992, the Working Group on Cooperation for Hemispheric Security had approved the study of three important issues: the security of small states; the relationship between the IADB and the OAS; and arms proliferation. Canada had already shown its interest in the third issue and its desire to propose a new framework through the concept of cooperative security, but the other two issues were also very important.

Canada was particularly interested in the security of small states in view of its close relations with Commonwealth and Francophone nations of the Caribbean. But, more importantly, many of the problems that small states faced in the hemisphere were compatible with the whole concept of cooperative security. For example, in its report on the issue of small states, the Commonwealth Group of the OAS suggested that some broad arenas for action could include a supportive and global environment, a flexible and diversified approach to economic development, effective development assistance, and a selective, but active, role for small states.[32] The threat to the security of small states from drug trafficking was also an important theme within cooperative security and one that greatly concerned Caribbean countries.

The issue of the IADB had been mentioned by Gooch in his 1991 speech, when he stated that Canada wanted to stimulate debate on the future mandate of the Inter-American Defence Board that would be relevant in the post-Cold War era and in a democratic hemisphere."[33] Indeed, Canada had shown its disdain for the IADB by not wanting to participate in it, even though it contributed approximately 12 percent of its budget. At first, Canada was excluded from participation because it had not signed the Rio Treaty, but later the rules were changed to allow any country to participate. Canada still refused. One reason for this refusal was no doubt the sensitivity in Canada to an institution in which the Latin American military played a central role. With Canada's promotion of democratization and the long history of military intervention with civilian governments in the region, participation in the IADB would not be a politically smart move at home. However, the IADB was also seen as irrelevant in its current structure, just like the Rio Treaty and the Pact of Bogotá. The Canadian government wanted it to be reformed, but it did not want to participate until it saw the nature of the reform. Finally, the IADB's ambiguous legal relationship to the OAS bothered Canadian policy makers. How much of an OAS agency was the IADB and how accountable was it? The answers to these questions were not at all clear to the Canadian government.

In a document entitled "Hemispheric Security: Arms Proliferation," written by Canadian Ambassador Jean-Paul Hubert in his role as rapporteur of the Working Group, the first explicit attempt was made to link traditional security issues and cooperative security, while suggesting that the OAS must find a permanent mechanism to study the complex issues of security.[34] As part of the framework of the problem of arms proliferation, Hubert included a section entitled "Building up on the Concept of 'Cooperative Security,'" in which he reiterated the importance of the concept and directly tied it into traditional security concerns. In this paper, it was clear that the Canadian government wanted something more permanent and with greater scope than the Working Group on Cooperation for Hemispheric Security. Indeed, the Canadian delegation seemed to want to focus discussion again on "cooperative security" rather than on the more meaningless concept of "Cooperation for Security in the Hemisphere," the former having a much broader set of meanings and pointing to a profound reconceptualization.

Hubert's report thus proposed that, besides the steps being taken on security issues for the next General Assembly suggested by others, "there may be a need to consider new ways of dealing with questions which require special and sometimes urgent attention. That, it is suggested, could take the form of a Committee on Cooperative Security, composed of all member states, for the purpose of ensuring regular consultations on the broader security agenda."[35] It was further suggested that there could be one or two general meetings of the Committee on broader topics, while one or two technical groups could meet in between. Hubert concluded his report by arguing that, in future, the issue of cooperative security should be built upon, and suggested that "Members may want to consider linking this issue to future work regarding, for example, the evaluation of the role and mandate of the Inter-American Defence Board."[36]

The continuing Canadian government support of both the limitation of arms proliferation and cooperative security was reiterated by the Secretary of State for External Affairs, Barbara McDougall, in her address to the 22nd General Assembly. McDougall expressed her satisfaction with the progress made on the issue of non-proliferation resulting from the General Assembly resolution of the previous year. She also reiterated her government's support and stated that "The scope of security has been broadened beyond traditional military concerns to include economic development, human rights, the fight against the illicit trade in drugs and environmental protection. Canada wants to see this work continue."[37] Indeed, Canada was successful in establishing the Special Committee on Hemispheric Security with the adoption of resolution 1180. However, the concept of "cooperative security" was still not openly recognized, although one of its greatest champions was Mr. Patiño, the chair of the Committee. The resolution stated that the General Assembly instructed "the Permanent Council to establish a Special Committee on Hemispheric Security to continue consideration of the agenda on cooperation for hemispheric security."[38] Cooperative security was not mentioned anywhere.

By the 22nd General Assembly in 1993, the issue of inter-American security seemed to be gaining momentum. Four important resolutions were passed by the General Assembly. The first, resolution 1236, was a response to the Permanent Council's report on "Cooperation for Security and Development in the Hemisphere: Regional Contributions to Regional Security," in which the General Assembly requested that the Special Committee on Hemispheric Security include other issues in its work plan, such as the relation between the UN and the OAS in matters of security, global and regional disarmament, and the "relationship between development, environment, disarmament and arms control."[39]

Resolution 1237 dealt with the convening of a meeting of experts on confidence- and security-building measures in the region. Resolution 1238 dealt with the exchange of information on defence spending and a register of conventional arms, and resolved to increase the ties between the UN and the OAS, as well as to "invite member states to provide to the conventional arms register set up in the Secretariat of the United Nations, on a regular basis, the information called for in the UN General Assembly resolutions 46/36 (L) and 47/52 (L)." The resolution also called for the consolidation of the Treaty of Tlatelolco (the treaty for the prohibition of nuclear weapons in Latin America and the Caribbean) by commending those countries that had supported it and urging all states to take the necessary measures to allow the treaty to enter into full force. Finally, resolution 1240 reiterated the necessity for a better definition of the legal-institutional relationship between the IADB and the OAS.

CANADA'S CONTRIBUTION: AN ASSESSMENT

Overall, the Canadian government has moved quickly to make security issues important to the OAS debate, as it had done with issues of democracy. But, although Canada was successful in establishing the Working Group and later the Committee and has been able to introduce issues in the field of arms proliferation, it seems to have been much less successful in promoting the concept of cooperative security and getting support for fundamental reform in the security field.

This is hardly surprising, however. Although cooperative security has much to offer, its broad inclusive base—which seems to make a security matter of everything—creates a great deal of apprehension and skepticism among politicians, military personnel, and academics. The issues that cooperative security points to seem important to most observers and participants, but there seems to be a reluctance by many countries to accept that these matters relate to security. This is, of course, part and parcel of the difficulty of adapting to the security realities of the post-Cold War world. In addition, uncomfortable military-civilian relations, the concern that many of the themes of cooperative security fall within the realm of national sovereignty, the fear that, once accepted, these themes will become the instruments of the powerful against the weak and promote interventionism on the basis of non-traditional security concerns—all these factors indicate an uphill battle for cooperative security.

It is clear that for Canada, cooperative security has great promise. It provides a new conceptual framework to replace the concept of security and doctrines of the Cold War era. It allows the government to address the concerns of many Canadian citizens interested in Latin America by promoting important Canadian internationalist values. Cooperative security also allows Canada to play an active role in the inter-American system and use its decades of experience in the UN, NATO, and NORAD, while not being tied to a military alliance against an undefined adversary. Canada's vast experience in security issues plus its non-threatening military role in the Americas make it an ideal interlocutor. However, learning the nuances and sensitivities of Latin American politics has not been an easy task for Canadian diplomats and politicians. The issue of security, and especially security reform, stirs up concerns that involve long-term distrust of U.S. motives in the region, military abuse of power, arms proliferation, border disputes, sub-regional military rivalries, and fear of insurgency movements, to name but a few.

The main challenge for Canada will be to sell the concept of cooperative security as one especially suited to the new era. Changing the mind-set of OAS members on security matters will be no easy task, but the adoption of the concept of cooperative security, with its focus on individual as well as global security, may become more appealing with time. One thing is sure, however: if the OAS does not address the inadequacy of its security instruments and institutions, which were quite useless even in the era they were intended for, it will become an irrelevant player in inter-American security, as it was throughout most of the Central American crisis of the 1980s. The members of the OAS must thus realize that fundamental reform is not only simply needed, but is needed desperately. Cooperative security, in this sense, is not an end, but only a beginning.

NOTES

1. For an excellent overview of the role of the OAS in matters of peace and security, see L. Ronald Scheman, *The Inter-American Dilemma: The Search for Inter-American Cooperation at the Centennial of the Inter-American System* (New York: Praeger, 1989) Chapter 3.
2. Jeffrey Stark, "Rethinking Security in the Americas," *North-South Issues* (Miami: North-South Center Press, 1992) 1-6.
3. Several authors have attempted to refine the concept of security to allow for new elements important to national security. Jeffrey Stark has distinguished between "positive" and "negative" aspects of security, the former being economic well-being, housing, health care, education, and environmental integrity, while the latter deals with threats to sovereignty, borders, and physical survival. H.P. Klepak has explained the difference as one between direct and traditional and indirect and non-traditional concepts of security. See Jeffrey Stark, "Rethinking" 4 and H.P. Klepak, "Canadian Security Interests in Latin America," in H.P. Klepak, ed., *Canada and Latin American Security* (Montreal: Méridien, 1993) 112.
4. Stark, "Rethinking" 1.
5. Stark, "Rethinking" 4.
6. David Dewitt (1994), "Cooperative Security: A Canadian Approach to the Promotion of Peace and Security in the Post-Cold War Era," *Canadian Defence Quarterly* 23(3): 11-18.
7. Dewitt, "Cooperative Security" 13.
8. Dewitt, "Cooperative Security" 15.
9. Canada, Department of External Affairs, *Foreign Policy for Canadians* (Ottawa: Queen's Printer, 1970).
10. See Brian Stevenson, *Domestic Pressures, External Constraints and the New Internationalism: Canadian Foreign Policy Towards Latin America, 1968-1990* (Kingston ON: unpublished doctoral dissertation, Queen's University, 1992) esp. Chapter 8.
11. Stevenson, *Domestic Pressures* Chapter 2.

12. Dewitt, "Cooperative Security" 15.
13. An annual assessment (called a report card) of Canada's performance in the OAS has been done by Canada-Caribbean-Central America Policy Alternatives (CAPA) and includes a detailed analysis and critique of Canada's involvement in the OAS during its first year.
14. See Colin I. Bradford, Jr. and Caroline Pestieau, *Canada and Latin America: The Potential for Partnership* (Toronto: CALA, 1971).
15. See H.P. Klepak, *Canada and Latin American Security*; see also H.P. Klepak, *Canada and Latin America: Strategic Issues for the 1990s*, ORAE Paper No. 54 (Ottawa: Department of National Defence, 1990).
16. Canada, Department of Foreign Affairs and International Trade, "The OAS and Peacemaking in the Americas," a speech by S.E. Gooch, Assistant Undersecretary of State for Latin America and the Caribbean at the Conference of Defence Associations, Seventh Annual Seminar, Ottawa (January 24, 1991) 2.
17. Speech by S.E. Gooch, "The OAS and Peacemaking" 17.
18. Speech by S.E. Gooch, "The OAS and Peacemaking" 18.
19. Speech by S.E. Gooch, "The OAS and Peacemaking."
20. OAS, OEA/Ser. P., AG/CP/Doc.513/91 Add 1, April 22, 1991.
21. OAS, OEA/Ser. P. 4.
22. OAS, OEA/Ser. P. 4.
23. OAS AG/RES 1121 (21-0/91) *Cooperation for Security in the Hemisphere: Curbing the Proliferation of Instruments of War and Weapons of Mass Destruction*, Resolution Adopted at the Eleventh Plenary Session held on June 8, 1991.
24. OAS AG/RES 1121, *Cooperation*.
25. OAS AG/RES 1123 (21-0/91) *Cooperation for Security in the Hemisphere*, Resolution Adopted at the Eleventh Plenary Session held on June 8, 1991.
26. Permanent Mission of Canada to the OAS, "Views of the Government of Canada on Curbing Weapons Proliferation," November 1991, mimeo.
27. Permanent Mission of Canada to the OAS, "Views of Canada on Cooperative Security," November 1991, mimeo.
28. Permanent Mission of Canada to the OAS, "Views of the Government of Canada on Curbing Weapons Proliferation," 8.
29. Permanent Mission of Canada to the OAS, "Views of the Government of Canada on Curbing Weapons Proliferation," 9-10.
30. Permanent Mission of Canada to the OAS, "Views of the Government of Canada on Curbing Weapons Proliferation," 1.
31. Permanent Mission of Canada to the OAS, "Views of the Government of Canada on Curbing Weapons Proliferation," 1-2.
32. Working Group on Cooperation for Hemispheric Security, Permanent Council of the OAS, OAS/Ser.G; CP/GT/CSH-91/92 add. 1 (April 15, 1992) 7-8.
33. Speech by S.E. Gooch, "The OAS and Peacemaking" 19.
34. Working Group on Cooperation for Hemispheric Security, OEA/Ser. G.
35. Working Group on Cooperation for Hemispheric Security, OEA/Ser. G. 6.
36. Working Group on Cooperation for Hemispheric Security, OEA/Ser. G.

37. Canada, Department of External Affairs and International Trade, "An Address by the Honourable Barbara McDougall, Secretary of State for External Affairs, to the 22nd Annual Conference of the General Assembly of the Organization of American States," Nassau, Bahamas (May 19, 1992) 2.
38. OAS, AG/RES 1180 (22-0/92) Cooperation for Hemispheric Security, Resolution Adopted at the Eighth Plenary Session held on May 23, 1992.
39. OAS, AG/RES 1236 (33-0/93) Report of the Permanent Council on "Cooperation for Security and Development in the Hemisphere: Regional Contributions to Regional Security," AG/RES 1179 and 1180 (22- 0/92).

8

CANADA'S INTERNATIONAL SECURITY POLICY

LA POLITIQUE CANADIENNE DE SÉCURITÉ INTERNATIONALE

Jill Sinclair

Abstract: Canada is recognized as a middle power on the international scene, despite its small population and rather limited resources. This reputation is due in large part to its activist multilateral stance and its search for a multiplier effect which both increases its influence and reduces costs in what it does internationally. Canadian foreign policy includes, nevertheless, a bilateral dimension which is crucial in dealing with the United States.

Since 1985 important changes have brought the strictly traditional, collective approach to security issues into question. Gaining ground is the idea of cooperative security, in terms both of content and procedure. The field has been broadened to include some non-traditional issues, and measures of deterrence have been replaced by procedures that aim at mutual assurance. The states in the international system are invited to discuss subjects that affect their own security, either directly or indirectly.

Canada pursues the development of "cooperative security" at both the regional and global levels. On the one hand, Ottawa promotes the United Nations as key to cooperative security. But the international security load today far surpasses the UN's capacity: needed are a clearer role and realistic mandates. On the other hand, Canada is working to reinforce various regional institutions active in cooperative security: in Europe within the OSCE; in Asia-Pacific within the ASEAN; and in the Americas as a member of the OAS.

Sommaire : Le Canada est reconnu sur la scène internationale comme une puissance moyenne, en dépit de sa faible population et de ressources plutôt limitées. Cette reconnaissance découle, en grande partie, de l'activisme multilatéral généralement caractéristique du Canada. En effet, la recherche d'un effet multiplicateur, accroissant le niveau d'influence et réduisant les coûts, est un élément essentiel de la politique étrangère canadienne. Cette dernière comporte néanmoins une dimension bilatérale, essentielle dans le cas des États-Unis.

Les changements importants survenus depuis 1985 ont remis en cause l'approche strictement traditionnelle et collective face aux questions de sécurité. La notion de sécurité est devenue coopérative, tant au niveau du contenu que des procédés. On a en effet élargi sa définition pour inclure certaines questions non-traditionnelles. On a aussi remplacé les mécanismes de dissuasion par des procédés visant l'assurance mutuelle. Les États du système international sont ainsi invités à discuter de sujets qui affectent, de près ou de loin, leur sécurité respective.

Le Canada s'efforce de contribuer au développement de la « sécurité coopérative » aux niveaux régional et global. D'une part, Ottawa fait la promotion de l'ONU en tant qu'institution-clé de la sécurité coopérative. L'ONU fait aujourd'hui face à un fardeau en matière de sécurité internationale dépassant ses capacités. Son rôle doit être clarifié et ses mandats devront être réalistes. D'autre part, Ottawa oeuvre au renforcement de diverses institutions régionales actives dans le domaine de la sécurité coopérative: en Europe, au sein de l'OSCE; en Asie-Pacifique, auprès de l'ASEAN; et dans les Amériques, en tant que membre de l'OEA.

NATURAL ALLIES?

THIS BRIEF CHAPTER sets out to highlight some of the main points behind Canadian thinking on the subject of international security. It hopes to provide a context for other papers written by Canadians for this book, this time from the vantage point of official thought at the Department of Foreign Affairs and International Trade.

As has been discussed elsewhere in this volume, Canadian international security policy is the result of a long process of development, reflecting historical and geographical realities that are part and parcel of the country's view of itself, its values, and its interests. Canadians see themselves as citizens of a fortunate country which should help advance causes that reflect their values while moving forward with their more objective national interests.

In many areas, these two thrusts blend easily. For example, Canadians' deep trust in democracy is supported both as a value in itself and as something that sustains international peace and development, objectives of obvious direct interest to Canadian foreign policy. The same can be seen with nuclear non-proliferation and several other arms control measures, areas in which national values and direct interest go hand in hand.

Canada is both a young and not-so-young country. Much of the nation's history has, of course, happened under the wing of European mother countries. But now, well over a century since Confederation, Ottawa has garnered much experience in international security affairs. During that period, Canada assumed an ever-increasing responsibility for its foreign policy, taking over full control in international affairs seven decades ago. Involved in no less than five international wars in this century alone, the country has discovered that it cannot isolate itself from those affairs, however much it may feel that its privileged position allows it—perhaps more than most countries—some latitude to pick and choose where it will place its main efforts.

The conceptual approach now largely adopted and resulting from Canada's historical experience, its geographical situation, and recent changes in the international environment is called "cooperative security." It is pursued on two levels, the global and the regional, and along two tracks, the multilateral and the bilateral. A word will first be said about these two levels and then the cooperative security concept will be discussed more fully.

CANADA'S INTERNATIONAL SECURITY POLICY

THE CANADIAN VIEW OF MULTILATERALISM AND BILATERALISM

Where Canadian international security policy is concerned, it is important to understand that the focus is essentially multilateral and this for a number of reasons, which might be termed, as Ambassador Jean-Paul Hubert put it, "by choice as well as by necessity." Canada is a small country, at least in terms of population. And while it may be a "middle power," its resources are limited. Despite this, it chooses to take an activist stance and thus looks for a multiplier effect in what it does internationally.

To gain the most from its reduced resources and basic conditions of national life, Canada thus tends to look for multilateral action. Indeed, more than once, Canada has been termed "the Great Joiner," and it is true that it is a member of a great many groupings, including NATO, the G-7, NAFTA, the OAS, the CSCE, the Commonwealth, and *la Francophonie*, to name but a few.

Multilateralism is, of course, expensive and, in order to be effective, requires that participants be present and active. It also often implies a global, regional, and even sub-regional presence. Canada wishes to further its agenda through global institutions, but knows that activity in regional ones is also essential. And while recognizing that the nation-state remains the essential bedrock of the international system, it still considers that certain elements of the state's sovereignty are being eroded due to globalization in its current form. A series of very significant problems reinforces this trend, including the environment, international crime, the illegal trade in drugs, fisheries, health—especially transnational epidemics—immigration, and a host of others. Their solutions require significantly interdependent approaches.

Canada accepts that there is something of a "comparative advantage" to dealing in multilateral structures and groupings with these and other matters such as conflict prevention, arms control, and human rights developments. It is clear that a growing number of countries share the view that seizing such multilateral opportunities is in those nations' own interests. This is felt to be the case because multilateral action allows a smaller country to influence others in more important ways and at less cost than through merely unilateral efforts.

This does not mean that there is no role for bilateral initiatives in Canadian foreign policy. Canada's geography and special situation vis-à-vis its giant neighbour require that considerable attention be paid to one central bilateral relationship. Close proximity to Russia across the North Pole, to France through St. Pierre and Miquelon, and to Denmark through Greenland necessarily adds other bilateral dimensions to Canada's international affairs. Its relations with its two mother countries are also deep, unique, and multifaceted.

All manner of other contexts also suggest to Canada the need for stronger and special bilateral links with key countries. Nowhere is this more obvious than with Mexico, with which Canada hopes to develop a strong trilateral connection through NAFTA and other North American initiatives, in addition to a bilateral one of great strength and originality based on shared perceptions of a vast range of issues.

It is true, nonetheless, that most Canadian specialists feel that the traditional emphasis on multilateralism has served the country well. For many, the asymmetries of North American life all but impose this preference on a country with Canada's basic characteristics. The result is that multilateralism as a fundamental preference in most Canadian foreign policy is taken as a given and is rarely questioned.

COOPERATIVE SECURITY

Recent years have been marked by a revolution in international affairs. As the great changes of the mid- and late-1980s became more evident, Canadian security policy makers began to question the utility of more traditional patterns of thought about collective security—and even about common security—as ways of addressing the complex challenges of the times. Gaining ground has been the idea of cooperative security.

This highly non-traditional approach involves a comprehensive view of international security that favours contact and dialogue among states, emphasizes democratic development, supports human rights, and accords priority to economic development. It posits that true security can no longer be viewed from an exclusively national perspective in which the interests of other states are seen as competitive and often threatening. It also rejects the notion that international affairs are zero-sum relationships where an advance by one country necessarily implies a loss by another.

This approach suggests that foreign policy—and especially defence policy—decision making should be done in a non-traditional context. The security interests of other countries should be considered when a country is furthering its own because a country's security cannot logically be considered outside the context of that of its neighbours and potential rivals. The argument is that, if one country's actions add to the sense of insecurity of other states, their logical reaction is to take action that will help restore their sense of security. However, such action is almost certain to be perceived as a threat and will thus, in turn, engender a reaction in kind. This spiral of events is hardly unknown in recent history or in the course of world events in general. And, although it can frequently be seen in alliance arrangements, strategic posture statements, or even trade and other economic accords, it is particularly evident in defence policy decisions involving military deployments and, even more so, in arms procurement.

The objective of cooperative security is to escape from this vicious cycle of action-reaction. This can be done only by a rather radical departure from traditional thinking in this field. As Canadian political scientists David Dewitt and David Leyton-Brown have put it, the proposed security architecture of cooperative security would:
- be multilateral;
- be geared toward reassurance rather than deterrence;
- complement, co-exist with, and in some cases replace bilateral security arrangements;
- promote both military and non-military security;
- be flexible and adaptive; and
- be based, ultimately, on the norms, principles, and practices of transparency in order to challenge the erosive characteristics of the security dilemma more effectively.[1]

The objective is not to do away with the pursuit of national interests or even power, but rather to allow this to be accomplished without endangering regional and even wider peace. The hope is to encourage countries to deal jointly with common concerns and eschew unilateral action. By acting together bilaterally and regionally, they should develop habits of cooperation and as a result confidence would grow among former rivals who would now, it is hoped, see themselves as partners.

FURTHERING THE COOPERATIVE SECURITY GOAL

Canada pursues the development of cooperative security at both the regional and global levels. This is seen as both necessary and obvious if the broader goals of furthering regional and wider security agendas are to be achieved.

It is felt to be absolutely essential that global instruments be developed to ensure the workability of cooperative security ideas, whether the issues being addressed are environmental standards, human rights commitments, or key global regimes, such as the Non-Proliferation Treaty or the Chemical Weapons Convention.

The UN is seen as the key institution and considered by Canada to be the only legitimate source of global action in the security area, as well as the main hope for creating a new international order where both peace and justice have a chance to flourish. There is a fundamental view that the UN needs strengthening if these goals are to be truly advanced. This requires the international community to give priority to putting the world body on a firm financial footing. It also means that the Agenda for Peace proposals must be taken more seriously, and that particular elements such as preventive diplomacy and early warning of potential conflicts must be given greater priority.

There is a need to strengthen the UN's ability to take effective action across the broad spectrum of its responsibilities for international security and stability. In this regard, it is important to bear in mind that the problem is not so much with the UN itself as with the international system. The role of the UN in vital areas such as conflict prevention and peacekeeping must be made clearer and more efficient. Work is needed to establish realistic mandates, as well as to clarify the myriad financial elements that these kinds of activities entail. Increasing the capacity of the UN to engage in "peacemaking" also requires thought and action, as do longer-term institutional development efforts to ensure that peace continues.

It is not too much to say that the burden of international security, humanitarian relief, and related operations—present and future—is simply too great for the organization at the present time. That is why the call of *Agenda for Peace* must be answered. And as is mentioned therein, the only logical place for the UN to turn for assistance is to regional organizations. While this is hardly a panacea for the difficulties encountered by the global body, there appear to be few alternatives.

Canada accepts the logic of the call to act in regional organizations in order to improve their capacity to shoulder part of the burden of security and stability. And, while it still places the main emphasis on the UN, Ottawa is working systematically to enhance the role of a wide range of regional organizations in the field of security. Partnerships between the UN and some of the regional bodies should be key, especially in the area of international security.

In Europe, Canada is actively promoting a role in international security for the Atlantic Alliance that goes beyond mere collective defence arrangements. Moves such as the Partnership for Peace, aimed at building real bridges between NATO members and the former signatories of the Warsaw Pact, have been initiated in recent years despite obvious challenges—for example, how best to reassure Russia that such measures are not aimed at reducing its legitimate role in Europe.

Meanwhile, the CSCE has moved forward in innovative ways to help with conflict prevention and management on this continent, distinguished historically by widespread and frequent warfare, in recent decades by peace, and in more recent years by growing instability, even violent disputes. Conflict prevention missions have been dispatched to a number of potential trouble spots on behalf of the CSCE. The post of High Commissioner on National Minorities has also been established within the CSCE to act as "an instrument of conflict prevention at the earliest possible stage."

In the vast Asia-Pacific region, Canada is working with the guiding principle of building habits of dialogue in parts of the world where, until now, no forum for multilateral security discussion has existed. While it has proven important not to attempt to simply transplant European models to this complex and often stressful set of situations, European experience has not been forgotten. Issues examined include: transparency measures such as information exchange; discussion of defence white papers and the processes behind them; and modest confidence-building measures such as notification of exercises and exchange of observers for such manoeuvres.

Canada is looking for a dialogue that includes all relevant partners, including China, Russia, and also, if felt useful, such states as India and Burma. This represents the widening of the mandate of an existing regional arrangement. The ASEAN/PMC process is part of this, as is the ASEAN Regional Forum, with which considerable progress was made in 1995. If Canada's objectives are met, cooperative security would be the dialogue's guiding concept. Its agenda would include non-traditional security matters, such as illegal immigration and drug trafficking, as well as environmental and resource problems, especially in the South China Sea.

In the Americas, the thrust of Canadian policy has been to make the OAS an effective focus for hemispheric security matters. In the early 1990s, Canada was at the forefront of moves to place security matters more centrally within OAS concerns. In addition, Ottawa pressed hard for the creation of a Committee of Hemispheric Security within the organization, and for that Committee's permanence, a status it achieved in 1995.

In specific areas, Canada has tried to take the lead in moving hemispheric security affairs forward. These have included the fields of confidence- and security-building measures, conventional arms transfers, non-proliferation, and de-mining, to name but a few. It has also included matters of broad governance.

In non-traditional areas, Canada has been active in support of the Inter-American Drug Abuse Control Commission (CICAD), the OAS agency responsible for dealing with the illegal drug trade. In addition, the Department of Foreign Affairs, the Department of National Defence, and the Royal Canadian Mounted Police have collaborated on a variety of programs aimed at improving the human rights situation in the Americas. Canada's enthusiasm for increasing the effectiveness of the OAS Unit for the Promotion of Democracy is likewise part of this non-traditional security effort.

All these initiatives have fitted well with an analysis of Canada's interests in the region which suggests that the country needs to belong to a hemispheric community that is democratic, prosperous, and peaceful. In this context, a broad definition of security has been accepted and acted upon in Canadian policy toward the hemisphere.

Finally, Canada is also active in security affairs in the international communities of which it is a member but which are not "regional" in any strict sense. This is especially true of the Commonwealth, where the North-South boundary is so obviously crossed and where Canadian interest has been constant in recent decades. The umbrella provided by this unique organization has allowed for activities ranging from the imposition of informal pressures on rivals in the settlement of disputes to direct intervention in electoral and peacekeeping/observer tasks, such as in Zimbabwe or Namibia. While such actions have been less obvious in *la Francophonie,* a more recently formed organization, there is no reason why this other grouping crossing North-South lines could not be valuable in the future.

It should be reemphasized that the basic aim of all this activity in support of regional organizations is not directed exclusively at them. Rather, it is intended to reinforce at the regional level what the UN is doing at the global level. Thus, it is hoped that the burden on the UN system will be reduced and international security as a whole will be furthered.

THE NON-PROLIFERATION AGENDA

It is worthwhile here to mention Canada's abiding interest in the international non-proliferation agenda which is in no way limited to the more obvious issue of nuclear proliferation. Rather, it includes nuclear, chemical, biological, and conventional weapons, as well as some delivery systems such as missiles.

Canadians feel that the current exceptional situation of generally reduced tensions, the end of the Cold War, the dissolution of most antagonistic blocs, and the widespread desire for reductions in armaments and the transfer of monies saved to pressing development tasks has given them a remarkable opportunity to make real progress in arms control in general and non-proliferation in particular. Ottawa has therefore been keen to maximize the potential offered by the present context and to attempt to move forward quickly in many of these challenging areas.

Canada worked hard in 1995 to bring about an indefinite extension of the Non-Proliferation Treaty. The reinforcement of safeguards under the International Atomic Energy Agency has also been a priority. Likewise, there is a major drive to bring the Chemical Weapons Convention, signed in January 1993, into force as soon as possible.

In the less dramatic but still crucial area of conventional arms, Ottawa is anxious to make progress with transfer issues. The main thrust for Canada in this field has been through support of the UN

Register of Conventional Arms, an instrument whose potential utility in its own right—and as a confidence-building measure—is felt to be considerable.

Needless to say, these efforts have their regional equivalents. Canada is seeking to reinforce non-proliferation agendas in the OAS, the CSCE, Asia-Pacific, and elsewhere, both for regional purposes and as a means to strengthen worldwide efforts.

GOVERNANCE AND PEACEKEEPING

Finally, two aspects of Canada's international security perspective should be examined: governance or good government, and peacekeeping.

As mentioned earlier, most thinking on cooperative security includes many issues usually considered within the rubric of governance: democracy, human rights, transparency, stability, economic development, and lack of corruption. Tenets of cooperative security hold that democratic governments tend to make war on one another less often than do non-democracies. Governments that respect human rights are more likely to be stable and command their population's loyalty than those that do not. Governments that are transparent have more chance of retaining the confidence of their population than governments that are not. Stability and economic development engender environments that are not conducive to political adventurism and war. Thus, the view is that these fundamental elements of good government will also anchor peace more solidly.

While Canadians consider that good governance is worth supporting under any circumstances, they also tend to see it as reinforcing regional and wider peace as well. And since peace is a vital objective of Canadian foreign and security policy, Canadian statements about this issue should not be seen as mere finger-pointing or irrelevant posturing: they are part and parcel of Canada's view of how best to ensure that peace is maintained.

Canada's role in peacekeeping is also often misunderstood by its international partners. Canada feels that participation in UN or other multilateral operations in support of legitimate national objectives is of value. The country has a long and distinguished history of involvement in peacekeeping and related missions, and has been in almost every UN operation of this kind mounted to date. Efforts to dampen disputes before they explode, to keep them under control and out of the competition between great powers, have been seen as a major means of reducing tensions and ensuring that "brush fire" wars remain contained.

Peacekeeping thus fits well into cooperative security thinking because, at its best, it is multilateral, largely transparent, and based on widespread consensus. It also seeks to reassure parties and potential parties to a dispute, promotes military and non-military security—at least if followed by peacemaking and peacebuilding efforts—and is flexible. For Canada, it offers a classic multilateral tool to increase its weight in the international system in ways supportive of its national goals.

Canada's international security policy thus places great emphasis on both global and regional institutions and processes. It believes that the UN must remain the crucial force in international security affairs if, in these uncertain times, the world Canadians desire is to be built. It is felt that regional and other multilateral organizations can operate in ways that will help relieve the burden on the global organization in such a way as to make the prospects for peace greater, both regionally and more widely.

In seeking to do this, however, it is worth remembering that the blame for failure cannot be placed on institutions. Because it is the nation-states of the international system that make up the UN and the regional organizations set up under its Charter, it is their responsibility to make the system work. Canada believes that the elements of cooperative security can represent a major step forward in the development of thought about international stability, peace, and security, and that they constitute a legitimate and innovative way of trying to come to grips with the major security challenges of today and tomorrow.

Dramatic change is already taking place. Canada must respond to it if it wishes to control the transformations of the international system and not be controlled by them.

NOTE

1. David Dewitt and David Leyton-Brown, "Canada's International Security Policy," in Dewitt and Leyton-Brown, eds., *Canada's International Security Policy* (Toronto: Prentice-Hall, 1995) 1-27.

III

THE WAY AHEAD

PROSPECTS FOR INCREASED MEXICAN-CANADIAN COLLABORATION IN THE SECURITY FIELD

PERSPECTIVES POUR UNE MEILLEURE COLLABORATION CANADO-MEXICAINE DANS LE DOMAINE DE LA SÉCURITÉ

H.P. Klepak

Abstract: The revolution in international affairs that has occurred since the end of the 1980s is forcing Mexico and Canada to thoroughly review the very basis of their defence and foreign policies.

Security is a field that both links and separates Canada and Mexico. Mexico confronts a geostrategic environment in which the sole—unanswerable—real threat is from the north. Its notion of security, therefore, diverges from strictly military considerations to encompass social and economic concerns, because the country's defence apparatus also assumes far less traditional roles. Likewise, Canada faces no real threat apart from the asymmetries of its relations with the United States, and it is generally comfortable with the expansion of the term security to some non-traditional areas in which its armed services are already involved.

Both countries' objectives converge in certain areas while they diverge in others. While Mexico wishes to retain close links with the rest of Latin America, for example, it also seeks to diversify its partners as a means of creating a counterpoise to the United States. Likewise, Canada is also attempting to distance itself from the U.S. while its privileged relationship draws it ever closer. Canada's multilateral efforts reinforce global or regional institutions and ensure a North American presence distinct from the U.S. vis-à-vis Latin America.

Elements of convergence on security issues are evident in the more traditional sectors, such as arms control, while the countries' policies do diverge in less traditional areas, such as peacekeeping. Nevertheless, Mexico and Canada would have much to gain from increased collaboration across several segments of the security field.

Sommaire : Suite aux bouleversements survenus à l'intérieur du système mondial, à la fin des années 80, le Mexique et le Canada doivent revoir en profondeur les fondements mêmes de leurs politiques étrangère et de défense.

La sécurité est un domaine qui, à la fois, rapproche et éloigne le Mexique et le Canada. Le Mexique fait face à un contexte géostratégique où la seule menace véritable viendrait du nord, et cette dernière ne pourrait aucunement être contrée. La notion de sécurité s'écarte donc de la dimension strictement militaire pour se rapprocher des questions économiques et sociales. L'appareil de défense sert ces fins en remplissant des rôles encore moins traditionnels. Le Canada, pour sa part, ne fait face à aucune menace véritable, si ce n'est l'assymétrie de sa relation avec les États-Unis. Lui aussi est généralement intéressé par la dimension « non-traditionnelle » de la sécurité, et son appareil de défense remplit certains rôles à cet effet.

Les objectifs des deux pays se rejoignent à certains niveaux alors qu'ils s'écartent ailleurs. Le Mexique espère à la fois maintenir sa relation étroite avec le reste de l'Amérique latine et diversifier ses partenaires, principalement pour s'assurer d'un contrepoids face aux États-Unis. Le Canada s'efforce lui-aussi de se distancer des États-Unis, bien que sa relation privilégiée l'en rapproche. Les efforts multilatéraux du Canada visent à renforcer les institutions globales ou régionales et à assurer une présence nord-américaine distincte des États-Unis auprès de l'Amérique latine.

Des éléments de convergence sont observés dans les secteurs traditionnels, comme le contrôle des armements, tandis que des éléments de divergence sont présents dans les secteurs moins traditionnels, comme le maintien de la paix. Néanmoins, le Mexique et le Canada ont tout à gagner d'une collaboration accrue dans plusieurs secteurs du domaine de la sécurité.

NATURAL ALLIES?

BUILDING ON THE DIFFERENT THRUSTS of the authors in this work, it is helpful at this stage to see whether there is room to propose, or expect, further Mexican-Canadian collaboration in the broad area of security affairs. This chapter will try to do this, first by reviewing how the two countries perceive the current context; then by asking what each hopes to see emerge from today's rather confused international picture, especially in the security area; and finally by assessing the potential of special areas of convergence and cooperation.

In a sense, this chapter attempts to bring together some of the ideas put forward at the workshop from which this book emerged, and to make a first cut at judging the likelihood and utility of some of the areas in which collaboration might be sought. The latter analysis is the result of the author's reflections on these matters and in no way reflects the views of others.

HOW DO THE TWO COUNTRIES PERCEIVE THE CURRENT CONTEXT?

As has been clear from the various assessments presented in this work, "change" seems to be the operative word for foreign policy and defence analysis in both Canada and Mexico. The extraordinary events of the last six years were not foreseen by either foreign or defence ministries in either country. Indeed, it would have been surprising if they had foreseen the revolution in international affairs, since the explosive changes of 1989 and after, which occurred first in Eastern Europe, then the Soviet Union, and finally more widely, were virtually unimaginable.[1]

The disappearance of a bipolar order, seemingly replaced, at least temporarily, by a unipolar one—especially in the security area—that shows signs of becoming in many senses multipolar, was swift, if not clear. Both countries found themselves involved in international relations far different from those they had known in recent decades. As several authors observed, it is not clear where current trends are leading, and it is not necessarily appropriate to be optimistic.

The main thrust of both countries' international policies had, after all, been remarkably straightforward until the end of the Cold War. While neither found itself without serious problems to address, both had, over time, developed foreign policies seemingly well suited to the realities that surrounded them. And while there were many obvious concerns, particularly in security areas, both Ottawa and Mexico City had mapped out policies that had stood the test of time during most of the post-World War II era.[2] This was, of course, not to last.

MEXICO

The development of Mexican security policy reflects the unique experience of that country, so well outlined by Raúl Benítez Manaut earlier in this volume. The traumas of the 19th and early 20th centuries gave way to remarkable stability and overall security in recent decades, a situation that, while threatened by recent events, has nonetheless shown the resilience of the Mexican system and its ability to address challenges.

It could be said that Mexico developed an exceptionally original security policy which philosophically reflected the country's unique position in Latin America. The very term "security" has been perceived differently in the country compared to both its generally accepted definition further north and its recent special evolution in many other countries of Latin America.

In no country, of course, is there a completely accepted definition of security. This is especially true in recent years when its scope has been expanded by so many in academic, diplomatic, governmental, and even military circles.[3] While some have tried of late, often with good reason, to circumscribe the bounds of security studies and maintain the close link with strictly defence issues, others have successfully pushed those boundaries outward to include areas as diverse as population movements, the environment, good government, health, drugs, natural disasters, and even climate.[4] In the post-Cold War environment, it proved possible to do this even in countries where the original context had held great sway. Canada is a case in point, Mexico even more so, having accepted to a much lesser extent the supposed dictates of the post-Cold War Western Hemisphere.[5]

Mexican views of security have not needed to change as greatly as those of others in recent years. Since it eschewed most of the ideas spawned by the Cold War and by domestic contexts in much of Latin America, the destructive National Security Doctrine popular among many regional armies in the past decades made little progress in Mexico. The idea of a great worldwide struggle against foreign and domestic enemies had much more difficulty making an impact on an army raised on the revolutionary myths of 1910.[6] And while no doubt more involved in internal security thinking and activity after the sad events of 1968, the army in no way became as viscerally anti-Leftist as all its counterparts, except Cuba's.[7]

The term "national security" having acquired negative connotations in much of Latin America, Mexican thinkers tended to gravitate toward notions such as the defence of sovereignty which seemed, in any case, more anchored in Mexican perceptions of the country and its challenges.[8] And this was for long blended with notions of economic security and development which have been the stuff of Mexican foreign, as well as security, policy for many years.

Thus, when new definitions of security began to circulate even before the end of the Cold War, Mexico was well placed to embrace them. Economic independence and security were already understood and championed by Mexicans, who could well articulate the links between the threat to the nation in defence terms and that coming from economic sources. Sovereignty and independence were seen as inextricably linked with economic security, and national legislation covering foreign investment and natural resources could not be understood without reference to these linkages.[9]

Knowing well that arming oneself for national defence was essentially meaningless in a strategic context that involved virtually no threat to the south and an unanswerable one to the north, Mexico found that it could concentrate on threats other than direct military ones.[10] Subtlety about issues of national defence and security was therefore the rule rather than the exception.

In addition, the use of the military in non-traditional roles provided a reinforcement for the inclusion of new "threats" in longstanding defence thinking. The Mexican Navy, for example, had never completely discarded the anti-contraband role it had inherited from the imperial naval authorities after independence.[11] Control of the national territory, and especially its borders, had long had a military component, especially in times of particular stress. And the Mexican military's role in civic action programs, assistance to the civil power, natural disaster relief, search and rescue, and even health had been marked since the Revolution and even before.[12]

Thus, for example, when new roles, such as fighting the drug trade, emerged, neither the state nor the armed services had great difficulty imagining the use of military resources in the struggle. Steadily expanding employment of the armed services, both alone and in support of police and specialist anti-drug forces, has occurred over more than two decades now. The level of such activity is remarkable, involving many thousands of troops annually and often several thousand at one time.[13]

Mexico had no difficulty following the U.S. example and declaring the illegal narcotics trade a threat to national security: as early as 1987, President de la Madrid did this for the first time in the country's history. This not only convinced Washington of the seriousness of Mexican intentions in this area, but also allowed the mobilization of the considerable resources needed to embark on the current anti-drug campaign.[14] Once again, the discipline, honesty, and cohesiveness of the military, its presence throughout the national territory and in Mexican air and sea spaces, and its weaponry, equipment, fitness, and training provided an invaluable reinforcement of national policy at home and abroad. And once again, this proved applicable beyond traditional military fields.[15]

Thus, one can say that Mexico was singularly ready for the challenges of redefinition that have come its way in the security area, even though the realities could hardly be comforting. As has been seen throughout this volume, change has been dramatic and costly. First economic crisis, then globalization and its attendant requirements for adjustment, have struck at the very heart of the Mexican national self-image. Traditions and national policies dating back even to before the Revolution have tumbled in the face of the stark economic and geopolitical realities of the post-Cold War world.

Abroad, non-interventionism—a pillar of Mexican foreign policy for many decades—now finds fewer takers. And independent foreign policies are rarer than ever as unipolar conditions and a single acceptable economic and political model appear to be the order of the day. Economic security concepts have been overtaken by events.

In response, Mexico has had, to a considerable extent, to turn its back on its historic cultural and political partners in Latin America.[16] It has had to acknowledge that diversification of trade and investment as a government policy is simply not viable. Even the independence of its foreign policy has had to be compromised on issues from Cuba to the Third World in general. And it has had to accept that a free trade area with the United States, whatever its political implications, was inevitable if Mexicans were to attain the prosperity they were insisting upon.[17]

At home, Mexicans have been obliged to dismantle the protectionist state built up since the end of the Revolution. National policies on natural resources and foreign investment have perished in the face of the dramatic need to open the economy and be accepted by the developed nations as a real partner, one that submitted to the most painful rules of belonging to the club. Even in terms of the political system, the need to modernize and open up was accepted, and the system became more democratic in the process. None of this was easy, and the political and economic pressure needed to bring it about was clearly enormous.

CANADA

If Canada, as a NATO, NORAD, and long-term British Commonwealth member was, in security terms, more tied to traditional notions than was Mexico, Ottawa was no less required to turn the page on the Cold War context than was Mexico City. The overall reaction to the improvement in East-West relations could hardly be other than cautious rejoicing. Canada, placed squarely between the United States and the Soviet Union, had long understood that, even if it was neutral, any central exchange of nuclear weapons between the two superpowers would spell its doom.[18] The removal of a direct potential military threat to North America, one that necessarily was considered to include Canada, was naturally an enormous boon in terms of reinforcing Canadians' sense of security, nationally and individually.

Indeed, the hopes of Canadians that the end of the Cold War would necessarily lead to an era of peace were only slowly abandoned as the post-Cold War era proved to be anything but peaceful. Defence budgets and preparations for conflict were allowed to slide dramatically in the immediate and subsequent aftermath of the events of autumn 1989. The number of deployable units, ships, and aircraft fell, although improvements to the Navy, planned long before, did make the situation appear less grim for that service.[19] Indeed, it can be argued that only the peacekeeping role, so well supported by almost all Canadians until very recently, was able to block the calls for further cuts to the country's armed forces in light of the end of the East-West stand-off.[20]

Be that as it may, Canadians have generally felt comfortable with the expansion of the term "security" to include many non-traditional areas. Peacekeeping itself, despite its close links to traditional roles that are part and parcel of Canadian military thought and strategic analysis, is to many quite far removed from preparation and training for war. Even further removed are assisting the police in fighting the drug trade, military humanitarian missions, natural disaster clean-ups, economic zone patrolling, and some elements of arms control verification.

The military has been generally pleased that such tasks, old or new, have so far been undertaken without excessive damage to its fighting capabilities. Most officers feel that peacekeeping is excellent training, especially for junior officers and senior non-commissioned officers (NCOs), and its more recent manifestations have often involved exposure to live fire as well, always a litmus test of armed forces' readiness for the real thing.[21] Fighting the drug trade within the limits of a national security doctrine that—unlike the U.S. and Mexican views—does not consider it a security problem, except perhaps peripherally, is reckoned to provide valuable training for all three services, especially for the Navy and Air Force.[22]

Military humanitarian missions have proven excellent not only for morale and recruiting, but also for active training in a wide variety of tasks. Natural disaster relief missions offer some of the same benefits for the military and are, of course, useful for search and rescue training, long a Canadian Forces (CF) responsibility. There are also many advantages to CF participation in patrolling economic zones and in arms control verification arrangements.

Canadians in general seem happy with the new roles of the armed services. Interestingly, it appears that Francophone Canadians are happier about the shifts than are Anglophones, although the majority of both groups generally favour the change.[23] They are, however, concerned that the new international scene will call upon the armed forces to become increasingly involved in seemingly interminable and hopeless conflicts far from their borders, where their direct interests would be less than obvious.[24]

However, the more or less traditional security agenda has not disappeared. If anything, the relative simplicity of the East-West struggle has given way to a wide and often bewildering spectrum of security issues. Beyond the already profound questions surrounding the internationally sanctioned use of force in peacekeeping and peace enforcement missions, others clamour for attention in new ways. The arrival of dozens of new states on the world scene, the spread of ethnic and religious conflict, the questioning of many of the international community's basic elements—all lead to confusion and uncertainty. Intelligence officers, long enmeshed in the minutiae of Warsaw Pact or Western military systems, now require greater flexibility, wide ranging interests, greater language and analytical capabilities, and many other skills that were needed less during the long Cold War. The Canadian Armed Forces, historically members of great international associations (the French and British Empires, the British Commonwealth, NATO) in which their own resources were small parts of the whole, now often confront the new challenges—which require national analysis rarely known in previous strategic situations—alone or nearly so.[25]

The key relationship with the United States has changed immeasurably, not only because of that country's relative growth in power and near-unipolar status, but also because of its central position in a developing inter-American free trade system. NAFTA has meant a connection with Mexico unimagined only a few years ago. Membership in the OAS, rejected for over a century by governments of every stripe, is now a fact of increasing significance. Canada now declares itself an "American country" after denying the fact to itself, for literally centuries.

The UN is no longer the organization it once was and loyal membership in it carries commitments that are perhaps greater than ever. The Commonwealth has all but lost its influence with the Canadian public, and *la Francophonie* has never had any of note, even among Francophones. The Canada of the 1990s sees new challenges and massive changes everywhere it looks. The major changes in perception this calls for are all the more needed as Canada finds itself at a crossroads marked by severe financial difficulties that require difficult decisions about where to place priorities, security or otherwise, in the coming years.

The decisions made so far on Canadian-U.S. free trade, the OAS, NAFTA, the European deployment of the Canadian Forces, peacekeeping limitations, and the like have often been painful and always made *faute de mieux*. Realism is the *mot d'ordre* in Ottawa almost as much as it is in Mexico City.

It would be helpful to look briefly now at Canada's and Mexico's objectives in the context of this post-Cold War world and the environments in which they find themselves. To discover whether there is potential for cooperation in the security field, it will first be necessary to seek out the aims of the two potential collaborators and then identify those elements that are security-related. Finally, areas of similarity or even commonality of aims can be considered.

MEXICO

In general, it seems that Mexico wishes above all to be allowed to implement the reforms that are necessary if it is to join the evolving international economic order and, most particularly, if it is to find a comfortable niche in the free trade area developing in the Americas. This implies political, economic, and probably social reform.

It is clear to most key decision makers in Mexico today that the country must become a functioning democracy much more along the lines of the Western model than it has been to date, and that this goal requires major reform of the state. While such reform is both more difficult and more long-term than the economic measures put in place have so far proven, there seems little doubt that this is the way all established political parties in the country view the future.[26] That there is resistance to such reform is not to be doubted, however, as the difficult years of 1994 and 1995 have shown. But that there is a determination to see the job through is also becoming clearer.[27]

In the foreign policy sphere, Mexico clearly wishes to retain the best of its long and impressive diplomatic history while adjusting to the realities of the end of the century. Its search for counterpoises to U.S. power and influence will surely continue, although in more subtle forms. Indeed, many Mexicans argue that this policy must be strengthened.[28] The rejection of unilateral interventionism on the part of their northern neighbour may also appear in less strident guise than in the past.

Mexico will certainly wish to retain close links with parts of the world outside the Americas and will fear too-exclusive Pan-American linkages. It will often eschew bilateralism where possible, although with a sense of realism: the U.S. connection will remain key. The country will seek to maintain the Latin American connection fundamental to its history and culture while accepting that this relationship can no longer be the defining one.

Sovereignty and independence will be reworked in the context of the newly developing world order, particularly the inter-American dimension. The value of international law in settling differences among states will still be proclaimed. Active links with the Third World, based on shared perceptions of development, will no doubt weaken, but this will not mean that Mexico will turn its back completely on its traditional, less-developed partners. Cultural independence will remain a priority, although the realities of the current world will greatly impinge on this area.[29]

Security objectives will likewise be a mix of constants from the past and initiatives reflecting new realities. Mexican sensitivities on security issues, stemming from a difficult and conflictual past, will in all probability be allayed less quickly than those on other issues.

The inter-American security "system" will retain features with which Mexico will be less than comfortable. The country will fear multilateral initiatives proposed by the United States in the security area: this was demonstrated at the Defence Ministerial of the Americas in July 1995, when Mexico merely sent its ambassador in Washington rather than a minister of defence as requested by the American hosts. The strongly held Mexican view of current trends can be summed up by the words heard so often in all Latin American defence ministries: *¿a dónde nos quieren llevar?* [Where do they want to take us?] And resistance to these efforts is strong. On the other hand, long-standing cooperative arrangements based on limited bilateral training accords, the IADB and the IADC continue. Fear of too many new duties being entrusted to the inter-American security system will keep Mexico interested, although concerned.

Peacekeeping, while officially welcomed, will remain a questionable area while there is major doubt about its philosophical basis, its legitimacy, and its objectives. Ideas such as democratic security, or pacts of democratic solidarity, will continue to be met with suspicion. Mexico will not soon or easily give way on issues so closely related to its long and deep commitment to non-intervention in the domestic affairs of sovereign states.[30]

The commitment of successive governments to arms control and disarmament is not likely to change either. While not as exposed as

Canada to the dangers inherent in nuclear strikes on North America, Mexico is well aware that the country would be enormously affected by nuclear conflict targeted at the United States.[31] The Tlatelolco process, already relatively successful, will retain its importance for Mexico. Elsewhere, the country will want to see peace anchored as firmly as possible in the new world order. Seeking to trade with peaceful and prosperous states—normally the best customers—Mexico will continue its tradition of active support and involvement in UN and other arms control and disarmament initiatives.

While many sensitivities remain in the field of drug trafficking, Mexico will wish to continue to be seen, especially by Washington, as helpful and cooperative on bilateral and multilateral levels. Both the UN and CICAD will continue to enjoy Mexican input. Given Mexico's problems and resources in this area, the security element of the anti-narcotics effort will likely remain to the fore for some time.

CANADA

Ottawa will not, of course, share all the objectives keenly sought by Mexico City. Canada also seeks a world of prosperous and peaceful states with which to trade and have profitable exchanges on all levels, but its interpretation of a policy for achieving progress in this direction will be somewhat different.

Canada will wish to remain a sovereign state in the face of globalization and the United States' increased ability to put pressures on the country. Ottawa will still wish to find potential counterpoises to undue U.S. influence on its future, but it will understand that the current context requires highly original initiatives to do so. Latin America and the NAFTA connection, while drawing the country closer to the United States, will also be used to provide some opportunities for multilateralism in the new inter-American context.[32] And while this will surely be fraught with dangers, it is probably the only option for Canada once its newly declared status as an "American" country is formally acknowledged.[33]

Canada will want an international order based on rules, where the weak or medium-ranked states will have recourse to accepted modes of action that will protect them—or at least attempt to—against the whims of the strong. In an era of protectionism, cynicism, and economic power politics of the worst kind, such a policy is surely well founded. Canada's approach to GATT and the WTO, peacekeeping, the UN, regional organizations, free trade and globalization, and international law in general—to name but a few areas of current interest—must be seen in this context.

Ottawa will seek reinforcement of GATT and the WTO, its sole multilateral hopes where truly international and global trade is concerned. It will wish to move forward quickly with regional arrangements that dovetail into wider global ones. To retain the potential for diversification of trade and wider linkages on which it must eventually base its future, it will seek to remain a player in Europe, Asia-Pacific, and even in the Commonwealth and *la Francophonie*. Thus, while accepting the rules of the inter-American system, it will work at keeping wider options open.[34]

The country will want to see minimum intervention in the affairs of others retained as a principle. At the same time, Ottawa has accepted that, in the post-Cold War world, the cession of some sovereignty to multinational bodies is essentially beneficial and can bring great economic and political advantages. Thus, Canada supports moves in the UN and other agencies to allow multilateral intervention in the domestic affairs of states when those countries clearly require help.

In the area of security, Canada wishes to see as much progress as the current, relatively positive environment allows in arms control and disarmament, confidence-building measures, international verification, and transparency as a whole. To move this agenda forward, Ottawa is active in an array of fora, sometimes in ways that do not address its national interests directly.

Reinforcement of the UN's ability to act to halt aggression or deploy peacekeeping contingents is, of course, a troubling issue, especially in light of events in Bosnia and elsewhere in the world. The international body's rapid reaction capability has been the source of considerable Canadian attention, and a major study on the subject has recently been completed. A rules-based international order, under which borders cannot be changed at the whim of the strong, is a clear goal. How to reach such a utopian state is the subject of widespread debate, however.

The UN remains Canada's great hope for the future. Regional organizations permitted by its Charter have a role—sometimes major, sometimes minor—to play. Canada, placed as it is between two formerly antagonistic blocs and with what David Haglund has called the "Wars of the Soviet Succession" perhaps only beginning, must favour major initiatives across the board in tension reduction, arms control, and disarmament. It must also favour the development of peacekeeping capabilities to "hold the ring" until peacemaking can take place.

In the Americas, Canada will particularly want to see peace and prosperity among its new partners in an expanded inter-American "system." If Canada is to feel comfortable in a hemisphere that it had largely ignored for centuries, the developing community of the Americas must have democratic government, peace among and within its constituent countries, and show signs of growing prosperity. The country's interest in security affairs in the hemisphere, slight before 1990 and only slowly perceived afterward, is at base a result of this state of affairs. If *golpes de estado (coup d'état)* again become the rule, if conflicts of the type of Peru-Ecuador 1995 spread, if poverty and inequalities continue to grow, it will be virtually impossible to convince the Canadian voting public to agree to closer links with countries of the region, much less to throw in its lot with them. This is, as it were, the bottom line of Canada's future in the Western Hemisphere and should be taken very seriously indeed.

CONVERGENCE

A reading of the above does seem to suggest a convergence of views between Canada and Mexico on a number of major issues of foreign policy, and some potential for collaboration on security matters. These two smaller North American partners do share a number of objectives and would presumably benefit from cooperation in achieving them.

Their main convergence of views appears to be on the world they wish to see evolve from the rather confusing post-Cold War context. As minor—or at best middle—powers, they both want to see an international order based on rules, not only in terms of political relations among states, but also on the economic front. As trading nations, each now sees wide-open markets as a good thing.

Both countries know that impoverished, warring countries tend to make poor trading partners, while wealthy, peaceful ones usually offer considerable scope for commerce. They also share strong humanitarian traditions, rejecting the idea of war as a means of settling disputes between states. Neither has a tradition of fighting except in the stricter sense of defence of territory and vital interests.

From these commonalities have come foreign and security policies that, while quite different in many ways—especially in the handling of the U.S. relationship—are nonetheless highly compatible, even complementary. Both have strong traditions of rejection of unilateral interventionism by the great powers and, given their geography, particularly by the United States. Each must accept the U.S. relationship as the bedrock of strategic thinking simply because of the obvious asymmetries of North American life. Each seeks multilateralism and far-flung contacts with the wider world, often specifically as a means of lessening the relative weight of Washington in national decision making. And, while both accept the need for closer economic integration in North America, Ottawa and Mexico City are virtually one on the issue of greater political linkages.

This wide range of generally converging views is clearly reflected in some areas of potential collaboration in the security field. Both countries have declared the other a priority for the coming years.[35] While this is not strictly a security connection, there is little doubt that, given the broadening of the concept of security and the importance of economic security, there are elements of the Canadian-Mexican relationship that fall within the definition.[36] Canada and Mexico are now the junior partners in a vast free trade area; much of the impetus for joining this group has come from the need for economic security for their highly dependent economies. But the scope for cooperation in both traditional and non-traditional security fields is felt to be considerable.

One of the seemingly most obvious areas for greater collaboration is that of arms control and disarmament initiatives on the world stage. Canada and Mexico have long been staunch supporters of the UN and have seen that body as a major priority in their foreign and security policies. Both have also considered the global organization to be an appropriate forum for a wide range of arms control and disarmament initiatives.[37] In what Canadian diplomat Gordon Vachon called "1995—watershed year for arms control," Mexico and Canada were well forward in the UN and other fora on a wide range of initiatives. They have almost always been in close accord on these issues, even though the degree of potential bilateral coordination between them has not been as close as some had hoped.

It should be possible for the two countries to do more toward arms control, given their common interests and similar perspectives. Providing support for further progress with the UN Arms Register could be one such field. Continued work on the Non-Proliferation Treaty is another. Current initiatives on small arms exports, de-mining, chemical and biological weapons, and a host of other matters may well provide areas of useful collaboration between Ottawa and Mexico City.

On the hemispheric level, the Security Committee of the OAS, which recently obtained permanent status, is an obvious forum for further cooperation. While Mexico and Canada come to these discussions with very different histories, they should be able to coordinate their approaches more effectively in the future, as their shared perspectives on so many inter-American security and wider issues become clearer to both.

Canada has much to learn from Mexico in institutions such as the IADB and IADC. While Mexico has a long connection with both, Canada is not a member of the IADB and is only now making its first contacts with the IADC. Both countries are keen to make their views known in the context of the need, expressed by most OAS members, to radically reform the IADB and to continue the reform of the IADC, so ably begun by the recently retired U.S. Army commander, General Harding. Here again, there is certainly room for the two smaller NAFTA countries to work together.

In a wider context, there is considerable pressure either to abandon the Rio Pact of 1947 or to replace it with something much less rooted in its original time frame. Ottawa did not want to sign the treaty when it joined the OAS in early 1990. Mexico signed the Pact, but its views on its evolution and use have often echoed Canadian concerns. It would certainly be of benefit to both countries to study the potential for improving the security aspects of the inter-American system and perhaps offer some new ideas for its future direction once basic documents like the Pact and Chapter 5 of the OAS Charter have been reconsidered.[38]

Mexico has shown less interest in current attempts to find confidence-building measures to help anchor the current, largely favourable security context in the Americas. Here again, there appear to be historical reasons for Mexico's perception that this is an area of potential pitfalls. Canada has enormous experience in this area, and it might be possible to move this agenda forward by means of a lengthy and detailed exchange of views between the two countries.

The Cuba question and other aspects of the Caribbean situation raise security concerns for Mexico in particular, but also for Canada. There is a real possibility that the Cuban situation could become a blood bath, that immigration issues could soon become security ones, and that both Canada and Mexico would be hard pressed to refrain from action of some kind. Should the transition from Castro be disrupted, the prospects for direct U.S. military intervention are high. Such a move would place Ottawa and Mexico City, both of which maintain formal relations with Havana and are traditionally receptive to ideological pluralism in the hemisphere, in a difficult position.[39] The Cuban situation, an emotional issue in both countries, could easily give rise to nationalist reactions. It may be helpful for the two countries to work together toward a solution to the current difficulties—difficulties that are likely to increase—caused by Cuba's reintegration into the Americas.[40]

On the issue of peacekeeping there has, of course, been some degree of divergence between the Mexican and Canadian positions in recent years. Mexico City has tended to be wary of what often appeared to be open-ended commitments whose legal—and even moral—basis seemed unclear. Mexican diplomats were particularly concerned that the expanded use of peacekeeping (defined broadly) in the post-Cold War era could become excessively intrusive in the internal affairs of states, thereby endangering deeply held traditions such as the rejection of interventionism. There is nonetheless some precedent for Mexican involvement: Mexico did provide police forces to Central American peace initiatives in El Salvador, and that mission (ONUSAL) was nothing if not intrusive.

Canadians, on the other hand, consider themselves the apostles of peacekeeping and feel that the slight diminution of sovereignty implied in its expanded role is a small price to pay for the significant increase in international security conferred by the new activism of the UN and some regional and other international organizations. No doubt this again reflects the very different historical experience of both countries with respect to their neighbours and international security ventures in general.

PROSPECTS FOR COLLABORATION

Canada would no doubt wish to see greater bilateral cooperation between the two countries in this area. Ottawa is well aware that Latin America in general, and Mexico in particular, has sizable armed forces, often of considerable professionalism. In these days of too many missions and too few countries contributing troops, the potential of some of Canada's new partners in the Americas would be worth tapping. Whatever the evolution of Mexico and Canada's views on these matters, it may be extremely useful for the two countries to exchange ideas. Mexico might even wish to send officers to the Lester Pearson Peacekeeping Training Centre in Nova Scotia.

In non-traditional areas (at least for Canada), there is probably much that could be gained from a closer connection. Both countries have a great deal of experience in natural disaster relief, search and rescue, and related activities. Mexico has vast experience with civic action programs as well. Canada is well versed in issues of the environment that closely affect the armed forces, matters that may well be of interest to Mexico at this time. Some work on these matters has already been done by the two capitals.[41]

In the anti-narcotics field, Mexico's armed forces have perhaps the most experience in the world. The Canadian Forces are much newer to this game and much less dramatically involved, although that involvement is growing and becoming more complex. Here again, it is difficult to believe that these two North American countries would not gain by looking closely at the other's experience. This could take various forms: visiting lecturers, exchanging officers, or Coast Guard liaison.[42] At the very least, it might be worth seeing whether greater bilateral collaboration within CICAD, the OAS body dealing with anti-narcotics issues, could bear more fruit.

All such cooperation could be seen as a reinforcement of multilateralism and, indeed, as a way of providing some distance vis-à-vis the overwhelming influence of Washington in the security fields. One cannot escape geography, but bilateral efforts aimed at maximizing linkages between Canada and Mexico would gain from the absence of asymmetries and historical baggage. In training, interoperability, military education, and other areas, it might at least be worth looking more carefully at mutually profitable initiatives.

This chapter has not sought to offer a dramatic way forward, or even to suggest that there is necessarily a great deal to be done immediately in the security field as far as bilateral Mexican-Canadian cooperation is concerned. Rather, it sought to underscore areas of commonality, or at least potential convergence of views, in security matters and to stimulate debate on where this might lead.

It appears, however, that there are diplomatic, military, and other security areas in which the two countries could find ways of broadening their rapidly developing relationship to their mutual benefit. In this regard, a closer study of the direction the two countries wish to take in security matters, and of the extent to which they can help one another, would be beneficial, even if both decided to limit the extent of their cooperation.

NOTES

1. Even the far-sighted and highly perceptive Hélène Carrère D'Encausse thought the Soviet disintegration process would be both longer in coming and less dramatic in its results. See her exceptional *L'Empire éclaté* (Paris: Flammarion, 1978).
2. See, for Canada, Paul Buteux, "NATO and the Evolution of Canadian Defence and Foreign Policy," in David Dewitt and David Leyton-Brown, eds., *Canada's International Security Policy* (Toronto: Prentice-Hall, 1995) 153-70. For Mexico, see Sergio Aguayo Quezada, "Los Usos, abusos y retos de la seguridad mexicana, 1946-1990," in Sergio Aguayo Quezada and Bruce M. Bagley, eds., *En Busca de la seguridad perdida: aproximaciones a la seguridad nacional mexicana* (Mexico: Siglo XXI, 1990) 107-45.
3. See, for Canada, Buteux, "NATO." For Mexico, see Aguayo Quezada, "Los Usos."
4. For a traditional view, see David Haglund, "Changing Concepts and Trends in International Security," in Dewitt and Leyton-Brown, *Canada's International Security Policy* 31-50. For new thinking, see Laszlo Valki, ed., *Changing Threat Perceptions and Military Doctrines* (London: Macmillan, 1992); and a series of works on particular elements on this new agenda. For drugs, there is Guy Delbrel, *La géopolitique de la drogue* (Paris: La Découverte, 1991). For immigration and population issues, see Nicholas Eberstadt (1991), "Population Change and National Security," *Foreign Affairs* 70(3): 115-31. For health issues, see among others Alan Whiteside and David Fitzsimmons, *AIDS—Economic, Political and Security Implications*, Conflict Study 251 (Southampton UK: Research Institute for the Study of Conflict and Terrorism, 1991). Linked to environmental issues is that of military humanitarianism, where the same caveats apply. See Thomas G. Weiss and K.M. Campbell (1991), "Military Humanitarianism," *Survival* 33(5): 451-65.
5. Josefina Zoraida Vázquez and Lorenzo Meyer, *México frente a Estados Unidos: un ensayo histórico, 1776-1988* (Mexico: EFE, 1989) 190-232.

6. Frederick M. Nunn, *The Time of the Generals: Latin American Professional Militarism in World Perspective* (Lincoln: University of Nebraska Press, 1992) 46-49 and 198-99.
7. Nunn, *Time of the Generals* 229-30.
8. See the prologue to Aguayo Quezada and Bagley, *En Busca* esp. 12-14.
9. Victor Flores Olea, *México entre las naciones* (Mexico: Cal y Arena, 1989) 30-35.
10. Mexico's official position in case of threatened invasion was a joining of forces between the armed services and the people. See José Luis Piñeyro, "Fuerzas armadas mexicanas y modernización militar," in Augusto Varas, ed., *La Autonomía militar en América latina* (Caracas: Nueva Sociedad, 1988) 267-88, esp. 272.
11. Adrian J. English, *Armed Forces of Latin America* (London: Jane's, 1984) 311-16.
12. See David Ronfeldt, ed., *The Modern Mexican Military: A Reassessment* (San Diego: University of California, 1984).
13. Mexico, *The Mexican Army and Air Force in the Campaign against Drug Traffic* (Mexico: Estado Mayor de la Defensa Nacional, 1991).
14. See the excellent Maria Celia Toro, "El Narcotráfico como amenaza a la seguridad nacional," in Aguayo Quezada and Bagley, *En Busca* 367-87. For a wider discussion of some of these issues, especially from a U.S. perspective, see Miguel Ruiz-Cabañas, "La Campaña permanente de México: costos, beneficios y consecuencia," in Peter H. Smith, ed., *El combate a las drogas en América* (Mexico: Fondo de Cultura Económica, 1992) 207-20.
15. For a wide-ranging look at the bases of Mexican military forces, see the interesting José Manuel Villalpando César, *Introducción al derecho militar mexicano* (Mexico: Porrúa, 1991) esp. 16-23, 53-60, and 128-30.
16. Jorge Castañeda, *La Casa por la ventana: México y América latina después de la guerra fría* (Mexico: Cal y Arena, 1993) 117-18.
17. See the striking article on Mexican willingness to accept the new rules of the game in Carlos Fuentes, "Nacionalismo e integración," in Carlos Arriola, ed., *Testimonios sobre el TLC* (Mexico: Porrúa, 1994) 147-57.
18. See Douglas A. Ross, "Arms Control and Disarmament and the Canadian Approach to Global Order," in Dewitt and Leyton-Brown, *Canada's International Security Policy* 251-86, esp. 257.
19. See this author's "Les Forces armées et l'armement au Canada," in S.J. Kirschbaum, ed., *La sécurité collective au XXIe siècle* (Quebec: Centre québécois de relations internationales, 1993) 197-214.
20. Alex Morrison, "Canada and Peacekeeping: A Time for Reanalysis?" in Dewitt and Leyton-Brown, *Canada's International Security Policy* 199-226. Some nuance is, however, needed in this, given the 1990 Oka crisis and other potential sources of domestic use of the armed services. See in the same volume, Desmond Morton, "No More Disagreeable or Onerous Duty: Canadians and Military Aid to the Civil Power, Past, Present and Future," 129-52, esp. 142-44.
21. Rod Byers, "Peacekeeping and Canadian Defence Policy: Ambivalence and Uncertainty," in Barry Hunt and Ronald Haycock, eds., *Canada's Defence:*

Perspectives on Policy in the Twentieth Century (Toronto: Copp Clark Pitman, 1993) 179-97, esp. 190-94. See also H.P. Klepak, "Education and Training for Peacekeeping Forces," in E. Gilman and D. Herold, eds., *Peacekeeping Challenges to Euro-Atlantic Security* (Rome: NATO Defence College, 1994) 111-25.

22. H.P. Klepak (1994), "The Impact of the International Narcotics Trade on Canada's Foreign and Security Policy," *International Journal* 49(1): 66-92.
23. James Finan and S.B. Flemming, "Public Attitudes toward Defence and Security in Canada," in Dewitt and Leyton-Brown, *Canada's International Security Policy* 291-311.
24. Pierre Martin and Michel Fortmann (1995), "Canadian Public Opinion and Peacekeeping in a Turbulent World," *International Journal* 50(2): 370-400.
25. See this author's "Changing Realities and Perceptions of Military Threat," in Dewitt and Leyton-Brown, *Canada's International Security Policy* 51-79, esp. 52-61.
26. See Luis F. Aguilar, "El TLC y el Pacto: doble reforma histórica," in Arriola, *Testimonios* 267-72.
27. *Latin American Regional Report Mexico* (June 8, 1995) 1.
28. See, for example, Aguilar, "El TLC y el Pacto" 270.
29. See Leopoldo Zea, "El TLC y la identidad nacional," in Arriola, *Testimonios* 207-09; in the same volume, Tovar y de Teresa, "La Cultura no se negocia ni se inscribe dentro del TLC," 211-16.
30. For more on this concept, see Juan Somavía and José Miguel Insulza, eds., *Seguridad democrática regional: una concepción alternativa* (Caracas: Nueva Sociedad, 1990).
31. See Aguayo Quezada and Bagley, *En Busca*.
32. *Toward a New World Strategy: Canadian Policy in the Americas into the Twenty-First Century* (Ottawa: FOCAL, 1994) 8-10.
33. H.P. Klepak, *What's in it for us? Canada's Relationship with Latin America* (Ottawa: FOCAL, 1994) 17-26.
34. See Rod Dobell and Michael Neufeld, eds., *Beyond NAFTA: The Western Hemisphere Interface* (Lantzville BC: Oolichan Books, 1993) 143-49.
35. For Mexico's view of Canada's priority, see José Navidad González Parás, ed., *La Política exterior de México en el nuevo orden mundial* (Mexico: EFE, 1993) 290-92. For the place of Mexico in Canadian priorities, see Canada, Department of Foreign Affairs and International Trade, *Canada in the World* (Ottawa: Queen's Printer, 1995).
36. Jorge Castro-Valle, "México-Canadá: hacia la consolidación de una nueva relación estratégica," in Mónica Verea Campos, ed., *50 años de relaciones México-Canadá: encuentros y coincidencias* (Mexico: UNAM, 1994) 35-43, esp. 38.
37. For Mexico, see González Parás, *La Política exterior* 97-99. For Canada, see Albert Legault and Michel Fortmann, *Une diplomatie de l'espoir* (Quebec: Les Presses de l'Université Laval, 1989).
38. For a discussion of these matters as viewed by both countries, see for Canada, Marcel Roussin, *Le Canada et le système interaméricain* (Ottawa: Les Presses de l'Université d'Ottawa, 1959); Frederic H. Soward and A.M.

MacAuley, *Canada and the Pan-American System* (Toronto: Canadian Institute for International Affairs, 1948). See also the historical chapters of H.P. Klepak, ed., *Canada and Latin American Security* (Montreal: Méridien, 1993). For Mexico, there is Zoraida Vázquez and Meyer, *México frente* 190-200. See also Hugo Luis Cargnelutti, *Seguridad interamericana* (Buenos Aires: Círculo Militar, 1993) 57-72.

39. See John Kirk, *Back in Business: Canada-Cuba Relations after 50 Years* (Ottawa: FOCAL, 1995); and both Cuba-specific chapters of Andrés Serbin and Joseph Tulchin, eds., *El Caribe y Cuba en la posguerra fría* (Caracas: Nueva Sociedad, 1994).
40. See this author's (1994) "Medidas de confianza mutua y reacercamiento entre Cuba y los Estados Unidos," *Estudios Internacionales* 27(107): 605-17; and (1995) "Cuban Security—Old Myths and New Realities," *Jane's Intelligence Review* 7(7): 334-35.
41. Castro-Valle, "México-Canadá" 38.
42. It may be worth noting in this regard that the Royal Canadian Mounted Police maintains a liaison officer in Mexico City.

10

WHAT CONCLUSIONS?

H.P. Klepak

Like many books of its kind, this one could end without a concluding chapter, not only because the various authors' chapters stand alone, but also because there is no absolute agreement on the answer to the question: "Are Mexico and Canada really 'natural allies'?" However, a brief conclusion will be offered on the basis of what appeared to be the consensus at the workshop.

There was general acceptance of a number of elements discussed. For example, there was no disagreement with the proposition, put forward explicitly by a number of participants, that the international security scene is changing with often dizzying speed and that new means of addressing it will be increasingly necessary in the future. All seemed to concur as well that a new world order of some kind, not yet fleshed out in all its various dimensions, is upon us; it offers many opportunities in the security area, but perhaps as many pitfalls for our two countries.

All agreed that Canada and Mexico need to get to know each other better if they are to recognize the extent to which their foreign and security policies may be compatible. And all felt that Canada and Mexico are clearly going to be much closer partners in the future.

There was, however, a pronounced lack of unanimity on several significant issues—for example, the question as to whether NAFTA necessarily meant a closer trilateral connection in the security field in North America. There were also doubts about the UN's interpretation of the concepts of peacekeeping, peacemaking, and peace enforcement.

There was division about how unipolar the world, the hemisphere, and indeed North America were going to be in the future, and how best to handle the evolving situations in this regard, especially in the security area. There was even some disagreement about what the term "security" should legitimately encompass, reflecting discussions—sometimes seemingly interminable—on this point in other fora.

How the UN, the OAS, and other multilateral bodies can best serve national interests, and how the two countries' foreign and security policies can best support those groupings, also brought diverse responses. Some felt that the global body, whatever its failings, would still be less dominated by a single power than the OAS was bound to be. Others felt that a reformed OAS could act as a significant agent of positive change in the hemisphere and should therefore be encouraged to change more rapidly.

The future roles of the European Union, Asia-Pacific and APEC, and even the Commonwealth and *la Francophonie,* were felt to be far from clear. Now that NAFTA is a reality, all participants felt that non-North American linkages will be of greater value than ever. But the extent to which those players could be made effective in the pursuit of both countries' goals was less certain.

Absolutely crystal-clear, however, was the belief that the sharing of a common neighbour of the power and influence of the United States is a very important unifier of approaches between the two countries. Some felt that this was the element of commonality upon which all others could be built and developed. How to handle the relationship with the United States remained a critical question of survival and prosperity for both countries, and a cornerstone of cooperation between Mexico and Canada that should be turned into concrete action wherever and whenever possible. The potential that this fact, and others, offers to both countries was felt by all to be considerable.

SELECT BIBLIOGRAPHY

Aguayo Quezada, Sergio, and Bruce M. Bagley, eds., *En busca de la seguridad perdida: aproximaciones a la seguridad nacional mexicana* (Mexico: Siglo XXI, 1990).

Aguayo Quezada, Sergio, *El Exodo Centroamericano* (Mexico: SEPFORO 2000, 1985).

Aguilar Camín, Héctor, *Subversiones silenciosas* (Mexico: Aguilar, 1993).

———, and Lorenzo Meyer, *A la sombra de la revolución mexicana* (Mexico: Cal y Arena, 1993).

Ai Camp, Roderic, *Generals in the Palacio: The Military in Modern Mexico* (New York/Oxford: Oxford University Press, 1992).

Allen, Robert S., *His Majesty's Indian Allies: British Indian Policy in the Defence of Canada, 1774-1815* (Toronto: Dundurn, 1992).

Amaral Gurgel, José A., *Segurança e democracia* (Rio de Janeiro: Biblioteca de Exército, 1975).

Angel Sánchez, Miguel, *Historia militar de la Revolución Mexicana en la época maderista* (Mexico: INEHRM, 1976).

Angeles, Luis, ed., *Los Desafíos de la globalización: económica múndial y sociedades nacionales* (Mexico: PRI, 1990).

Archer, Christon I., *The Army in Bourbon Mexico, 1760-1810* (Albuquerque NM: University of New Mexico Press, 1977).

Arciniegas, Germán, *O.E.A. La suerte de una institución regional* (Bogotá: Planeta, 1985).

Arriola, Carlos, ed., *Testimonios sobre el TLC* (Mexico: Porrúa, 1994).

Axelman, H.M., and John Kirk, *Cuban Foreign Policy Confronts a New International Order* (Boulder CO: Lynne Rienner, 1991).

Bagley, Bruce M., *Contadora and the Diplomacy of Peace in Central America* (Boulder CO: Westview, 1987).

———, (1983), "Mexican Foreign Policy: The Decline of a Regional Power?" *Current History* 82(488):406-10.

———, (1981), "Mexico in the 1980's: A New Regional Power," *Current History* 80(469).

Bean, Frank D., et al., *Mexican and Central American Population and U.S. Immigration Policy* (Austin TX: University of Texas Press, 1989).

Benítez Manaut, Raúl, *México a cincuenta años de la expropriación petrolera* (Mexico: CIIH-UNAM, 1988).

———, (1992) "La ONU y el proceso de paz en El Salvador," *Revista Mexicana de Política Exterior* (34).

———, and Lilia Bermúdez, *Viejos desafíos, nuevas perspectivas. México-Estados Unidos y América latina* (Mexico: UNAM-Porrúa, 1988).

———, and Ricardo Cordova Macias, eds., *México en Centroamérica. Expedientes de documentos fundamentales, 1979-1986* (Mexico: CIIH-UNAM, 1989).

Bermúdez, Lilia, *Guerra de baja intensidad. Reagan contra Centroamérica* (Mexico: Siglo XXI, 1987).

Berton, Pierre, *Why We Act Like Canadians* (Toronto: McClelland and Stewart, 1985).

Blanchard, Peter, and Peter Landstreet, *Human Rights in Latin America and the Caribbean* (Toronto: Canadian Scholars' Press, 1989).

Boils, Guillermo, *Los militares y la política en México: 1915-1974* (Mexico: El Caballito, 1975).

Bradford, Colin I., Jr., and Caroline Pestieau, *Canada and Latin America: The Potential for Partnership* (Toronto: CALA, 1971).

Bradging, David, ed., *Caudillo and Peasant in the Mexican Revolution* (Cambridge: Cambridge University Press, 1980).

Brzezinski, Zbigniew, *Out of Control* (New York: Charles Scribner's Sons, 1993).

Camilleri, Joseph, and Jim Falk, *The End of Sovereignty?* (Hants U.K.: Edward Elgar Publishing, 1992).

Canada, Department of External Affairs, *Foreign Policy for Canadians* (Ottawa: Queen's Printer, 1970).

———, Department of Foreign Affairs and International Trade, *Canada in the World* (Ottawa: Queen's Printer, 1995).

———, House of Commons Standing Committee on External Affairs and National Defence, *Canada's Relations with Latin America and the Caribbean* (Ottawa: Queen's Printer, 1982).

———, Royal Canadian Mounted Police, *National Drug Intelligence Estimate 1988/1989* (Ottawa: Queen's Printer, 1990).

———, Senate Standing Committee on Foreign Affairs, *Meeting New Challenges: Canada's Response to a New Generation of Peacekeeping* (Ottawa: Queen's Printer, February 1993).

Canada 21 Group, *Canada and Common Security in the Twenty-First Century* (Toronto: Centre for International Studies, University of Toronto, 1994).

Cargnelutti, Hugo Luis, *Seguridad interamericana* (Buenos Aires: Círculo Militar, 1993).

Carrère D'Encausse, Hélène, *L'Empire éclaté* (Paris: Flammarion, 1978).

Castañeda, Jorge, *La Casa por la ventana: México y América latina después de la guerra fría* (Mexico: Cal y Arena, 1993).

———, *México y el orden internacional* (Mexico: El Colegio de México, 1981).

Cavalla, Antonio, *Geopolítica y seguridad nacional en América* (Mexico: UNAM, 1983).

Child, Jack, *The Central American Peace Process, 1983-1991* (Boulder CO: Lynne Rienner, 1992).

Cline, Howard, *The United States and Mexico* (New York: Atheneum, 1971).

Comblin, Joseph, *Le pouvoir militaire en Amérique latine* (Paris: Delarge, 1977).

Conn, Stetson, et al., *The United States Army in World War II: The Western Hemisphere. Guarding the United States and Its Outposts* (Washington: Office of the Chief of Military History, 1964).

Contreras, Carlos Lopez, *Después de la Guerra fría* (Caracas: Editorial Nueva Sociedad, 1990).

———, *El sentido de una tarea* (Santiago: Comisión sudamericana de paz, 1990).

Cordera, Rolando, *El Reclamo democrático* (Mexico: Siglo XXI, 1988).

Cornish, Vaughn, *A Geography of Imperial Defence* (London: Sifton, 1922).

Daudelin, Jean, and Edgar Dosman, eds., *Beyond Mexico* (Ottawa: Carleton University Press, 1995).

Delbrel, Guy, *La géopolitique de la drogue* (Paris: La Découverte, 1991).

del Carmen Velazquez, María, *El estado de guerra en Nueva España, 1760-1808* (Mexico: El Colegio de México, 1950).

del Olmo, Rosa, *Los Discursos de la droga* (La Paz: HISBOL, 1989).

de Windt Lavandier, Cesar, *La segunda guerra múndial y los submarinos alemanes en el Caribe* (Santo Domingo: Universidad Central del Este, 1982).

Dewitt, David (1994), "Cooperative Security: A Canadian Approach to the Promotion of Peace and Security in the Post-Cold War Era," *Canadian Defence Quarterly* 23(3):11-18.

———, and David Leyton-Brown, eds., *Canada's International Security Policy* (Toronto: Prentice-Hall, 1995).

———, et al., eds., *Building a New Global Order: Emerging Trends in International Security* (Toronto: Oxford University Press, 1993).

Dobell, Rod, and Michael Neufeld, *Beyond NAFTA: The Western Hemisphere Interface* (Lantzville BC: Oolichan Books, 1993).

Dosman, Edgar J., *Latin America and the Caribbean. The Strategic Framework—A Canadian Perspective*, ORAE Paper No. 31 (Ottawa: Department of National Defence, 1984).

Driscoll de Alvarado, Bárbara, and Mónica Gambrill, eds., *El Tratado de Libre Comercio: entre el viejo y el nuevo orden* (Mexico: UNAM, 1992).

Dziedzic, Michael J., *The Essence of Decision in a Hegemonic Regime: The Case of Mexico's Acquisition of a Supersonic Fighter* (Austin TX: Ph.D. dissertation, University of Texas, 1984).

Eayrs, James, *Growing Up Allied* (Toronto: University of Toronto Press, 1980).

———, *In Defence of Canada*, Vol. II, *Appeasement and Rearmament* (Toronto: University of Toronto Press, 1965).

Eberstadt, Nicholas (1991), "Population Change and National Security," *Foreign Affairs* 70(3):115-31.

Eccles, W.J., *France in America* (New York: Praeger, 1972).

Eguizábal, Cristina, ed., *América latina y la crisis centroamericana: en busca de una solución regional* (Buenos Aires: Grupo Editor Latinoamericano, 1988).

English, Adrian J., *Armed Forces of Latin America* (London: Jane's, 1984).

Estrada, Genaro, *Obras completas* (Mexico: Siglo XXI, 1988).

Fauriol, Georges, *Latin American Insurgencies* (Washington: National Defense University, 1985).

Flores Olea, Victor, *México entre las naciones* (Mexico: Cal y Arena, 1989).

Fuentes, Gloria, *El Ejército Mexicano* (Mexico: Grijalvo, 1983).

Fukker, Eraham, *The Democracy Trap* (New York: Outlon Books, 1991).

Galeana de Valadés, Patricia, *Las Relaciones Iglesia-Estados durante el Segundo Imperio* (Mexico: UNAM, 1991).

Gilman, E., and D. Herold, eds., *Peacekeeping Challenges to Euro-Atlantic Security* (Rome: NATO Defence College, 1994).

González Casanova, Pablo, *La Democracia en México* (Mexico: ERA, 1965).

———, *Los militares y la política en América Latina* (Mexico: Oceano, 1988).

———, ed., *México hacia el año 2000: desafíos y opciones* (Caracas: Nueva Sociedad, 1989).

Gordillo, Octavio, *La revolución en el Estado de Chiapas* (Mexico: INEHRM, 1986).

Graham, Dominick, *The Price of Command: A Biography of General Guy Simonds* (Toronto: Stoddart, 1993).

Graham, Gerald, *The Empire of the North Atlantic: The Maritime Struggle for North America* (Toronto: University of Toronto Press, 1958).

Granatstein, J.L., *The Generals: The Canadian Army's Senior Commanders in the Second World War* (Toronto: Stoddart, 1993).

———, *How Britain's Weakness Forced Canada into the Arms of the U.S.* (Toronto: University of Toronto Press, 1989).

———, *Ties that Bind: Canadian-American Relations in Wartime from the Great War to the Cold War* (Toronto: Hakkert, 1977).

Grant, George, *Lament for a Nation* (Ottawa ON: Carleton University Press, 1968).

Green, Rosario, ed., *México y la paz* (Mexico: SRE, 1986).

———, and Peter Smith, eds., *Foreign Policy in U.S.-Mexican Relations* (San Diego CA: Center for U.S.-Mexican Studies, 1989).

Grinspun, Ricardo, and Maxwell Cameron, eds., *The Political Economy of North American Free Trade* (Montreal: McGill-Queen's University Press, 1993).

Haar, Jeffrey, and Edgar Dosman, eds., *A Dynamic Partnership: Canada's Changing Role in the Americas* (Miami: North-South Center, 1993).

Habeeb, William Mark, *Power and Tactics in International Negotiation* (Baltimore MD: Johns Hopkins University Press, 1988).

Haglund, David, ed., *The New Geopolitics of Minerals* (Vancouver: University of British Columbia Press, 1989).

Haglund, David, ed., *Latin America and the Transformation of U.S. Strategic Thought, 1936-1940* (Albuquerque NM: University of New Mexico Press, 1985).

Harris, Stephen, *Canadian Brass: The Making of a Professional Army, 1860-1939* (Toronto: University of Toronto Press, 1988).

Harris, William V., *War and Imperialism in Republican Rome, 327-70 B.C.* (Oxford: Clarendon Press, 1985).

Hassig, Ross, *Aztec Warfare* (Norman OK: University of Oklahoma Press, 1988).

Haycock, Ronald G., *Sam Hughes: The Public Career of a Controversial Canadian, 1885-1916* (Waterloo ON: Wilfrid Laurier University Press, 1986).

Heller, Claude, ed., *El ejército como agente de cambio social* (Mexico: FCE, 1980).

Herrera-Lasso, Luis, et al., *México y la seguridad hemisférica* (Mexico: Centro Latinoamericano de Estudios Estratégicos, 1990).

Hilliker, John, *Le Ministère des affaires extérieures du Canada*, Vol. 1, *Les années de formation, 1909-1946* (Quebec: Les Presses de l'Université Laval, 1990).

Hitsman, J. Mackay, *Safeguarding Canada, 1763-1871* (Toronto: University of Toronto Press, 1968).

Holmes, John, *The Better Part of Valour: Essays on Canadian Diplomacy* (Toronto: McClelland and Stewart, 1970).

Hunt, Barry, and Ronald Haycock, eds., *Canada's Defence: Perspectives on Policy in the Twentieth Century* (Toronto: Copp Clark Pitman, 1993).

Inoguchi, Takashi (1992), "Japan's Role in International Affairs," *Survival* 34(2):71-87.

Jamieson, Alison, *Drug Trafficking 1992: A Special Report* (Southampton UK: Research Institute for the Study of Conflict and Terrorism, 1992).

Jockel, Joseph, *No Boundaries Upstairs* (Vancouver: University of British Columbia Press, 1987).

Johnson, John J., *The Military and Society in Latin America* (Stanford CA: Stanford University Press, 1964).

Jorden, William, *Panama Odyssey* (Austin TX: University of Texas Press, 1984).

Katz, Friedrich, *La Guerra secreta en México,* Vol. 1 (Mexico: ERA, 1982).

Kennedy, Paul, *Hacia el Siglo XXI* (Barcelona: Paz y Janés Editores, 1993).

———, *The Rise and Fall of the Great Powers* (London: Fontana, 1988).

Keohane, R.O., and J.S. Nye, *Power and Interdependence* (Boston: Little Brown, 1977).

Kirk, John, *Back in Business: Canada-Cuba Relations after 50 Years* (Ottawa: FOCAL, 1995).

Kirschbaum, S.J., ed., *La sécurité collective au XXIe siècle* (Quebec: Centre québécois de relations internationales, 1994).

Kitching, George, *Mud and Green Fields* (St. Catharines ON: Vanwell, 1992).

Klepak, H.P., (1995), "Cuban Security—Old Myths and New Realities," *Jane's Intelligence Review* 7(7):334-35.

———, (1994), "Medidas de confianza mutua y reacercamiento entre Cuba y los Estados Unidos," *Estudios Internacionales* 27(107):605-17.

———, (1994), "The Impact of the International Narcotics Trade on Canada's Foreign and Security Policy," *International Journal* 49(1):66-92.

———, *What's In It For Us? Canada's Relationship with Latin America* (Ottawa: FOCAL, 1994).

———, ed., *Canada and Latin American Security* (Montreal: Méridien, 1993).

———, (1992), "Canada's Pull-Out May Mean More than Losing a Brigade," *Jane's Defence Weekly* 16(15):614.

———, *Canada and Latin America: Strategic Issues for the 1990s,* ORAE Paper No. 54 (Ottawa: Department of National Defence, 1990).

———, and G.K. Vachon, *A Strategic and Economic Analysis of Canadian National Interests in Latin America* (Ottawa: Department of National Defence, 1978).

———, *Potential Regional Strategic Considerations Regarding Nuclear Proliferation in Latin America,* ORAE Paper No. 57 (Ottawa: Department of National Defence, 1975).

Krauze, Enrique, *Siglo de Caudillos: biografía política de México, 1810-1910* (Mexico: Tusquets, 1994).

Kruijt, D., and Edelberto Torres, eds., *América Latina: militares y sociedad* (San José: FLACSO, 1991).

Lake, Anthony (1994), "Confronting Backlash State," *Foreign Affairs* 73(2):45-56.

Lanctôt, Gustave, *Le Canada et la Révolution américaine* (Montreal: Beauchemin, 1965).

Lasswell, Harold, *Politics: Who Gets What, When, How* (New York: McGraw-Hill, 1936).

Latel, Brian, *Mexico at the Crossroads: The Many Crises of the Mexican Political System* (San Francisco: The Hoover Institution, 1986).

Leal Buitrago, Francisco, and Juan Gabriel Tokatlian, eds., *Orden mundial y seguridad: nuevos desafíos para Colombia y América Latina* (Bogotá: Tercer Mundo, 1994).

Legault, Albert, and Michel Fortmann, eds., *Prolifération et non-prolifération nucléaires* (Quebec: Centre québécois de relations internationales, 1992).

———, *Une diplomatie de l'espoir* (Quebec: Les Presses de l'Université Laval, 1989).

Lieuwen, Edwin, *Mexican Militarism: The Political Rise and Fall of the Revolutionary Army, 1910-1940* (Albuquerque NM: University of New Mexico Press, 1968).

Littuma, Alfonso, *Doctrina de seguridad nacional* (Caracas: Ministerio de Defensa, 1966).

Lowenthal, Abraham, *Partners in Conflict: The United States and Latin America* (Baltimore MD: Johns Hopkins University Press, 1987).

Lustig, Nora, *Mexico: The Remaking of an Economy* (Washington: Brookings Institution, 1992).

Mabry, Donald J., ed., *The Latin American Narcotics Trade and U.S. National Security* (New York: Greenwood, 1989).

MacKenzie, David (1991), "The World's Greatest Joiner, Canada and the Organization of American States," *British Journal of Canadian Studies* 1:203-20.

Mahan, Alfred Thayer, *The Influence of Sea Power upon History* (Englewood Cliffs NJ: Prentice-Hall, 1980).

Martin, Pierre, and Michel Fortmann (1995), "Canadian Public Opinion and Peacekeeping in a Turbulent World," *International Journal* 50(2):370-400.

Martínez, Leopoldo, *La intervención norteamericana en México, 1846-1848* (Mexico: Panorama, 1989).

Martínez, Orlando, *The Great Landgrab* (London: Quartet, 1975).

Martins, Dean, *Non-Proliferation Policy and Nuclear Threshold States: The Case of Argentina and Brazil* (Kingston: Unpublished master's thesis, Queen's University, 1990).

McKenna, Peter, *Canada and the OAS* (Ottawa ON: Carleton University Press, 1996).

Medina, Luis, *Historia de la Revolución Mexicana. Período 1940-1952. Civilismo y modernización del autoritarismo*, Vol. 20 (Mexico: El Colegio de México, 1979).

Mercado Jarrín, Edgardo, *Un sistema de seguridad y defensa sudamericano* (Lima: CONCYTEC, 1990).

Merle, Marcel, *Le nouvel ordre international et la guerre du Golfe* (Paris: Economica, 1991).

Mexico, *The Mexican Army and Air Force in the Campaign against Drug Traffic* (Mexico: Estado Mayor de la Defensa Nacional, 1991).

———, *Plan nacional de desarrollo, 1989-1994* (Mexico: Secretaría de Planificación y Presupuesto, 1989).

———, *Política exterior de México: 175 años de historia* (Mexico: Secretaría de Relaciones Exteriores, 1985).

———, *Plan nacional de desarrollo, 1983-1988* (Mexico: Secretaría de Planificación y Presupuesto, 1983).

———, *México demográfico. Breviario, 1980-81* (Mexico: Consejo Nacional de Población, 1982).

———, *Plan Global de Desarrollo, 1980-1982* (Mexico: Talleres Gráficos de la Nación, 1980).

———, *El ejército mexicano. Historia de los orígenes hasta nuestros días* (Mexico: Ministerio de la Defensa Nacional, 1979).

———, *Memoria de la Secretaría de Relaciones Exteriores*, September 1941-August 1942 (Mexico: SRE, 1942).

Meyer, Jean, et al., *Historia de la Revolución Mexicana. Período 1924-1928. Estado y sociedad con Calles*, Vol. 11 (Mexico: El Colegio de México, 1977).

———, *La révolution mexicaine, 1910-1940* (Paris: Calmann-Lévy, 1973).

Meyer, Lorenzo, *Su Majestad Británica contra la Revolución Mexicana, 1900-1950* (Mexico: El Colegio de México, 1991).

Meyer, Lorenzo, *México y Estados Unidos en el conflicto petrolero, 1917-1942* (Mexico: PEMEX, 1988).

———, *Historia de la Revolución mexicana. Período 1928-1934. El conflicto social y los gobiernos del maximato*, Vol. 13 (Mexico: El Colegio de México, 1978).

Moneta, Carlos, ed., *Civiles y militares: fuerzas armadas y transición democrática* (Caracas: Nueva Sociedad, 1990).

Morris, M.A., *Expansion of Third World Navies* (London: Macmillan, 1987).

———, and Victor Millán, *Controlling Latin American Conflicts: Ten Approaches* (Boulder CO: Westview, 1986).

Morris, Richard, *Documentos fundamentales de la historia de los Estados Unidos de América* (Mexico: Libreros Mexicanos Unidos, 1962).

Morton, Desmond, *A Military History of Canada* (Edmonton: Hurtig, 1990).

———, *Ministers and Generals: Politics and the Canadian Militia, 1868-1904* (Toronto: University of Toronto Press, 1970).

Moyano Pahissa, Angela, *La Resistencia de las Californias a la invasión norteamericana, 1846-1848* (Mexico: Consejo Nacional para la Cultura y las Artes, 1992).

Mullin, James, *Breaking Through Together: Prospects for Canada-Latin America Partnerships in Science and Technology* (Ottawa: FOCAL, 1995).

Muñoz, Héctor, ed., *El Desafío de los '90: anuario de políticas exteriores latinoamericanas, 1989-1990* (Caracas: Nueva Sociedad, 1990).

Murray, David R., ed., *Documents on Canadian External Relations, 1939-1941: Part II*, Vol. 8 (Ottawa: Department of External Affairs, 1976).

Navidad González Parás, José, ed., *La Política exterior de México en el nuevo orden mundial* (Mexico: EFE, 1993).

North, Liisa, ed., *Between War and Peace in Central America: Choices for Canada* (Toronto: Between the Lines, 1990).

Norton, Mary Beth, *The British-Americans* (Boston: Little Brown, 1972).

Nugent, Daniel, ed., *Rural Revolt in Mexico and U.S. Intervention* (San Diego: Centre for U.S.-Mexican Studies, 1988).

Nunn, Frederick M., *The Time of the Generals: Latin American Professional Militarism in World Perspective* (Lincoln NK: University of Nebraska Press, 1992).

Nunn, Frederick M., *Yesterday's Soldiers* (Lincoln NK: University of Nebraska Press, 1985).

Nye, Joseph S., *Bound to Lead: The Changing Nature of American Power* (New York: Basic Books, 1990).

———, (1974), "Transnational Relations and Interstate Conflicts: An Empirical Analysis," *International Organization* 28(4):961-96.

Ogelsby, J.C.M., *Gringos from the Far North: Essays in the History of Canadian-Latin American Relations, 1866-1968* (Toronto: Macmillan, 1976).

Ojeda, Mario, ed., *Las Relaciones de México con los Países de América Central* (Mexico: El Colegio de México, 1985).

———, and René Herrera, *La Política exterior de México hacia Centroamérica* (Mexico: El Colegio de México, 1983).

———, *Alcances y límites de la política exterior de México* (Mexico: El Colegio de México, 1980).

Ornstein, Norman J. (1992), "Foreign Policy and the 1992 Election," *Foreign Affairs* 71(3):1-16.

Palma, Hugo, *América latina: limitación de armamento y desarme en la región* (Lima: CEPEI, 1986).

Pellicer, Olga ed., *La Política exterior de México: desafíos en los ochenta* (Mexico: CIDE, 1983).

———, and José Luis Reyna, *Historia de la Revolución Mexicana. Período 1952-1960. El afianzamiento de la estabilidad política*, Vol. 22 (Mexico: El Colegio de México, 1978).

———,(1965-66), "México en la OEA," *Foro internacional* 6(2-3).

Piñeyro, Jose Luis, *Ejército y sociedad en México: pasado y presente* (Mexico: UAP-UAM.A, 1985).

Preston, Richard A., *The Defence of the Undefended Border: Planning for War in North America, 1867-1939* (Durham NC: Duke University Press, 1967).

Queuille, Pierre, *L'Amérique latine, la doctrine Monroe et le panaméricanisme* (Paris: Payot, 1969).

Rangarajan, L.N., ed., *Kautilya, The Arthashastra* (New Delhi: Penguin, 1987).

Robinson, Alan (1990), "La conexión mexicana," in *América Economía* 4(40).

Rochlin, James, *Discovering the Americas: The Evolution of Canadian Foreign Policy towards Latin America* (Vancouver: University of British Columbia Press, 1994).

Rodrigo Jauberth Rojas, H., ed., *La Triangulación Centroamérica-México-Estados Unidos ¿una oportunidad para el desarrollo y la paz?* (Mexico: DEI, 1991).

Roett, Riordan, ed., *Mexico's External Relations in the 1990s* (Boulder CO: Lynne Rienner, 1990).

——, ed., *México y Estados Unidos: el manejo de la relación* (Mexico: Siglo XXI, 1989).

Ronfeldt, David, ed., *The Modern Mexican Military: A Reassessment* (San Diego: University of California, 1984).

——, et al., *Mexico's Petroleum and U.S. Policy: Implications for the 1980s* (Santa Monica CA: RAND Corporation, 1980).

Roosevelt, Franklin D., *The Roosevelt Reader: Press Conferences and Letters of Franklin D. Roosevelt, 1882-1945* (New York: Rinehart, 1957).

Roper, John, "Shaping Strategy Without the Threat," *Adelphi Papers 257* (London: The International Institute for Strategic Studies, 1990-91).

Rosen, Boris, ed., *México y la paz. Testimonios 1810-1896.* Vol. 1, *El Estado* (Mexico: Centro de Investigación Científica Jorge L. Tamayo, 1986).

Rouquié, Alain, *Amérique latine: Introduction à l'Extrême-Occident* (Paris: Seuil, 1987).

——, *El Estado militar en América Latina* (Mexico: Siglo XXI, 1984).

Roussel, Stéphane, et al. (1994), "Le Canada et la sécurité européenne, 1943-1952: à la recherche de l'équilibre des puissances," *Canadian Defence Quarterly* 23(4):23-27.

Roussin, Marcel, *Le Canada et le système interaméricain* (Ottawa: Les Presses de l'Université d'Ottawa, 1959).

Rupesinghe, Kumar, ed., *Internal Conflict and Governance* (New York: St. Martin Press, 1992).

Saldivar, Americo, *Ideología y política del Estado Mexicano, 1970-1976* (Mexico: Siglo XXI, 1980).

Santos Caamal, Mario, Rear Admiral (1985), "México frente a Centroamérica. Un concepto estratégico nacional en acción," *Armada de México* (51).

Sarkesian, Sam, and John Mead Flanagan, eds., *U.S. Domestic and National Security Agendas* (London: Greenwood Press, 1993).

Saxe-Fernandez, John, *Petróleo y estrategia. México y Estados Unidos en el contexto de la política global* (Mexico: Siglo XXI, 1980).

Scheman, L. Ronald, *The Inter-American Dilemma: The Search for Inter-American Cooperation at the Centennial of the Inter-American System* (New York: Praeger, 1989).

Schoultz, Lars, *National Security and U.S. Policy in Latin America* (Princeton NJ: Princeton University Press, 1987).

Schrader, Peter, ed., *Intervention into the 1990s* (Boulder CO: Lynne Rienner Publishers, 1992).

Sepúlveda, Bernardo, "México y Centroamérica," *Revista Mexicana de Política Exterior* (10) (1986).

Serbin, Andrés, *Medio ambiente, seguridad y cooperación regional en el Caribe* (Caracas: Nueva Sociedad, 1992).

———, and Joseph Tulchin, eds., *El Caribe y Cuba en la posguerra fría* (Caracas: Nueva Sociedad, 1994).

Silva-Michelena, José, ed., *Latin America: Peace, Democratization and Economic Crisis* (London: Zed Books, 1988).

Slaten, Robert, et al., eds., *Global Transformation and the Third World* (Boulder CO: Lynne Rienner Publishers, 1993).

Smith, Peter H., ed., *El combate a las drogas en América* (Mexico: Fondo de Cultura Económica, 1992).

Smith, Wayne S., *The Closest of Enemies* (New York: Norton, 1987).

Sokolsky, Joel J. (1995), "Great Ideals and Uneasy Compromises: the United States Approach to Peacekeeping," *International Journal* 50(2):266-93.

Somavía, Juan, and José Miguel Insulza, eds., *Seguridad democrática regional: una concepción alternativa* (Caracas: Nueva Sociedad, 1990).

Soward, Frederic H., and A.M. MacAuley, *Canada and the Pan American System* (Toronto: Canadian Institute for International Affairs, 1948).

Stacey, C.P., *The Military Problems of Canada* (Toronto: Ryerson, 1940).

———, and Barbara Wilson, *The Half Million: The Canadians in Britain, 1939-1946* (Toronto: University of Toronto Press, 1987).

Stanley, George F., *Canada's Soldiers: The Military History of an Unmilitary People* (Toronto: Macmillan, 1960).

Stark, Jeffrey, "Rethinking Security in the Americas," *North-South Issues* (Miami: North-South Center Press, 1992).

Stevenson, Brian, *Domestic Pressures, External Constraints and the New Internationalism: Canadian Foreign Policy Towards Latin*

America, 1968-1990 (Kingston ON: Unpublished doctoral dissertation, Queen's University, 1992).

Strange, Susan, *States and Markets* (London: Pinter, 1988).

Sutherland, R.J. (1962), "Canada's Long Term Strategic Situation," *International Journal* 17(3):199-223.

Tello, Carlos, and Clark Reynolds, eds., *Las Relaciones México-Estados Unidos* (Mexico: FCE, 1981).

Tobler, Hans-Werner (1971), "Las paradojas del ejército revolucionario: su papel social en la reforma agraria mexicana, 1920-1935," *Historia Mexicana* 21(1):38-79.

Toward a New World Strategy: Canadian Policy in the Americas into the Twenty-First Century (Ottawa: FOCAL, 1994)

United Nations Development Program, *Informe sobre Desarrollo Humano, 1994* (Mexico: Fondo de Cultura Económica, 1994).

Valadés, José, *México, Santa Anna y la guerra de Texas* (Mexico: Diana, 1979).

Valki, Laszlo, ed., *Changing Threat Perceptions and Military Doctrines* (London: Macmillan, 1992).

Varas, Augusto, ed., *La Autonomía militar en América latina* (Caracas: Nueva Sociedad, 1988).

———, ed., *Paz, desarme y desarrollo en América latina* (Buenos Aires: Latinoamericano, 1987).

Veneroni, Horacio L., *Estados Unidos y las fuerzas armadas de América latina* (Buenos Aires: Periferia, 1973).

Verea Campos, Mónica, ed., *50 años de relaciones México-Canadá: encuentros y coincidencias* (Mexico: UNAM, 1994).

Villalpando César, José Manuel, *Introducción al derecho militar mexicano* (Mexico: Porrúa, 1991).

Wager, Stephen, *The Mexican Military Approaches the 21st Century: Coping with a New World Order* (Washington: Strategic Studies Institute, 1993).

Walt, Stephen M., *The Origins of Alliances* (Ithaca NY: Cornell University Press, 1987).

Weiss, Thomas G., and K.M. Campbell (1991), "Military Humanitarianism," *Survival* 33(5):451-65.

White, Richard Alan, *The Morass: United States Intervention in Central America* (New York: Harper & Row, 1984).

Whiteside, Alan, and David Fitzsimmons, *AIDS—Economic, Political and Security Implications*, Conflict Study 251

(Southampton U.K.: Research Institute for the Study of Conflict and Terrorism, 1991).

Wiarda, Howard, ed., *Rift and Revolution: The Central American Imbroglio* (Washington: The American Enterprise Institute, 1984).

Wisolsky, Steven, *Breaking the Impasse in the War on Drugs* (New York: Greenwood Press, 1986).

Womack, John, Jr., *Zapata y la Revolución mexicana* (Mexico: SEP-Siglo XXI, 1985).

Zermeno, Sergio, *México: una democracia utópica. El movimiento estudiantil del 68* (Mexico: Siglo XXI, 1985).

Zoraida Vázquez, Josefina, and Lorenzo Meyer, *México frente a Estados Unidos: un ensayo histórico, 1776-1988* (Mexico: EFE, 1989).

——, *Vigésimo Aniversario del Tratado de Tlatelolco* (Mexico: OPANAL, 1987).

——, *Madero y su obra. Documentos inéditos publicados con motivo del XXV aniversario de la grandiosa Revolución mexicana, 1910-1934* (Mexico: Talleres Gráficos de la Nación, 1934).

CONTRIBUTORS

Raúl Benítez Manaut is a researcher with the *Centro de Investigaciones Interdisciplinarias en Humanidades, Universidad Nacional Autónoma de México* (UNAM), Mexico City.

Paul Buteux is professor of political science, and Director of the Centre for Defence and Security Studies, at the University of Manitoba, Winnipeg.

Jorge Chen Charpentier, Ambassador, is Director General for Asia and Africa at the *Secretaría de Relaciones Exteriores*, Mexico City, and professor of international relations at the *Instituto Tecnológico Autónomo de México* (ITAM), Mexico City.

Jorge Castro-Valle K., Ambassador, is a former minister-counsellor at the Mexican Embassy in Ottawa, and currently Director General for North America at the *Secretaría de Relaciones Exteriores*, Mexico City.

Luís Herrera-Lasso, Ambassador, is Consul General of Mexico in San Diego, California.

Hal P. Klepak is professor of strategy and international history at the Royal Military College of Canada, Kingston, and Director of the Governance and Security Program at the Canadian Foundation for the Americas (FOCAL) in Ottawa.

Jill Sinclair is Director for Arms Control and Disarmament at the Department of Foreign Affairs and International Trade, Ottawa.

Brian Stevenson is coordinator of the Canadian studies programme, and associate professor in the department of international relations, *Instituto Tecnológico Autónomo México* (ITAM), Mexico City. He is also visiting Imperial Oil/Royal Bank associate professor of international business at the University of Alberta, Edmonton.